Strange Reciprocity

Strange Reciprocity

Mainstreaming Women's Work in Tepoztlán in the "Decade of the New Economy"

Sidney S. Perutz

It is a joy to share Tepoztlán with you—

¡Viva! Sidney

LEXINGTON BOOKS

A division of

ROWMAN & LITTLEFIELD PUBLISHERS, INC.

Lanham • Boulder • New York • Toronto • Plymouth, UK

LEXINGTON BOOKS

A division of Rowman & Littlefield Publishers, Inc.
A wholly owned subsidiary of The Rowman & Littlefield Publishing Group, Inc.
4501 Forbes Boulevard, Suite 200
Lanham, MD 20706

Estover Road
Plymouth PL6 7PY
United Kingdom

British Library Cataloguing in Publication Information Available

Library of Congress Cataloging-in-Publication Data

Perutz, Sidney S., 1933–
Strange reciprocity : mainstreaming women's work in Tepoztlán in the "decade of the new economy" / Sidney S. Perutz.
p. cm.
Includes bibliographical references and index.
ISBN-13: 978-0-7391-1628-9 (cloth: alk. paper)
ISBN-10: 0-7391-1628-2 (cloth: alk. paper)
eISBN-13: 978-0-7391-3026-1
eISBN-10: 0-7391-3026-9
1. Indian women—Mexico—Tepoztlán—Economic conditions. 2. Women—Employment—Mexico—Tepoztlán. 3. Indians of Mexico—Commerce—Mexico—Tepoztlán. 4. Tepoztlán (Mexico)—Economic conditions. I. Title.
F1219.3.W6P47 2008
331.4089'9707249—dc22

2008015325

Printed in the United States of America

∞™ The paper used in this publication meets the minimum requirements of American National Standard for Information Sciences—Permanence of Paper for Printed Library Materials, ANSI/NISO Z39.48-1992.

The daily things we do
For money or for fun
Can disappear like dew
Or harden and live on.
Strange reciprocity:
The circumstances we cause
In time give rise to us,
Becomes our memory.

—*Philip Larkin*

"It now appears to me that women's place in human social life is not in any direct sense a product of the things she does, but of the meaning her activities acquire through concrete social interaction."

—*Michelle Rosaldo*

Contents

Introduction: Keywords and Organization of the Book

> Women are often pictured as being pulled in and out [of] the labor market merely as a result of capital's interests and strategies. This takes no account of women's own resistance and struggles that, while clearly subject to significant constraints due to their subordination in society, derive from a strategy of their own.
>
> —Lourdes Benería and Martha Roldán, 1987

"Keywords," in Raymond Williams' (1983:14–15) sense, are not "eternal categories" but active records of "important social and historical processes" which "in practice" turn out to be "inextricably bound up with the problems [they are] being used to discuss." A "*vocabulary*" shared with others when acted upon, keywords indicate connections people are making to "the area in which meanings of *culture* and *society* have formed." Interred in a dictionary, they cease to be signposts to ways people confront particular formations of "problems"—such as the simultaneously oppositional and mutually essential relationship between "society" and "capital" and "subordination" and "resistance" brought up in the passage from Benería and Roldán.

The keywords integrated into this frontpiece lay the ground for disinterring connections to the problems of meanings and relations and solutions to the problems taken up throughout this study of women's work in and against the socioeconomic culture often glossed as free market capitalism or *globalization*. I observe workplace exchanges of valued things as both signifiers and carriers of the contradictions—fusions of tensions and dependencies—interweaving women's work processes, the institution of gender, and international capital's interests and strategies. I seek to make explicit women's ways of turning profoundly gendered global economy constraints into profoundly gendered global economy strategies of their own. Or not.

RESEARCH SITES

"Anthropologists study processes—connections and sequences among events—not isolates and fixities" (Sanjek 1994:31). Women's work processes are the processes studied in this feminist anthropology of work. To call oneself *feminist* is to commit to "a sex-related emancipatory project" (S. Smith 1997:691). Because it is a feminist anthropology, forefronted as the process within processes is *gender*: the coercive ways individuals and alliances of individuals construct and regulate sexual differences and preferences. Committed to achieving a *feminist standpoint* (Harding 1991:127)—a politics and science anchored in the logic of "knowing" (D. Smith 1987) women's value/values creating practices—emphasized is the "performance" (Butler 1990) of gender, *gendering*: asymmetrical exchanges of valued things.

Women's configurations of paid and unpaid work processes in the central Mexican *municipio*, municipality, and town of Tepoztlán—"the *pueblo*"—are the gendering sites researched.[1] The ethnographic present is 1990 to 2000, the period Mexicans (increasingly ironically) call the "Decade of the New Economy." The testimony of many women of the pueblo is that during these years, women's roles in the labor force, the practices of everyday life, and the political arena changed more rapidly and profoundly than during any other period in the turbulent modern history of the ancient municipio.

Michel de Certeau[2]—a frequent visitor to Tepoztlán—made us aware that ways "consumers" make use of economies imposed by dominant orders bring into play "a way of thinking, invested in a way of acting, an art of combination which cannot be dissociated from an art of using" (1984: xv). However, he did not specify the gender dimensions accruing as "users' fees" (Elson 2006:60): fees uniquely imposed on women as members of a distinctively subordinated working class—distinctive because inequities are imposed upon women who possess and share real power precisely at points where they activate this power. Fundamental to the twenty-first century emancipatory project is to empirically isolate relations of causation binding users and users' fees into capital's current economic strategy synthesized by Guy Standing (1989) as "global feminization through flexible labor" (see chapter 1).

To Vandana Shiva (1999:21), "the first wave of globalization" hit during the earliest stages of European colonization of the terrains subsequently identified as the Third World. Residents of one of the first New Spain regions to be colonized industrially, citizens of Tepoztlán—Tepoztecans—were one of the earliest populations of the occupied world to have their labor globalized. *Tepoztecas*—women of Tepoztlán—were among the first New World labor forces to be globally *feminized*: a concept I expand to incorporate not only a complex of personal and public asymmetries systemically weighted against multitasking women but also working women's ways of challenging gender inequities.

Men, *Tepoztecos*, were impressed into the new *production economy* (called *production*)—the sector that creates *commodities*: standardized goods and services intended for exchange in a market. Barred by laws and customs from the Europeanized production sector, Tepoztecas coped by taking advantage of diasporas of foreign and indigenous men in need of care. They invented a *reproductive* or *consumption economy*: the sector that creates and distributes goods and services for private use, often on a face-to-face and caring basis. Its organization correlated to a survivalist need for cash, extensive domestic obligations, and the requirement to take up subsistence activities formerly performed by the decimated male population.

Worksite transactions here fuse a deep history of global feminization with the gendered present women are deploying to construct a more equitable future. Tepoztecas never stopped adjusting to waves of colonizing systems that depend on gendering "in order to be global" (Basu and others 2001:943).

The social actors-economic agents of this study are members of a venerable, vulnerable, and truly globalized working class. They are market and street economy merchants, teachers, butchers, accountants, nurses, domestic, restaurant and shop employees, and so on and on. As makers and keepers of a long-functioning society and its basic cooperative unit—the parent/child household—they create and allocate many of the goods, services, and ideas essential to a collective way of being in and acting on capital's interests and strategies. They are women going to work across all zones, sectors, and domains of Tepoztlán's segment of Mexico's New Economy, with its transnational flows (or undertows) of people, technologies, things, crises, currencies, crimes, aspirations, and the gendered work processes that are the focus of this book.

Though frequently derided as elitist, *jargon*, "the use of a new term or definition," is often "the necessary form of a challenge to other ways of thinking or indicating new and alterative ways" (R. Williams 1983:176). Ahead, I use New Economy jargon to give a production-reproduction context to arts of combinations explored in the chapters that follow.

On the surface, the 1990s segue into the "Lost Decade" of economic growth of the 1980s, a period marked by deprivations that raised questions about the ability of ordinary Mexicans to survive (Benería 1992:83). But, necessarily, out of crises came potentially "progressive transformation of the condition of struggle" (Elson 1992:29). I begin then by specifying the "new" in Mexico's New Economy, not as a "finished and coherent template" but as the texts and contexts of "new economic becomings" (Gibson-Graham 2005:137).

The idea of *economy* denotes ways individuals coalesce to produce and reproduce each day and over time the goods and services that make a collective life possible. *Capitalism* is a world-systems interlinked idea based on buying labor power to *produce*, to convert natural and human resources into things that can be sold for a greater value than labor and other costs of reproducing techniques and relations of production. *Capital* (as used by Benería and Roldán) is the *firm*—the force empowered to coordinate two mechanisms of *accumulation*: profit making on a progressively expanding scale. These forces are (1) the *market*—an institution where *value* (to economists, a synonym for price per unit produced) is set in response to the supply-and-demand of items exchanged—and (2) the allocation of *resources*—physical and human goods and services that can be used to accumulate (Coase 1937).

Though integral to all exchanges in the shared world, capitalism is not the global economy. Exploring the *global economy* as all the values everyone everywhere purposefully creates and *experience* as cogent responses to essential conditions, the central concern of this book is value/values creating women's experiences of the neoliberal variant of capitalist *development*: broadly, economic growth with structural and behavioral changes.

In his inaugural address, U.S. President Truman described "the problem" of "developing underdeveloped areas" with the term *development.* Though "solutions"—instituted development—have taken many different directions, economist Amartya Sen (1983) identifies the "major strategic themes" of all instituted development initiatives as industrialization, rapid capital accumulation, mobilization of the unemployed and underemployed, and an increasingly economically active or *technocratic* state.

In the context of an economic policy, *liberalization* describes a program aimed at moving a country in the direction of a Free Market trading system. The current development orthodoxy of *neoliberalism*[3] "deifies" the combination of *open* (free) markets and fiscal stabilization (Cardoso and Helwege 1995:181) (which in practice has proven to be yet another dialectical contradiction). Development is not the outcome of processes but of *structures*—objectively knowable, generalizable rules and elements framing a social *system*: the "stretching" of organizing relations across time-space (Giddens 1984:377). Orthodox *economists*, overwhelmingly neoliberal and male, calculate development as growth in the Gross National Product (GNP), all final (consumed) goods produced by a nation in a single year. Technological advances (called *supply siding*) that allow more output without more or far better, less input (called *productivity*); control of the national money supply; unfettered inflows and outflows of capital; and the increased consumption of goods and services—*consumables* (G. Becker 1991)—that must be purchased directly or indirectly in global market systems are recursively the means and destination of the development industry.

La Crisis

To recap the events that came to be known as The Crisis, unable to pay the interest on a US$62 billion (or considerably more, say $82 billion) debt, in July 1982 Mexico closed its foreign currency exchange, thereby rendering pesos and centavos, the Mexican currency, worthless in money markets. In order to receive U.S. dollar (USD) loans from developed world lenders to service its massive debt to developed world lenders, President de la Madrid agreed to neoliberalize Mexico, to shift from an inward (closed) to an outward (open) oriented development model (Pastor 1993; Lustig 1998). The objective of "structural adjustments policies" (SAPs) was to bring the economy into stable equilibrium. According to economists, stabilization (or balancing) happens when the demand and the supply of money, producers, and products are generally equal. Only Adam Smith's "Invisible Hand," the mechanism that sets the price for economic goods (goods that are scarce because they must be purchased) can achieve and sustain general equilibrium (which by definition cannot be experienced "generally").

During the 1990 to 2000 decade, Mexico entered the second, more radically transformative phase of the neoliberal model of development. Despite "spurts" of GNP growth, even in the dynamic export-manufacturing sector, into the 1990s aggregate (macroeconomic) growth was "mediocre"; and, with huge increases in income inequality, poverty, and repression, for most Mexicans, a "mirage" (Monsiváis 2006:15). As is the established pattern of the grid of women's work-gender-and-development, the mirror image of spectacular results flowing to an already empowered few was the intensification of the feminization of work processes. Because it was a decade when gender had never been more integrated into globally interlinked capitalism (Salas and Zepeda 2003:523), it was also a time when gendering had never been more "unfinalized" (Bakhtin 1981), more made, remade, and unmade as intensely "interested" (in Dewey's sense) women transacted it.

A Catastrophic Equilibrium

Mexico's regime of "authoritarian populism" (Stevens 1974) that radiates from a dictator/president through a pyramid of "patron-client" (ordinate/subordinate, capital/labor) relations fits the profile of the system most likely to enforce conditions that suppress "the people's" dissent. Thus despite the incalculably high social costs and macroeconomic failures, Mexican presidents continued (and continue) to implement reforms designed to (1) open internal and external trade to foreign firms and investors; (2) control wages and the credit and money supply; and (3) privatize state industries, social welfare, communal land, and other public goods and infrastructures (Székely 2006).

Balancing exports and imports is deemed vital to *transition*, from a *closed* (protectionist), natural resource-dependent economy to an *open* (free market-driven) industrial economy, which has little direct input from raw resources. Achieving equilibration was predicated on intensive utilization of Mexico's *comparative advantage* (to other nations) of the proximity of a reservoir of cheap, efficient labor to U.S. consumers of manufactured commodities. The pace of Mexico's first top-down revolution (Centeno 1994)—it became the U.S.'s second largest trading "partner"—made it "a paradigmatic example of liberalization" (Middlebrook and Zepeda 2003:3). Meanwhile, most Mexicans experienced the 1980s as unprecedented deprivations.

Exporting conglomerates with access to international capital and/or allied with foreign firms prospered spectacularly. By no means incidentally, market-freeing reforms deepened Mexico's chronic—and chronically group-specific—problems of insufficient modern sector jobs, world class inequality of wealth and income, and an oppressive, corrupt, seemingly endlessly "ruling party" (known as "the PRI"). Achieved then by inversions of advantages and disadvantages was that order of balancing Colin Hay (1995) describes as "a catastrophic equilibrium."

Disciplines and Antidisciplines of the Neoliberal Project

Though disguised by politicized statistics, evident by 1988 was that Mexico's development regime was "a self-defeating macroeconomic strategy" (Nadal 2003:65). Nevertheless, Presidents Carlos Salinas (1988–1994) and Ernesto Zedillo (1994–2000)—both Ivy League-educated in big economy matters—initiated and sustained the Decade of the New Economy. Each expanded policies that had (1) impoverished masses of Mexicans; (2) increased already grotesque income and opportunity inequities; (3) set real wages and the ratio of job creation below 1970 levels; (4) regressively affected already low levels of food consumption, health care, education, and other human and infrastructural essentials; and (5) hugely intensified the feminization of one of the world's most feminized labor forces (Judisman and Eternod 1995).

For a population that had already overused its managing to manage resources in surviving the "Debt Crisis" years, intensification did not simply raise the level of devastatingly wrong-way reforms, urgently required was the invention of a new synthesis of the dialectical pair de Certeau (1984) identifies as the "disciplines" and "antidisciplines" of "the practice of everyday life." Here two preeminent scholars of ordinary Mexico contextualize the terms of the new synthesis Mexicans invented between 1990 and 2000.

John Gledhill characterizes Mexico's neoliberal model as "a peculiarly disadvantageous form of integration into the global economy managed by a technocratic elite, backed by force when hegemony crumbled, on behalf of a transnational capitalist alliance that covers both the legal and illegal economy" (2005:388). While not minimizing the hardships of absorbing SAPs, Scott Cook stresses that accommodating the post-North American Free Trade Agreement (NAFTA) "neoliberal project" became the context of a "broad-based, multifaceted transformation of the Mexican economy, society and culture" (2004:1).

Disciplines Gledhill enumerates were highly visible in Tepoztlán during my fieldwork. Yet through it all, staying-on women coped by accommodating the neoliberal project: up to a point. Therefore, this research integrates a feminist standpoint into Cook's paradigmatic way of studying late modern Mexico: The "commodity culture[s]" Mexicans create in the interstices of dominant economy openings-and-closings must be the sites of twenty-first century research. We need then to know a great deal more about the concrete operations and costs involved in turning neoliberal disciplines into neoliberal antidisciplines.

As to disciplines, SAPs came into households as (1) loss of jobs in formerly protected regional industries; (2) sharply diminished enforcement of labor and environmental laws; (3) the removal of subsidies on 200 consumption necessities; (4) the transfer to households of welfare services and social income no longer supplied by the public or private sectors; and (5) supply-siding strategies that made working women's vulnerabilities central to trading networks.

About antidisciplines, as a direct result of social and economic policy decisions, women have been compelled to expand participation in a severely degraded labor market while assuming domestic obligations that now include replacing essential services, commodities, and social protections no longer subsidized by the state. Women as members of a distinct working class were ever more disproportionately challenged; yet also more creatively widening "loopholes" in "hegemonic hierarchies" (Bakhtin 1984). Recent statistics leave no doubt that the decade was "a "disaster" for most Mexican women (Griffith and Ickowitz 2003:583). But case studies from Tepoztlán indicate that it was also a time when women's work processes have never been more in movement.

Analytical Aims

Anthropologist June Nash (2005a) asserts that using women's experiences "cultivated in the immanent roles assigned to subordinates in the world system" as the primary empirical base results in analyses that differ substantively from studies that fail to document the *scientific* (reasonably verifiable) importance of gender to globalization. Expressed in the chapters ahead are my four analytical objectives: (1) Factually, I seek to show how women's adaptive work processes interconnect labor and capital, households and firms, and male and female work cultures. By doing so, I establish a longitudinal and task-specific framework for my second aim. (2) Politically, I intend to show how it comes about that the neoliberal project can have simultaneous negative and positive effects on women's ability to create and align social and material value. (3) Methodologically, I demonstrate that the practice approach of feminist studies can challenge and transform ahistorical theories of what constitutes productive work. (4) Critically, I reread through a feminist lens male/female dichotomies—such as modern/traditional, productive/reproductive, and global/local—that disadvantage women as users and makers of the global economy.

ORGANIZATION OF THE BOOK

I agree with Daniel Miller and Christopher Tilly (1996:5) that the idea of the economic extends "to all relationships between people and things irrespective of time and space." But to respond to priorities expressed by Tepoztecas in their practices and reiterated in conversations with them, I have narrowed the idea to the production-and-reproduction of material life.[4]

In chapter 1, I elaborate the "strange reciprocity" that conceptually frames this book. I discuss the Gender Mainstreaming Platform adopted at the Fourth UN World Conference on Women, the reasons cited for the failure to realize the goal, and the feminist project to use the material realities of women's experiences to achieve it. The final section describes the fieldwork that is the basis of this book.

Chapters 2 and 3 contextualize key discourses, many already introduced. Chapter 3 draws on the rich ethnography of Tepoztlán, integrating the still provocative ideas of economist Albert Hirschman and philosopher Mikhail Bakhtin to develop a trope I call "the market/fortress dialogic." Chapter 4 describes the environment and relates Tepoztlán's turbulent path into the twenty-first century to women's resolve to achieve gender equity.

Though still gender-biased, Mexican statistics are far more useful than when scholars recognized them as distortions disadvantaging women. Chapter 5 counterpoises formal statistics against my own work process-informed observations to establish gendering patterns.[5]

In matching caregiving tasks Tepoztecas classify as "housework" to specific constraints, chapter 6 proposes a gender-centered reevaluation of "labor flexibility," capital's pivotal supply siding strategy. Chapters 7 through 13 situate specific Tepoztecas in a wide range of local-global work processes. Chapter 7 describes three historically primary female occupations: domestic employment, shopkeeping, and school teaching. Chapters 8 through 11 show how women use and are used by exchanges in an ancient marketplace now fifteen minutes from Sam's Club.

"Tepoztlán is not for sale! Tepoztlán will not surrender!" This mantra introduces the subject of chapter 12: the feminization of the work of preserving community. The context is the No to the Golf Club resistance struggle, a social action well suited to examining Nash's (2005a:145) crucial question: Will women's increasingly "individualized and privatized" paths to political empowerment erode the "collective perspective" essential to emancipation? First, I narrate women's interventions in a struggle waged against a transnational elite intent on privatizing communal land. Next, I disaggregate women of the movement—women introduced in previous chapters in other work capacities—into distinct interest groups. Finally, I discuss the aftermath, balancing gains for women against a politically protected status quo.

The last chapter uses women's work processes to challenge gender biases integrated into dominant development theories and agendas. I conclude with a brief discussion of feminist theorized alternative approaches to transforming development policies and projects that have proven to be primary sources of gender inequality at work.

Chapter One

Mainstreaming Women's Work Processes: A Strange Reciprocity

> Of course, we identify problems to study, and these constitute beginnings or points of entry into complex processes. But it is the processes we must continually keep in mind.
>
> —Joan W. Scott, 1991

"Jobs! Jobs! Jobs! Decent jobs! That is what we women of Tepoztlán want!" (Doña Paola, homemaker-shopkeeper). This book describes, analyzes, and gives a history to women's work processes in Tepoztlán during the middle and late 1990s, a time when Tepoztecas were entering paid employment in unprecedented numbers. The surge corresponds to the increasingly radical implementation of development policies strongly privileging the production of goods for foreign exchange. While succeeding on its own market-opening terms—in the 1990s Mexico was Latin America's largest exporter—in Tepoztlán, as throughout Mexico, reforms massively failed to translate into "decent jobs": reasonably secure careers paying a wage commiserate with the material and social needs and priorities of the worker.

For example, in 1993, five Tepoztecas were earning slightly more than the US$2.25 per day official minimum salary in a factory/home operation assembling belts for The Gap. Classified as temporary workers, they were unprotected by Mexico's comparatively progressive but "systematically suppressed" labor laws (La Botz 1992:3). One day, an "On Strike" banner had been hung out, though the women were still working their usual eight-hour day. Before long, the Japanese contractor moved the operation to China.

Primary data in chapter 5 establishes that between 1990 and 2000, overwhelmingly, Tepoztecas were employed in the lowest paying, most sex typed, dead end, and unprotected jobs. But with male unemployment and underemployment and inflation rates at staggering highs, wives, mothers, and daughters, their households, and the pueblo place a high value on women's cash contributions, however meager and precarious. Yet at all levels—teachers (formal/quasi-regulated economy), housefront merchants (informal/unregulated economy), shop owners (self-employed)—participation was strengthening rather than decreasing occupational segregation by "sex/gender" (Rubin 1975), a job characteristic that universally and enduringly predicts work process discrimination against women (Anker 2001).

It was also a time of drastic reductions in government spending on social programs and small farming. Consequently, increased *economic activity*—officially counted activity—did not entail a reduction in women's responsibility for most types of the official *economic inactivity* of "chores for one's own household." To the contrary, Tepoztecas were compelled to intensify gratis caregiving to replace entitlements no longer coming from the public, from private sectors, or from the daily provisioning labor of men migrating out at a greatly intensified rate.

Empirically confirmed are the high material and social costs to women of combining paid and unpaid caregiving. Seldom estimated are the advantages accruing to public and private sector economies. Susan Himmelweit's (2000:52) flow chart demonstrates why the fragmentation of women's caregiving labor significantly enhances profits. "Care," whether paid or unpaid, Lee Badgett and Nancy Folbre (2001:336) remind us, "is costly" to governments, to industry, to households, and to the individuals giving it.

Tepoztlán has often been researched as prototypical of small-scale societies in transition from dependency on "backward"—traditional, low-tech, natural—resources to "forward"—modern, high-tech—resources. The work processes described ahead indicate that Free Market Tepoztlán is prototypical of Mexico's major job growth sector, the *shadow economy*: "income generating activities that are not regulated by the state in social environments where similar activities are regulated" (Castells and Portes 1989:12). First identified by Ivan Illich (1981) as an essential element in capital's "war" against subsistence activities, the diverse activities lumped as "homemaking" are by far the major category of Illich's "shadow work."[1]

A vast literature makes it impossible to deny that gender is integral "at every aspect of international capitalism" (Fernández-Kelly and Wolf 2001:1243). Gender inequality at work is enforced and resisted as it cuts across paid and unpaid worksites (Katz and Correia 1997). Articulating how job gendering constitutes and in turn is constituted by women's multilayered work processes is at once the problem, the point of entry to the problem, and the destination of this critical feminist study of women's ways of creating and aligning value and values.

WOMEN, GENDER, AND DEVELOPMENT

Experts in the field of women, gender, and development have long viewed wage earning in the competitive market as the most achievable route for closing gender gaps. Yet up to now, salaried employment though likely necessary for most women, has not proven sufficient to empower women as public and private decision-makers in an economy that necessitates inequitable employment.

Recent interdisciplinary studies reveal a high correlation between unequal gender systems, on the one hand, and control over discretionary income and assets[2] that can be converted to cash, on the other. I argue that the reason why women's economic activity has not eliminated gender inequality at work is the "strange reciprocity" explored in this study. In order to create and integrate social and material value, Tepoztecas are compelled to turn to their advantage the very ideologies and technologies that simultaneously make them central to capital's interests and strategies while constraining their access to resources—goods, services, information, prestige, accumulated wealth—that can be exchanged at prices set by and for powerful men.

Conflicting Logics of Reciprocity

Many influential theorists argue that to make headway against rampant twenty-first century injustices, we must integrate our knowledge systems. One major theoretical division that has had a profoundly negative impact on women's labor processes is that between the disciplines of economics and anthropology over the concept "reciprocity." An understanding of reciprocity as a willingness to sacrifice one's own "interests" (at least in the short run) to those of others is a common entry point. Paradoxically, consensus both illuminates ruptures between economics and anthropology and exposes shared gender biases.

The Economic Approach

Orthodox economists study how aggregates of empowered consumers allocate their resources among scarce commodities. They use variations of rational choice theory to explain the logic/illogic of reciprocity (to economists, "altruism") and all other exchange systems (Albelda 1997). Classical, neoclassical, and now neoliberal economics defines "rationality" as the ability of individuals to choose actions that will produce maximum benefit ("utility") to them, and assumes that transacting in an open market system is the most efficient means to "maximize utility." An individual's "preference" or "taste" for reciprocity, categorized as a nonmarket exchange system, is by definition not likely to be "optimizing" and thus not economically rational, except when deployed by a cunning and cogent individual to achieve a properly rational, that is, selfish, goal. Fundamental to all these assumptions is the ideology of organizationally separate production/reproduction domains.

The Anthropological Approach

In the 1940s, economic historian Karl Polanyi brought the term "reciprocity" into anthropology as one of three standard exchange modalities. (The other two are "redistribution" and "marketization.") However, most anthropological approaches are rooted in Marcel Mauss's 1925 literary masterpiece *The Gift*, which limits reciprocity, "gifting," as an exchange system to "primitive" societies. Mauss encompasses but extends beyond the technically economic to the political, the covetous, the religious, the sensual, and all other spheres of human interaction. Given that women perform a lot of work across all these spheres, so far, so good. But the bad news is that *The Gift* comes out of a chain of canonical carriers of superior/inferior binary propositions that have never served working women's interests well. This dichotomizing tradition descends from the Greeks to Descartes through the Enlightenment and Structuralism to Foucault, Lacan, and other post (now post-post) modernists and structuralists, and development theorists (Meier and Rauch 2005).

The two interpretations bring into view two seemingly irresolvable logics, represented by "Economic Man" and "Social Man" (*sic* is not appropriate in either case). At the same time, basic elements of both long tended to relegate women's work to the economically nonrational. However, feminist thinkers also advance contradictory logics along an axis of "difference": gender and sex, the self and the social, the queer and the straight (Moore 1994).

Feminist Approaches

Insisting on the interdependency of women's work and the dominant economy, by the 1960s, feminists were disputing both left and right stereotypes. Rejecting the passive victim ideology, Annette Weiner (1976) reinterpreted weaving as potentially empowering. Keeping a prestigious object is a way to gain status within one's group; but giving shows that the owner has "the right to power." Demonstrating that by gifting Oceanic women translate kinship ties into political authority, she linked gifting and *agency*: the power to realize a desired end. However, postculturalism soon supplanted Weiner's institutionalism. Stressing the fluidity rather than the continuity of social energy, to Marilyn Strathern, "To ask about the gender of the gift [is] to ask about the form that domination [and hence resistance] takes in [a particular society]" (1988:xii). The politics of difference displaced "red feminist" analyses of women's work processes as sites of political struggles (Ebert 1995).

Perceiving domestic and extradomestic labor as distinct orders of value creation, Genevieve Vaughan contends "a basic distinction" in their logics is required (2007:4). Drawing on Judith Butler (1993) to describe this distinction, Jenny Cameron (1997) argues that once gender is understood as "a constant, but never final, process of becoming," even such voluntary tasks as making sandwiches for a partner's lunchbox can be evaluated as "a social activity" that empowers rather than oppresses women. The *Women and the Politics of Place* (Harcourt and Escobar 2005) movement is an important new academic tool for destabilizing "hegemonic globalization discourse" by making space for "different" forms of transactions, labor, and enterprises (Gibson-Graham 2005:137). But to standpoint feminists, the core of the problem continues to be the failure to ground the logic of reciprocity in the realities of women's experiences, a distortion that leaves uncounted nonmarketed forms of women's work, estimated to contribute perhaps one-half of all economic value. Also expunged by definition is a vast amount of work women perform in the global market system, types of employment that conform to women's caregiving obligations and to the neoliberal project but that leave even fulltime salaried women economically dependent.

Up to now, most feminist interpretations have proven to be to some extent valid (or at least not falsifiable); but none has been sufficient to erase gender inequities in an economy that punishes women for performing and compounding paid and unpaid caring labor. An economic system that requires women's combinations of unpaid and underpaid labor in order to reproduce the system requires a new logic of reciprocity. With Carla Freeman (2001:1025), I argue that while contemporary feminists must continue to stress "the realm of culture and meaning," to specify the significance of gender to "globalizing modes of consumption and production" feminists must privilege "the realm of labor and production." Only a materialist feminism that is cultural and a cultural feminism that is materialist can challenge the explicitly and implicitly gendered policies and programs by opening them to women's transnationalized arts of using an economic system loaded against them.

Cross-pollinating Feminisms

To be sure, there are now multiple feminisms rather than feminism (Redclift 1997:223). Yet feminists do fundamentally share a belief that the work women perform as producer-reproducers of the processes that make an economy possible is at once the cause and the effect of their domain-radiating subordination. Clearly, we stand to gain methodological and analytical value from a cross-pollination of feminist anthropology and feminist economics.

So far, while many feminist economists have embraced the practice approach of feminist anthropology few anthropologists have taken advantage of the fine-grained science coming out of feminist economics. This book aims to integrate the two (and other) innovative knowledge systems in order to promote mainstreaming gender equity across all levels of economic development policies and projects.

Authenticity and Women's Work

Why do I call gender mainstreaming a "strange reciprocity," as does Larkin in his poem quoted on page v? As a critical thinker, I share his perception that inevitably, hegemonic hierarchies structure people's ways of exchanging needs and desires. Moreover, as "Power/knowledge" (Foucault 1980) systems dialectically reproduce each other, called up for questioning is the way we think about what Sartre (in *Nausea*) calls our *authenticity*, our real me: being in-itself, for-itself, and for-others. The issue has become increasingly central to the human sciences, as systematic controls over the "local" have become at once more overriding and more "global." However, as I interpret Larkin, he puts forward self-alienation as the inescapable outcome of living in and acting on the hegemonic world. To the contrary, I use Tepoztecan women's goal-oriented ways of positioning themselves in global economy constraints to prove that a woman's sense of herself is never exclusively a function of the systematic injustices she is compelled to accommodate. Women's work processes undermine the "globalization scripts of powerful men" (Gibson-Graham 1996) and hierarchical taken-for-granted dichotomies that subordinate them. However devalued, whether paid or unpaid, value/values creation makes women *authentic* economic agents-and-social actors. Late modern women—from Argentina's mothers of the disappeared to Long Island soccer moms—are *insisting* on making the personal political. There is, then, reason to hope that in time Irene Tinker (2006) will prove to be right that in the process of challenging they are making empowerment happen.

As Tepoztecas work against the grain of what Mexico's New Economy seems to have in mind for them to forge small economies for themselves, their families, and pueblo, they are also restructuring the big economies of the winners. Still, it remains in dispute whether increasingly unevenly burdened women can invent ways of inverting, "standing beside," openly "disagreeing" with, and even "rebelling" against (Bakhtin 1984:4) the "double edged process" of patriarchal globalization (D. Wolf 2001:1246). While I think (and statistics confirm) that many critiques go too far in equating private acts of resistance with victory over the system, the example of Tepoztecas does strongly suggest that women's antidisciplines can be a form of empowerment *within* the system. Heeding Lila Abu-Lughod (1993:204), I use resistance "as a *diagnostic* of power" while always keeping in mind Larkin's insight that resistance is never in a position of exteriority to power.

Recently Mercedes González de la Roche (2006:97–8) has redirected her extended inquiry of "the availability of *resources in poverty*—primarily, hard work—to the growing "*poverty of resources*." "The deep restructuring over the last two decades has severely undermined" Mexicans women's capacity to convert constraints into strategies. The key resource of women's power to labor to "achieve well-being and income levels commensurate with their needs" may already have been stretched to its limits. Achieving gender equity is then ever more urgent. It was this sense of urgency that delegates infused into the Beijing 1995 World Conference on Women and into the unanimous adoption of the Gender Mainstreaming (GM) Platform for Action.

MAINSTREAMING GENDER

Mainstreaming a gender perspective is "the process of assessing the implications for men and women of any planned action [and] a strategy for making women's as well as men's concerns and experiences an integral dimension of the design, implementation, monitoring, and evaluation of policies and programs in all political, economic, and social spheres so that women and men benefit equally. [The] ultimate goal is to achieve gender equality" (UN 1995).

Since its inception, the United Nations has been concerned with the well-being of women and children, the population most at risk of deprivations and violence (Jain 2005). The focus has been on alleviating women's poverty, long attributed to the inequitable organization of the society in which they lived. It was not until Beijing that the UN formally used the term "gender" to engage world-systems constraints subordinating women.

Key objectives laid out in the Platform leave no doubt that the substitution of "gender" for "women" was far from nominal. Rather, the use of gender signals the UN's acceptance of a defining feminist analytical shift in the 1980s. Peggy Antrobus (2004:147), an influential activist, states that the substitution was not only a way of emphasizing the asymmetrical division of labor as an outcome of social, political, and material rather than biological processes. An equally and ever more important intended reference was to the requirement to interlink women and men's inequalities.

Principal feminist objections to the term "women" were that it tended to freeze women in the low economic status role of consumption work and represent them as passive victims. Feminists wanted to press the argument that gender has many points of origin because constructed across all institutions: the family and the household, yes, but also the community, the government, the legal system, the church, the market. In addition, in the 1980s, it became clear that globalization scripts were "enticing or forcing women" (Harding 2000:243) into underpaid and unpaid labor. Further, Sandra Harding argues that women's current marginalized roles in development are a form of "dedevelopment," a condition she views as "necessary" for developing the underdeveloped "South" in ways that divert resources directly to men in the overdeveloped "North" (2000:244).

Beyond Beijing?

The subsequent widespread adoption of the GM project—even by donors as "long resistant to gender issues" as the World Bank (WB) (Jaquette and Summerfield 2006:17)—verifies that Beijing did succeed in making gender equity a cutting-edge concern across the massive development industry. However, despite explicit institutional guidelines requiring "attention to gender issues at the initial planning stage," the International Monetary Fund (IMF) and other donor agencies simply added gender into preexisting gender-blind policies (Radcliffe and others 2004:401). In fact, Umud Dalgic's study reveals pre-Beijing WB "developmentalist discourse" had already become "noticeably gendered" in response to the "gendered needs of the global market" (2007:27). The generic name for this shift in development policy is the variety of programs referred to as "microfinance."

Follow-up reports by 145 member states confirm that gender is prominently on the agendas of governmental and nongovernmental (NGO) agencies. Nevertheless, no major advances have come toward the International Labor Organization (ILO) goal of "nourishing decent and productive jobs" for women. Instead, in her "handbook for policy-makers and other stakeholders," Mariama Williams (2003) details the integration of gender biases into the "complex web of multilateral trading systems:" alliances that enforce conditions that marginalize economic women.

Luis Gutierrez (2007) summarizes the situation thusly. Positive changes have come, mainly in education and health. However, the "progress that has been made toward gender equity in women's empowerment is partial, has benefits and costs, and may not be sustainable." As to realizing GM goals by 2015, "Realistically, the obstacles would seem to outweigh the incentives."

"Beijing and beyond" conferences identify little correlation between GM programs—notably including the current magic bullet of microloans from financial institutions—and achieving sustainable equity. Some activists in the field view these loans as an efficient way of bringing capital-constrained women into the very economy that makes them materially dependent, thus activating a "dedevelopment" agenda that appears to be essential to international capitalism and has been so at least since the Industrial Revolution (and in Tepoztlán, since the Spanish Conquest).

We find, then, that on the one hand, the huge increase of women employed in the world market system has elevated women's salaried labor to a "macro imperative" (Loutfi 2001). On the other side, women's progress toward equal agency in the creation, distribution, and consumption of world marketable goods and services continues to be halting at best and even wrong way: in the developed world (Rubery 2005), the developing world (Spivak 2000), and the indigenous world (Keating 2004). In sum, a stream of cross-cultural evaluations confirms that gender equality continues to lag far behind the "ascendant rhetoric" of transformative change (Hirschmann 2006:71).

Enduring Problems Endure

Dishearteningly, the reasons that development manager/scholar David Hirschmann cites for the "notable scaling down" of mainstreaming reprise themes stated as long ago as Ester Boserup's 1970 catalyzing analysis of *Woman's Roles in Economic Development*. Like Boserup, Hirschmann stresses bureaucratic ineptitude in attributing failures to "patriarchal biases that create misperceptions" of the roles of men and women in development (2006:72). He notes that the "character and representation" of these biases have changed markedly, toward promoting enterprises for homemakers on the fringes of the global market. But these seemingly progressive changes make it all the more profoundly disturbing that decision-makers continue to approach the issue of decent jobs as "gender blind in orientation and gender neutral in effect" (M. Williams 2003:xiii).

To Benería, the "enduring problem" stems "from the way 'work' has been identified both in theory and in conventional statistics, as a paid economic activity linked to the market" (2001:87). Randy Albelda (1997:105) deconstructs the "antifeminism" of analyses that brought women's work into orthodox economics. Gender gap evidence from environments as different as, say, Bangladesh and Sweden confirms participation in an economy structured by gender "cannot transcend power relations." "Empowerment," argues post-development theorists Parpart, Rai, and Staudt (2004: 4) "requires attention to the specificities of struggle over time and place."

Listening and Learning from Enlightened Women

Again reprising Boserup, Hirschmann (quoting Goetz 2001:285) specifies the fundamental problem thusly: "'Claims to know' which are based on women's experiences have not carried much weight." Certainly, the standpoint canon that women's practical experiences of resistance to repression and oppression constitute authoritative knowledge is often contested, and not only by the heavily male-dominated development establishment. Even some vanguard theorists reject feminist standpoint epistemology as more politics than positivist science (Walby 2001).

In contrast, June Nash (2005a:145–46) accords women's perspectives "the significance of a new enlightenment, overtaking the seventeenth-century Enlightenment." She asserts—as do I—that "women's everyday experiences [must be] examined, extrapolated, and extolled" as "the fount" of humanist insights and the "touchstone of reality." And she identifies the task remaining—as do I—as incorporating "these understandings in collective action."

As women insert themselves into global trading networks they open up new opportunities within "new relations of inequality, subordination, and exploitation" (Feldman 1992:5). Thus, Mexicanist Sylvia Chant concludes: "governments, NGOs, and international agencies might be best advised to [support] bids for empowerment that emerge from women themselves" (2006:105). Practitioners confronting mainstreaming in the field stress that the starting point of all projects must be the "first-do-no-harm" imperative of activist feminism. "We must pay close attention to the contradictions, problems, and complicating moments of local encounters with processes of globalized capitalism" (Keating 2004:427).

THE FIELDWORK BASIS OF THIS BOOK

Fittingly, then, this study is based on participant observation, anthropology's "paradigmatic way of studying the social world" (Burawoy 1991:3). The participant observation incorporated into this book began during the years I worked alongside women of the developed and developing world, first in the for-profit economy and later as an unpaid advisor to women's enterprises and cooperatives. In the U.S., Kenya, Taiwan, India, Japan, the Philippines, British Columbia, France, and other venues, my colleagues ranged from superrich and superpoor consumers to corporate executives, the self-employed, global factory workers, and homeworkers juggling childcare with tying strings on Christmas ornaments.

From all this work, the practical lesson that I took with me when I began to study women's work processes from the anthropology of work perspective was "For women, unlike men, the question of gender is never absent" (Elson and Pearson 1986:77). Despite formidable degrees of difference in access to productive resources, at no point did even the most empowered or capable women I knew escape the rules, regulations, and coercive mechanisms of gender. Indeed, it was because I saw that gender affected the whole array of production-reproduction variables that I became deeply conscious of the formal structure of women's work processes: that input/output logic economists identify as "rationality."

Participant observation in Tepoztlán began in June 1993. Most of the fieldwork described in this book came from two visits in 1994, three in 1995, and several more between 1996 and 1998. I resided in Tepoztlán at different times of the year in order to be present at a range of special events. During the early period, my objective was to find my way around women's new worlds of work. As I located actors in specific sectors, I was also making contacts that enabled me to conduct participant observation in homes, schools, and commercial enterprises. Of course, I tried to be as peripheral as possible. However, a significantly revealing fact is that the women included in this book welcomed having their economic contributions taken seriously, as they themselves did. For most, it was the first time.

My first local contacts were made through feminist activists I met in Cuernavaca, where I had earlier conducted fieldwork with a group of craft producers. This was how I came to rent a room in the Revolution Avenue bungalow of Doña Juana, age seventy-five, a woman greatly esteemed in the community. Long a widow, Doña Juana combined part-time market and street economy vending with daily janitorial work in the nearby clinic-residence of perhaps the most prominent family in Tepoztlán and the only municipio woman holding a formal political office. Members of this family actively cooperated with my project. With these endorsements, I soon integrated into many work sites.

In 1994, I met Claudine, a twenty-two-year-old woman then studying to earn a certificate to teach English at the elementary-school level. Her mother, Doña Julia, long separated from Claudine's father worked fulltime as a cook at a hotel. I became very close to her mother, her younger sister (still attending the local middle school), and her slightly older sister, a nurse. This sister married in 1995 and soon had two children; the relationship gave me insights into the lifestyle of a young family trying to integrate the various aspects of their lives as they struggle to secure a middle-class lifestyle. Each of Claudine's parents has nine brothers and sisters, all have families, and all live in Tepoztlán. These two large, socially diverse extended families opened their homes to me. I shared ceremonies and rituals as well as daily life with six and sometimes seven generations of stakeholders. I was able to do in-depth interviews with twenty of the female members of these two families. "What is it they want?" asked a mystified uncle interviewed in his wife's shoe store. He was one of the male family members who cooperated in my project. During most of my fieldwork, I was a guest in Claudine's home.

"My house is your house" came true for me. (Neighbors and family knew me as a friend because they knew that Julia had given me a door key.) Thus, I began to move with relative ease into many sectors of Tepoztecan society. Integration, as it turned out, was especially problematic at this time because of the political turbulence, the No to the Golf Club struggle that erupted at the end of 1994. Tepoztecans were justifiably wary of outsiders gazing, making notes, recording interviews, and taking photographs.

Another rewarding contact was with Doña Carmen, age forty-two. In addition to her morning newspaper route, she ran the local office of a cultural center sponsored by the state, and tended to the needs of the many social scientists coming and going. Although a "foreigner"—she was born in Mexico City—she seemed to know the intimate history of almost everyone, including the enclaved residents of the villas encroaching across the municipio. She also assisted me in enlisting a pool of qualified assistants for various projects. As political insiders, she and her journalist husband helped me to sort out entangled local politics.

In 1996, I began to work closely with Margarita, age twenty-two, and her household of three children, a husband, and ninety-something grandmother who shared with me her nonstandard views about being a Tepoztecan wife and mother. Association with this family informed my work in many ways by giving me the chance to study an upwardly striving household and a homemaker resolved to establish herself in the waged economy.

Rita's grandmother, Claudine's three grandparents, and other senior residents permitted me to tape-record accounts of the well-remembered village in Mexico. I asked them to describe their daily lives; this resulted in a great deal of information about the Revolution and descriptions of material possessions. These accounts contradicted earlier accounts of rejection by the folk of the modern and very high incidence of grinding poverty.

Of course, members of the real family made famous by anthropologist Oscar Lewis as the "Martínez" family were especially valued interviewees. A few people who worked with a well known but seldom read Lewis still live in Tepoztlán. I encountered few people who had ever even heard of Robert Redfield, the first modern anthropologist of Tepoztlán. Then, startlingly, a market merchant I was interviewing turned out to have worked for the family. ("We called him 'the man who is always taking notes,'" the child nursemaid turned ninety-four told me.) In particular, Redfield's meticulous attention to cyclical *fiestas* made him a valuable source for calibrating continuity in participation patterns. I discovered that rituals were almost uncannily as he describes them; this made contextual changes even more interesting. It is important to point out that a wife and child accompanied both Lewis and Redfield. The stability of the community enabled me to retrace their historical footsteps, paths that made me aware of the pivotal (still inadequately acknowledged) research roles played by Margaret Park Redfield and Ruth Lewis.

Highly informative were exhibits, books, papers, and photographs in private collections, libraries, and museums and, of course, the extensive published and unpublished literature on this intensively studied municipality. Visits to Prehispanic and Colonial period sites helped to situate formative processes in time and space. I worked in the Cuernavaca census bureau and attended a number of lectures, seminars, and conferences.

El Centro, the downtown quadrant, was the spatial focal point of the study. Because of my own extensive career, I knew my way around developing-world markets overwhelmingly staffed by women I could engage as living links to the global economy of which I had been an active part. As a public space, it was open ethnographic territory where I observed and participated in a range of transactions, including working in various stalls. In 1994, I prepared a detailed map that reflected the spatial, temporal, and historical use patterns across the quadrant. I used the map to grid my research in the central district.

I spent many hours observing and interacting with merchants, suppliers, and consumers. A series of questionnaires emerged that were the basis for structured interviews with more than fifty vendors. Some interviews were during business hours, since one object was to isolate gender as a transactional factor. I also conducted interviews in a range of other commercial and professional sites. Usually, an assistant (paid) who wrote down what interviewees had to say accompanied me. I also surveyed all classes of consumers. While the intimate culture of households is not a focus of this study, I did research households as work sites. Daily interactions clarified commodities exchanged and illuminated modes and relations of exchange.

To accumulate different perspectives on a range of issues, I administered a number of other surveys. Two that duplicated studies done by a Mexico City newspaper, one with "mothers" and the other with "young people," allowed me to compare Tepoztecans' views to those of Mexico City residents. Interviews with men focused on interpretations of gender-appropriate work. Other interviews centered on intra-household labor divisions. I also investigated interactions in the *tanda,* the rotating credit association. Survey assistants represented a wide demographic range.

Hands-on participation was of paramount importance. I worked in several market businesses (without pay, of course) and went on buying trips with merchants to regional market centers. I followed several commodity chains and production/distribution circuits. I visited schools and participated in and/or closely observed mobile commerce, home sited work, and workshop operations. I interacted with office workers, nurses, a librarian, volunteers, transportation and hospitality sector workers, and so on and on. I closely observed women's fiesta activities as work sites. (Often women gathered in house gardens to prepare delicacies particular to each fiesta.) Other community events I joined by invitation included a health-conscious cooking class for brides, seminars sponsored by an environmental group, and (sporadically) an exercise class. I often worked in the public library, the setting for many after-school activities; enchantingly including Friday afternoon guitar lessons given by one of Tepoztlán's fabled balladeers.

Because the No to the Golf Club protest movement took place during my fieldwork, I became closely involved in the complex rituals of Tepoztecan politics. By invitation, I observed several strategy-setting meetings and attended two highly charged encounters with government officials leading the campaign to impose this multimillion-dollar private commercial development. In addition to following newspapers, magazines, special publications, and television, I conversed with local political leaders and went on mass marches to Cuernavaca and Mexico City. (I had to be very careful not to seem to be participating in demonstrations, which were under close official scrutiny and from which foreigners are officially barred.) I interviewed political analysts, reporters, human rights officials, movement leaders, the parish priest, and two Golf Club supporters shunned by the community. A close observer kept a daily Golf Club journal for me throughout the movement. Along with 2000 and beyond censuses, I have integrated several post-2000 visits into the research.

Chapter Two

Articulating Tepoztecas into Commodity Culture(s)

> An *articulation* [is] an active insertion of a practice into a set of contextual relations that determine the identity and effects of both the texts and the contexts [and] will always have political consequences.
>
> —Lawrence Grossberg, 1988

By the late 1960s, feminists in the field had begun to isolate "women's work"—doing almost anything anytime for little or no pay (Mies 1986)—as the "central operating premise," indeed, "the very basis" (J. Smith 1984:309) of the fastest growing sectors of the "new international division of labor" (Froebel and others 1978). Commodity by commodity, academics and activists "challenged the dominant scripts of globalization by elaborating the gendered assumptions and effects that are generally invisible in mainstream theories" (Bergeron 2006:991).

"THIS TIME SHOW US LIKE WE REALLY ARE!"

Into the 1990s, two competing theses continued to frame studies of women's roles in Latin American development. Broadly, the division was between right (neoclassical/neoliberal) and left (neomarxist/postmarxist) feminists. The integration/equalization thesis holds that women gain empowerment when gainfully employed in the dominant economy. The marginalization/exploitation thesis holds that low-status jobs solidify women's subordination. However, as transnational capital's reliance on women's systematically subordinated labor intensified, neither thesis seemed to articulate with women's material realities. Increasingly, theorists of women's work joined

Diane Elson and Ruth Pearson to insist, "It is precisely the relations through which women are 'integrated' into the development process that need to be problematized and investigated" (1986:67). As to these relations, "the set of social arrangements characterizing women's lives as nonwage workers are incorporated into the very ground of the economy," states world-systems theorist Joan Smith (1984:309).

Innovative Latin American studies focused on "the gendered character of the work process at all levels" (del Alba Acevedo 1995:82; Cooper et al. 1989). Much of this "nascent post-binary" (Redclift 1997) literature carried forward another message contained in Elson and Pearson's groundbreaking study. The material realities on transnational "factory floors" present not only new problems but also new possibilities for turning constraints into emancipatory strategies. Even feminists dismayed by the failure of the huge increase in women's participation in salaried employment to result in transformative changes judge "any connection with the world of employment" a much better option than "redundancy" (Fernández-Kelly and Wolf 2001:1248). Julie Nelson cautions colleagues that they must differentiate between production processes that afford many women options they would not otherwise have and "the overzealous marketization, corporate irresponsibility, and abuses of economic power that we see in the world around us" (2006:1067). The archive of feminist studies makes it clear that we must focus on the gendering of women's work processes if we are to "bring home the lived realities of these mammoth forces" (Freeman 2001:1010; Chiñas 1993; Alba and Cabrera 1994).

"Alternative policies" must be grounded in the material realities of women's experiences of transacting "'development,'" states Benería (2003:ix). This book articulates the problems and possibilities and Tepoztecan women's readings of them as *transactions*—"changes in the status of a good or service between people" (Plattner 1994:209)"—during a period when devastating crises merged into sporadic recoveries.

By the end of 1994, the municipio faced the reinforcing catastrophes of its deepest modern depression and perhaps the greatest post-Conquest threat ever to the rights of stakeholders to control the allocation and development of its resource bases. The combination could not but intensify women's "triple challenges" (Moser 1993): (1) participation in a highly degraded labor market, (2) increasing claims on their unpaid labor, and (3) frontline engagement in a hazardous resistance struggle that *had* to be won. Contradictory mixes of socialization made aligning these challenges (barely) possible and extremely costly. "Multilateral and resilient" techniques of managing to manage that enable women to more clearly assess "global issues" (Nash 2005a:144), had never been more critical to the survival of the basic institutions of the pueblo, nor more challenged.

"This time show us like we really are!" This mandate from homemaker and market merchant Doña Clara acknowledges that Tepoztlán is very likely the most researched community in Mexico—and that there is much understanding of women's work processes yet to achieve. The definition of *productivity* as output per unit only when it flows into the macroeconomy still disconnects much of women's paid as well as unpaid work from what is officially counted as *economic*: the particular types of labor men perform to earn (at least in theory) a "family wage" (a wage sufficient to provide a family of five with the basic necessities). Plotting Tepoztecas into their multistructured production systems is a starting point for showing them as they really are.

Ordinary Commodity Cultures

In Mexican literature, the "supplementary" work women, particularly women of the provinces, perform has generally been outside positivist scientific analyses altogether. In reality, as the male breadwinner became Helen Safa's (1995) ever more "mythic" patriarch, ever more capital-intensive ways for gaining a family wage were ever more family-unit intensive—an adaptation to turbulence that in the context of neoliberal capitalism more profoundly than ever before conditions the supply-of-and-demand-for specific forms of women's labor. The globalization of the production and consumption economies pushed and pulled Tepoztecas into such generally low-yielding specializations as undercapitalized self-employment, processing of often rapidly perishable commodities, artisan-scale manufacturing, third-tier distributive trades, and especially the under and unremunerated person-to-person delivery of public and personal services.

In place and industry-specific studies broken down by ethnicity, economic class, and gender, economic anthropologist Scott Cook has set a research path for moving past entrenched dichotomies. "Culture is ordinary": extending Raymond Williams's influential slogan to the articulation of the cultural and the material, Cook demonstrates that to develop and survive, ordinary Mexicans must use the structures that distance them from their "historical economies." Stressing that NAFTA has hugely intensified this dependency, he insists that we integrate them into the dominant economic order. Disarticulating "indigenous" Mexicans out of "exogenous forces and experiences" disguises the reality that capitalism and class stratification are not "external disturbances" (Cook 2004:206).

In any exchange system, commodities are things that "must be not only produced materially, but also culturally marked as being a certain kind of thing" (Kopytoff 1992:64). Indeed, "things" have never been more "heavily semiotic" than in postindustrial commodity cultures (Lash and Urry

1994:193). Then, the localization of global disruptions is where "cooperative units of ordinary Mexicans imagine, produce, exchange, allocate, and consume true commodity cultures" (Cook 2004:141).

Regarding the econometrically unruly category of *social reproductive* labor—the private labor that produces goods and services that maintain individuals and society as a whole—Cook argues that "the process of social reproduction, which is culturally informed, and class and gender differentiated" (2004:141) must be given equal emphasis with the process of production. Since the disturbances of late capitalism mean that much reproductive work requires using the market, problematizing the production of things with use value requires, in David Shumway's words, acknowledging that "the use-value of such goods cannot be reduced to this function" (2000:14). Commodity cultures as a whole way of life that are also a way of struggle are the setting of this research.

Then to show Tepoztecas as they really are, I try to integrate (1) the political-economic alliance in control of the tradable resources of the global commons: the *state* and the *firm*; (2) the family/household as a core institution and its gender, age, and dependency-graded labor force: the *hogar*; (3) the people, the place, and their ways of producing and reproducing value and values: the *pueblo*; and (4) the multiform tasks a situated woman performs as a social actor and an economic agent: *women's work*.

Doing (Almost) Everything Right

With the 1990s theoretical turn to the "participatory strategy" (Maguire 1996), economists began to take women's employment more seriously. Yet many projects designed to empower women through participation in the fringes of the global market are still being carried out in the patriarchal tradition of a steadfastly "androcentric" and production-centric development industry (Benería 2003). Very much a case in point is Mexico's liberalization model, which has proven to be intensely regressive when measured by private consumption levels (Nadal 2003:58).

Discouragingly, by the widely accepted criteria of human capital theory—the market value of a person's capacity to produce tradables is the measure of what developmentalists call "human capital" (T. Schultz 1995)—many Mexican women including Tepoztecas have done most things right. They have increasingly entered wage labor in dominant economy growth sectors; they have become risk-taking entrepreneurs; they have lowered their fertility levels; they are spending more years in school; they are healthier, less likely to die from preventative and reversible diseases (except for "women's diseases"); and they have intensified their grassroots and formal political and human rights activism. Yet Mexican women's economic position deteriorated as they became more concentrated in low-wage sectors and low-wage jobs within sectors. Not women's human capital but their social capital, often a function of activating fictions, is driving the post-Beijing gender and development discourse. In sum, given the overexposure of Tepoztecas as producer-reproducers, Mexico's New Economy could not but intensify the inequalities sustained by the work women perform.

FORMATIVE PROCESSES

This section contextualizes gendering at work as those "conditions of existence (but also of coexistence, maintenance, and disappearance) in a given discursive division" Foucault excavates as "formative processes" (1993:38).

Work Processes

Two decades ago, Veronica Beechey criticized contemporary feminists' "endeavors to constitute our concepts with little reference to concrete evidence about women's employment" (1986:130–31). Recently, Patricia Fernández-Kelly (2001) reiterated Beechey. Even though gender is apparent in every aspect of international capitalism, studies of globalization continue to pay "scant attention" to material connections between women's work processes and "the varying effects of 'structural adjustment policies'" (1243). In the centering term "work process" I incorporate the task actually performed; the techniques, resources, and capabilities a worker enlists; and the value that the worker, her transaction partners, and the dominant economy accord to the producer and the product: a thing, a place, a person, a concept. As in the old economy that Tepoztecas are intent on moving beyond, value creation in Tepoztlán's New Economy continues to be structured hierarchically from the outside in and the inside out by gender.

Gender Processes

Like a work process, a "gender process" too is an entire system of power, knowledge, and desire: gender is everywhere, in everything. However, in the work process framework of this study I use "gender" mostly to refer to the social and material constructions of women's individual and collective inequalities at *work*: "the purposeful exertion of physical and mental faculties to accomplish something" (Gamst 1984:58).

"The paradox of gender," states Judith Lorber, "is that it must be made visible" (1995:82). Gender cannot be reduced to or read off from biology, class, or any dynamic. Because it is a "complex process," gender must be disaggregated as it articulates with "multiple other independent processes interacting with each other in a great many ways" (Waldrop 1992:11). Case studies indicate that as an analytical tool, gender does not "merely identify" structures of inequality, "it actually *constitutes* them" (Oyewumi 1998:1059). The issue is then to articulate gender as a formative process into "interplays of transmission, resumptions, disappearance, and repetitions" (Foucault 1992:5).

Disaggregating Global Feminization through Flexible Labor

To labor scholar Guy Standing, the convergence of international capital's new "politico-economic strategy" with "the erosion of labor regulations" and the massive entrance of women into the labor force was "no coincidence" (1989:1077). With the phrase "global feminization through flexible labor," he disaggregated women, dialectical contradictions of this new geohistorical gender and development relationship. Feminists have demonstrated that on the one hand, multitasking women's vulnerabilities are central to capital's supply siding strategy: reducing operating costs while increasing productivity and widening market penetration. At the same time, adjustments that hugely increase both their need for cash and their responsibility for gratis caregiving limit women's access to both *tradables*—commodities exchangeable at prices set in world labor, product, and financial markets—and *nontradables*—goods and services that are not usually profitably exchangeable in the market.

Standing's concern was with the patterned overuse of Third World women in border-crossing industrial world firms in search of cheap, nimble-fingered, and compliant labor forces. My concern is with the unremunerated, informal, and quasiformal tasks that dominate women's multifaceted work processes. My "factory floors" are social realms and local labor markets: spaces where "the understandings of capitalist firms" assimilate with "the needs and understandings of a particular community" (J. Collins 1995:185).

What are the consequences to Mexican women in general and Tepoztecas in particular of the "new and unprecedented way [that] labor processes and relations are on the move, distant and *almost* perfectly concealed" (Rothstein 2000:6). This section disaggregates the terms of this new symbiosis of gender inequality and capitalist development.

Globalization

By now, it is clear that globalization happens to different people in differentiated forms and combinations—and happens not only to people and labor processes but also to neighbors and neighborhoods, to slow and fast food, to rivers and mountains, and, so on and on. In Mexico, regionally and household specific complexes are anchored in the ruling ideas of privileged classes of men with a deep, deeply gendered history.

The neoliberal wave of globalization involves the reorganization of "the structures of companies and business behavior" (Smeets 1999:11). Coalitions of supranational and national firms outsource value-adding stages of production to individuals and groups of individuals in the borderlands and the badlands of capitalism. As well, footloose firms aim to neo-colonize spaces where two paralleling shifts of restructured capitalism merge. Contrasting the old centered economy and the new decentered economy, John Myles (1990:276) identifies de- or post-industrialized capitalism as (1) limited growth at the top and massive growth at the bottom of the wage scale accompanied by an accelerating decline in the middle; and (2) the incorporation in unprecedented numbers of new demographic classes of women into the labor market mainly at unprotected, low-status levels of the service sector. These *breaks* within but not *from* capitalism per se—capitalism as it really is—are also the sites where women must open loopholes.

Feminization

The concept of feminization has been used to analyze women's absolute and comparative (to men) inequality at work since Diane Pearce (1978) demonstrated that the work women perform makes them "poor in their own right." That feminization turned out to be "*produced* by capitalist economic and political policies and practices" (Morgan 2002:4) in combination with work site-specific norms and priorities set a new research horizon. As global capitalism spread into all 'underdeveloped' arenas, feminist theorists targeted the reorganization of gender at work at the intersecting levels of macro-agent/micro-agent and male/female divisions. Occupation and task-level studies of labor forces have revealed that the dramatic increase in women's gainful employment is only one of multiple job-gendering contexts. Consequently, in this study, "feminization" refers to reinforcing complexes of the social, political, and economic institutions that consubstantially integrate and subordinate a woman within a specific workspace. But to standpoint feminists, feminization must also emphasize *breaks* in the uneven division of labor and assets that occur as knowing women purposefully manipulate the New Economy to transform their own and their families' existence and ultimately, uneven capitalism per se.

Flexibility

Gender is highly visible in a primary carrier of feminization: flexibility. Flexible techniques that diminish fixed costs and that enable producers to respond rapidly to changes in demand—whether genuine technological advances or buying pattern shifts—drive the changes. Due to factors such as training, steady employment even during slack periods, and benefits, labor used to be the highest relatively fixed production cost. To achieve functional flexibility, firms implement job-displacing technical innovations and status-reducing working conditions. A dramatic increase in part-time labor, "the plunder of wages by capital and labor unions" (Roman and Velasco Arregui 1997:103), the commercialization of social services, the war against subsistence, and the flood of desperate homemakers into the labor market that has created intense competition for scare jobs: these flexibilities are the control systems of Mexico's variant of global capitalism.

Problematic is that profit enhancing strategies such as impoverishing wages, outsourcing, and temporary jobs translate into forms of employment that enable dependent homemakers to assimilate increasingly disparate production-reproduction obligations. In short, by manipulating reorganized capitalism per se, pragmatic women have been active, indeed zealous, participants in feminizing specific task and occupation categories.

Once constituted as a dependent homemaker (or even a potential homemaker), women, especially women of the periphery, become the "optimal labor force" (Mies 1986) whether in or out of the waged labor force. We encounter these *transaction costs*—costs incurred when operating in a too free market—in asset-constrained women's techniques for responding to new mechanisms of control over their power to labor: in the intense competition for jobs in the lowest paying, more insecure service sectors; in undercapitalized self-employment; and a heightened reliance on self-provisioning and gratis caregiving. Women accept the new terms of the "mutual accommodation between patriarchy and capitalism" (Hartmann 1979) to compensate for daily uncertainties and for wages that are insufficient to reproduce a family and often even the worker herself.

Caring Labor

As to neo-liberalized caring labor, the outsourcing of human services to private suppliers has been the main thrust of Mexico's "counterrevolutionary" social reforms (Laurell 2003:320). Now unpaid and underpaid women are the primary suppliers of care. As Nancy Folbre argues, because caring, "whether for love or for money," implies "responsibility" and solidarity, it "threatens the underpinnings of neoclassical economics: rational Economic Man maximizes a utility function that does not include consideration for any other person's welfare" (1995:74). Fetishized as "consumer preferences," orthodox theory all but ignores the ways that caregiving interacts with gender, age, ethnicity, and preexisting advantages to distort all market and development processes.

That commonly female-typed occupations are the most rapidly increasing and lowest paid employment category *within* the dominant economy means that gendering must be disaggregated not as an outcome of "differential growth or decline" but as an integral aspect of "new techniques of capital accumulation and managerial control over production" (Massey 1995:10). Then to show Tepoztecas as they really are, I focus on the work processes women activate to create social and material value in an economy in which significant gender constraints and strategies are infused into every aspect of the production-reproduction system.

Chapter Three

Local-Global Constellations

> [T]he new constellation formed by the coming together of global integration and apparent cultural fragmentation is the contemporary horizon against which the project of contemporary feminist must be rethought.
>
> —Seyla Benhabib, 1999

This chapter explores anthropological concepts that have been used to describe Tepoztlán. The chapter introduces a prototypical member of the New Economy working class: a Tepoztecan homemaker. Using the testimony of homemaker-market merchant Doña Luz, I consider the ways her resistance strategies entrap her in reordered regimes of dominance. I begin with a consideration of two key ethnographies that allow us to observe Tepoztecas and anthropologists at work during formative years.

A CONTROVERSIAL BACKGROUND

In 1926, anthropologist Robert Redfield had entered the starkly beautiful mountain community of Tepoztlán on horseback, aiming to salvage from the rising tide of modernization the customs, practices, and "mores" of an ancient central Mexican "folk." In 1943, anthropologist Oscar Lewis arrived by automobile, aiming to extend Redfield's (1930) by now iconic "small community study" to a twentieth-century village-world-system profoundly in transition.

"Upon my arrival in the village it seemed in many respects as Redfield had described it" (1951:xi). But if little had changed at its still "impoverished" surface, Lewis had caught citizens in the midst of accommodating a chain of great and everyday transformations.

During the years between, the municipio population had increased from around 4,000 to more than 7,000, and there had been three decisive changes. (1) The Mexican government had implemented constitutional reforms that endowed stakeholders with collective control over the resources for producing a livelihood and for reproducing their unique sociocultural patrimony. (2) Mechanized grinding mills were reducing by hours the labor countless generations of Tepoztecas had devoted each day to transforming corn into the staple food of *tortillas*. (3) In 1936, the first-ever highway had opened. Seventeen kilometers of asphalt christened the "Pathway to Progress," connected the municipio and Cuernavaca, the capital of the state of Morelos, and a central Mexican hub. The new bus line reduced to some twenty jolting minutes the arduous first stage of the expedition across the Sierra of Tepoztlán to world markets.

Clearly, these adjustments were structural enough to create significant differences in the production-reproduction systems the two anthropologists encountered. However, almost at once Lewis detected glaring errors in Redfield's "facts" that could not be explained away by interim revisions. To a discipline obsessed with establishing itself as a falsifiable science, the misrepresentations were of considerable moment because they fit worrisomely neatly with the theoretical agenda that doctoral candidate Redfield had gone to the field to validate.

Frames

To Wittgenstein, "all seeing is relative to 'frames'—to presuppositions, assumptions, and values" (Jones 1975:393). Two ways of seeing that into the twenty-first century have dominated Mexican economic models frame Redfield and Lewis' small community monographs. As structuralist thinkers, both men studied institutions, social structures, to determine how the parts functioned to maintain the social whole and the likely result of ruptures in institutionalized relations. Redfield adopted a liberal, later "modernization," stance. His way of seeing evidenced the Chicago School of Sociology approach of setting up equivalences of unlike phenomena in order to contrast two types of "will": Schopenhauer's "Natural will" of country folks and "Rational will" of city dwellers. (See Wilcox 2006.)

As a Marxist-Leninist, Lewis picked-up on nascent Latin American "dependency theory" that views "the violent condition of the underdevelopment" of the periphery as a plotted outcome of the "overdevelopment" of the colonizing core (Chilcote and Edelstein 1985). As a Marxist, he took class conflict as the driving force of social formation. As a Leninist, he cast off Marx's disparaging "sack-of-potatoes" interpretation of "peasant" economies. Within their own precapitalist terms, rural workers were rational. Ironically, this rationality doomed them to transition into a bleak capitalism that required their dedevelopment.

Redfield's Frame

"While the villagers live by agriculture, the village lives by trade. It is essentially a market" (1972:19). In these words, Redfield begins to construct an evolutionary primitive-modern progression that would become "one of the main pillars" (Kearny 1996:50) of modernization theory and in the 1980s, of Mexico's fiercely neoliberal project.

By representing the small, periurban town of Tepoztlán as an all but idyllic and all but self-sufficient farming village, he could explore the "natural" division of labor by sex, age, and prestige as an expression of what was necessary for cohesive exchange in a "primitive little community" (Redfield 1961). Thereby, he rationalized patriarchy and other 'traditional' systems of control. Like his model nineteenth-century theorists (notably Toennies), he vacillated between admiring the common sense ways of the folk and exposing tradition as an obstacle to progress. Contrasting the integrating norms and rhythms—the "cradle to grave arrangements" (1961:4)—of a landed peasantry with the entrepreneurial ways of an urban, industrialized society, he identified low-productivity systems that would have to be reorganized by "rationally-willed" outsiders if the folk were to progress to the core modernization goals: technological control over nature and the accumulation by enterprising individuals of financial and human capital. Women's work processes he put forward as a textbook example of the natural, the pre-modern.

Lewis's Frame

"The world in which Tepoztecans live is filled with hostile forces and punishing figures which must be propitiated" (Lewis 1960:86). In his restudy, Lewis presented the mountain-walled municipio as a "fortress" where citizens contrived physical and structural survival in the treacherous world of the Mexican folk, but at great cost to communitarian and interpersonal relations.

Classic Marx/Engels patriarchy—the power that men who control the means of producing and allocating a livelihood have over the labor of dependent women, children, and other men—constituted both the punishing and the propitiating force. He judged Tepoztlán a quasi-feudal rather than an economic class-differentiated society. Households, on the other hand, he presented as economic-class divided by unequal access to productive resources. As what constituted a tradable agricultural or commercial resource modernized, and as the historically subordinated found paying jobs in non-family enterprises, the material sources of patriarchal power seemed to be in jeopardy. In contrast to Redfield's (on balance) optimistic view of competitive capitalism, like Marx, Lewis believed that the spread of individuating capitalism would in the short run increase rather than decrease internal and external schisms.

Readily discovering that Tepoztlán had never been agriculturally self-sufficient and that well over half the households still did not have access to private farming land, Lewis promptly demolished Redfield's foundational "ownership society" premise. Chronic food and land scarcity had given rise to the "violence, disruption, cruelty, disease, suffering and maladjustment" (Lewis 1951:428) that Redfield bracketed.

Hobgoblins and the Unit of Analysis

Anthropologist of Tepoztlán Claudio Lomnitz (1982) suggests the on-the-ground scarcity of communitarianism led both men to change their primary unit of analysis. Both focused on the parent/child household as the basic cooperative unit, rather than on the institution of the community. Thereby, the two studies made visible the work processes of betwixt-and-between women well before the feminist era. In large part, thanks to collaborating wives, we glimpse women and children, as well as men, using new technologies—material, social, and intellectual resources—to mitigate an impoverishing reliance on marginal farming conjoined with meagerly waged employment (mainly outside the municipio), small commerce, and women's consumption work.

"Consistency," to Donald (now Deidre) McCloskey, "is not the hobgoblin only of little minds; it is more particularly the hobgoblin of little masculine minds" (1993:89). The Economic Man centrism that anchors the theories they unpacked led both scholars to interpret "progress" as industrialization and explore market openings as (probably) worth the trauma. But what stood out to scholars of gender was that despite left/right Grand Theory divergence, both monographs were shot through with such stratifying hobgoblins as culture/nature, market economy/family economy, forward/backward.

Moreover, both men "blamed" irrational homemakers. Even women's gratis caring labor was put forward as designed *by them* to perpetuate the very systems that oppressed and repressed them. What stands out now is their continuity with "interconnected webs of dualistic meanings" (Jennings 1993:121) that update the Economic Man biases Paula England finds in "the deep theoretical structure" of orthodox economics (1993:37).

Taking Off

By the mid-1950s, adaptations to technological advances had begun to bring a significant change in "the calculus of force-relationships," from what de

Certeau (1984) calls *tactics* to what he calls *strategy*. Tactics—such "murmurings of the everyday" as "talking, reading, moving about, shopping, cooking, etc."—are the "clever tricks" that consumers must constantly manipulate in order to "turn to their own ends forces alien to them"; a strategy assumes control over an operational base from which to generate "relations with an exterior distinct from it" (1984:xvii-xx). Or as taxi-driver and oral historian Don Arturo put it: "It is from this period that Tepoztlán took off."

New Economy reconfigurations of women's work had begun to emerge during the time Lewis was composing his epic community study and led him to modify his earlier downgrading of women's work. In 1951, observing that women's "strong preference" to work outside the home was fueling impatience with the "limiting ways" of the folk, he predicted that the first citizens to activate revisions would be the homemakers. And by 1956, when he made his last recorded visit, already many Tepoztecas had invented openings for themselves in the new production-consumption system.

Among the transition bases he recorded were an international tourism industry; a technological revolution that commercialized farming; a vanguard elementary school; access to radio, movies, and other information and propaganda sources; contract labor for men in agriculture in the U.S. and Canada; jobs mainly for men in the region's burgeoning manufacturing and commercial complex and in a local construction industry; and the accelerated expansion of an increasingly polarized modern consumer sector. Looming as the greatest revision of all was the superhighway that would open in 1963 to put Tepoztlán forty-five motorized minutes due south of the rapaciously radiating metropolitan system of the Federal District, in which is located Mexico City.

Was the New Economy he encountered in its take-off stage too aggressively advancing across a developing-world village? "Tepoztlán today poses many questions which can be answered only with time" (Lewis 1960:103) and the testimonies of the new working class, the Tepoztecan homemaker.

THIS IS A NEW ECONOMY HOMEMAKER

"What is your occupation?" To this query, all but a few of my interviewees responded, "homemaker," (*ama de casa*). Many women went on to qualify the métier: "I am a homemaker and a teacher homemaker;" "I am a homemaker and a domestic worker;" and so on and on. Women can be a proper *ama de casa* even if she owns and operates a chain of restaurants. Still other women told me, "I am a fulltime homemaker"—including women making crucial cash contributions to households with resident male breadwinners.

What does it mean to be a New Economy Tepoztecan homemaker? And how and at what cost is this goal achieved? When in a 1995 interview Doña Luz told me that she was "a market merchant and a homemaker," she added "And that's the rub, *la friega*."

As Luz deftly scoops sardine and coffee-can measures of beans and rice out of gunnysacks for homemakers shopping in her makeshift stall in an open-air market of no importance, it seems as if her operation could not be more irrelevant to the macroeconomy of the winners. However, Luz's rub involves continuous friction among an economic, a social, and a political sphere. Though a skilled, third-generation merchant, Luz struggles to find a way around Mexico's extreme free market reforms that hugely disadvantage buyers and sellers dependent on daily wages: most Tepoztecans. As a microentrepreneur, she must absorb the devastating effects of the merging of economic crises and restructuring at both supply and demand points.

Smaller regional wholesale markets where she knew her way around have all but vanished into mammoth urban depots that receive products from all over the world at prices established in First World markets. At a time when she cannot afford to be closed even for a day, she must extract time from other responsibilities to travel more often and farther away to buy domestic (and sometimes even locally grown) goods. Increasingly stiff competition from transnationally mobile producer-distributor capitalists and competitors struggling to survive is cutting her out of the distribution stage. With the privatization and collapse of regional industries that employed many Tepoztecans, under and unemployment were at a modern high. Luz said, "People must still buy my beans since few of them have the time or money to go away to shop in supermarkets. But they buy less." While her purchasing costs increase, she cannot raise her selling prices enough to cover them. Nor can she craftily substitute lesser quality goods because her clients are astute and suspicious buyers. So she works more unpaid hours in an attempt to make up for lagging profits.

To detail her domestic production obligations, Luz's husband has never been a dependable breadwinner. Now he has "medical problems" (which she attributes to his "hard life and hard living"). His contributions are even more uncertain at a time when sustaining the household has become more challenging and humanly stressful than ever before. Multi-digit inflation makes the cost of such now unsubsidized necessities as shoes and bus fare much more than she can accumulate. She attempts to compensate with greater expenditures of her unpaid time and power to labor.

She told me that she sees her primarily obligation as keeping her four children in school "as long as possible." But already one son has dropped out of elementary school to work fulltime, and she doubts that she can ever make enough to give any of her children a "proper" education: that is, a base for getting a job in advanced capitalism.

In acknowledging that her clientele is to some extent captive, Luz is recognizing that her enterprise depends on two forms of protectionism: the pueblo has excluded chain businesses, including supermarkets and fast and slow food franchises; and as a member, she is eligible to rent space for a few pesos in the public market. This dependency on the pueblo is the context for the third dimension of Luz's rub: the work of citizenship.

The right of all citizens to use communal land to gain a socially acceptable livelihood (addressed in the next chapter) has come under increasing threat from short-term national and international investment capitalists. As a tourism center, Tepoztlán is one of the sites whose resource base the government has attempted to put "on sale," to quote ads in airline magazines. Sharply diminished local funding means that citizens must aggressively fight a blatantly corrupt establishment to ensure even a minimum of the basic services and shelter Luz requires if she is to "balance and perform her multifaceted roles" (Tinker 1995:261).

In multiple ways, New Economy reforms are the contexts of each component of Luz's triadic rub. Market-opening liberalization policies degrade her extradomestic production. As protected First World and privileged Mexican firms penetrate ever more deeply into her homemaking and citizenship obligations, Luz must continually merge her human and social capital in order to invent ways to confront a host of world market-driven problems that constrain her ability to realize her multidimensional goals.

However, a feminist standpoint must emphasize Doña Luz's testimony—her continuum of labor processes—and not the inevitability of the labor feminization script. For "if the gendered significance of a technology lies in the interpretive framework within which it is constructed, then there is a possibility of deconstructing and subsequently reconstructing the technology" (Grint and Woolgar 1995:71).

A Market/Fortress Dialogic

William Roseberry (1995:152) asserts that because Redfield and Lewis confronted their own "present," ethnographers can use their research to construct "a more critical, engaged work." This section describes and engenders a frame for combining their seemingly irreconcilable discourses. In fact, Redfield (1961) also proposed an approach to integrate the market/fortress contradiction as a "complex truth." In an essay in which he both acknowledged and explained away his "objective" blemishes, he characterized the two studies as "a dialogue" of "dialectical viewpoints" that are fundamental to all "human wholes" (1961:137). But when the objective is to mainstream gender equity into the neoliberal project, the dialogue is of that complex order Bakhtin describes as "dialogic"—"discourse that lives on the boundary between its own context and another alien context" (1981:284)—as it is also Luz's rub.

Authentic Tepoztlán survives, against all odds, because its institutions remain strong enough to be a base for defending control over commodity culture resources against a succession of hugely empowered takeover plots. So adapting the market/fortress narrative to the feminist fundamental of the interdependency of the productive and reproductive spheres, I chart Redfield and Lewis's insights and blind spots into this study of Tepoztecan women's ways of using new sets of contradictions to create new emancipatory possibilities.

To plot gender into the market/fortress dialogic, I adapt Albert Hirschman's (1958) paradigmatic analysis of the advantages that "unbalanced development" offers to "group-focused" societies (versus societies that place a much higher value on individualism than on mutuality). I begin by understanding late Tepoztlán's commodity culture[s] as what he called a linked "chain of disequilibria": of "the forward" (strategic/outward/productive/global) and "the backward" (tactical/inward/reproductive/local) sectors. In contrast to the orthodox canon that economic growth and behavioral modifications must be "balanced," he concluded that "sustainable development" happens not as an across-the-board rupture with "a whole traditional way of life," but as the integration of modernizing technologies into preexisting power systems. What makes linkage possible is a "binding agent," a force that harmonizes "hidden, scattered, and conditionally available elements" that facilitate "the cooperative component" he found particularly accessible and essential in cohesive but undercapitalized economies.

Elaborating (1958:100) on this development "inducement mechanism," Hirschman made this argument. Local agents in control of indigenous commodities find it in their interest to propagate their continued use. Thus maintaining a hierarchy of control over local resources is essential to bringing "into being active forces that [utilize the traditional] as input in new economic activities catering to new economic actors. Though the "production functions" he has in mind cannot but enhance the power of local patriarchs, once given equal standing, work in the consumption economy can become far more effective in producing commodities intended for exchange as well as for use. I emphasize that because I do not have in mind self-abnegating caregiving but the type of labor that is the binding force of free market capitalism, women's overlapping economies can reach their potential as a unifying force essential to the dialogic truth that is the late modern pueblo.

Post-binary Discourses

Here I situate my dialogic approach in Latin American feminists' "post-binary" (Redclift 1997) discourses that have shifted "analyses of female labor force participation in the market economy to the complexities and dynamics involved in women's work in and out of the household" (del Alba Acevedo 1995:66).

This literature in general and Mexican studies in particular verifies gendering as both constituted and implicated in "a whole array of sites" (French and James 1997:4). Lynn Sikkink (2001:1) argues, "Workers are informed by the conditions of their households and must align their work to the needs and rhythms of the household to which they belong." Increasingly, public/private separations are rejected because all too often the outcome of the "breaking down" of the divide has been "continued subordination, but of a different kind" (Cubbit and Greenslade 1997:53).

A core concern is the intensification of the negative consequences of the terms on which Mexican women incorporate into flexible capitalism (G. Chávez et al. 1994; Gonzáles Marín 1996:5). Chant (1990) shows that each region, community, and household has unique sets of constraints and coping resources. And Mary Jo Vaughan (2001) positions the authoritarian state as a coercive force interlinking all levels of domination and resistance to domination.

Like all feminisms, Latin American feminism has been both challenged and enriched by "postmodern insights that highlight the contingent and contradictory expressions of patriarchal relations" (Feldman 2001:1106). Post-theorists seek to counterpoise reflexivity and subordination without "lapsing" into biology (Hawkesworth 1997). Feminist archeologists reject "the cleaned-up folk model" long imposed by "Western intellectuals" (Pyburn 2003:8). Taking gender as "something one does" (Joyce 2000:7), they continue to uncover commodity cultures in Prehispanic Mexico and people them with reflexive women. But, states Susana Narotzky, the most transformational new direction is the development of the science for repositioning reproduction on at the very least an "equal methodological standing" with production (1997:39).

The new geography of Latin American women's work processes led Patricia Fernández-Kelly and Saskia Sassen to ask, "Why are women playing such a conspicuous role in the reconfiguration of the global economy?" (1995:99). "Recasting women in the global economy," they detect movement toward emancipation through the labor market but not as "a steady trend"; instead, advances have proceeded along "a course of halting contestation, negotiation, resistance, and compromise requiring repeated adjustments at the material and ideological levels" (120).

Perceiving this same pattern, my research strives to draw in "the multiplicities and ambivalences of gendered identities" discerned by Nanneke Redclift (1997:225). Toward the goal of mainstreaming gender into Tepoztlán's post-NAFTA commodity cultures, I focus on women's binding agency as a series of potentially transformative relationships in which "the macroprocesses of power, those that play out in individual lives, can only be fully understood at the level of society as a whole" (Hartsock 1997:371).

Chapter Four

Women's Work In and Out of Economic Space and Time

> The history of gendered labor [is] not a set of ideas developed separately from the economic structure but a part of it, built into the organization and social relations of work.
>
> —Ava Baron, 1991

Rising abruptly south of Mexico City are the snowy peaks framing the "cold country" of Central Mexico. Further south, the Sierra of Tepozteco marks the entrance into the small, densely populated state of Morelos, which also includes the "temperate country" and the "hot country" of the lowlands. At altitudes ranging from 1,200 to 3,500 meters, the municipio of Tepoztlán straddles all three zones (Aguilar 1992). Located in Morelos' craggy-peaked northern highlands, by the 1960s its spectacular scenery and agreeable climate, together with its proximity to population centers, its historical and cultural treasures, and its authenticity had made it a popular destination for excursionists as well as weekend dwellers in villas. But then Tepoztecans have always been involved in transcontinental drifts.

A KEY AREA

Morelos was a "key area" in Prehispanic core/periphery commodity-driven symbioses (Crespo and von Metz 1984; Hirth 1984; Hassig 1993). Its labor forces, which could reproduce themselves in intensely challenging circumstances, were crucial resources extracted by a succession of "conquest-states" (M. E. Smith 1994). In a region with a six-month dry season, with no irrigation, even when the rains came, only one annual crop could be produced. In the rain-dependent highlands, in which is located Tepoztlán, even the 15 percent of the land suitable for temporal farming was suitable only for making *milpa*, small fields intermingling corn, beans, squash, and peppers: crops that while essential to subsistence tend to be comparatively undervalued in the market.

It seems that during Aztec times, irrigation was being engineered to the more tradable resource-endowed lowlands. This pattern intensified during the Spanish occupation and the emergence in the nineteenth century of a Mexican nation-state. The primary commodities that made Tepoztlán important to indigenous superpowers—the intellectual, artistic, industrial, and commercial skills of its population—were anachronistic in New Spain. Until the Mexican Revolution (1910–1921), the systematically underdeveloped highlands were exploited for its cheapened labor and its forests, diverted to lowland *haciendas*, plantations, controlled by an oligarchy that rarely left Mexico City and was dependent on the vagaries of world markets (Chevalier 1964) and a Spanish court in turmoil. Aware that development schemes imposed by outsiders have "fostered not industrialization, but poverty," highlanders, reports Guillermo de la Peña (1986:4), conceive of their history as "an on-going conspiracy" that they continue 'to stubbornly resist" by refusing "to become fully organized in terms of modern firms."

Morelos' modern day economy radiated out of the valleys in which are located the industrialized cities of Cuautla, to the southeast, and Cuernavaca, to the northwest. During the years of the "Mexican Miracle" of aggregate growth (6 percent per annum), the increasingly authoritarian state's investments in manufacturing, agribusiness, and upscale tourism subsidized a new oligarchy of insider traders seated in Mexico City (many with luxurious second homes in Cuernavaca). Even though much of northern Morelos benefited, Lomnitz argues that modernization increased its dependency on the Mexico City establishment (1992:70).

Nevertheless, Tepoztlán contrived to retain the means of gaining a relatively autonomous and conceptually, if ever less materially *campesino*, rural toiler, livelihood. "People from outside say 'They are no longer campesinos' but make no mistake, we are still a community of campesinos," said Doña Benita, "and that is why we have survived." No Mexican citizenry is more celebrated for the steadfastness of their resolve to detect and resist conspiracies than are the stakeholders of Tepoztlán.

THE LATE MODERN PUEBLO

"Almost a world in a nutshell" (C. Chávez et al. 1990), the 1,300m^2 municipio cuts across five microclimates. In an interior (at its widest point, 279m^2) fragmented by small mountains (locally called *cerros*) and ravines are fifty-seven settlements inhabited in 2000 by 32,921 Tepoztecans. Within a radius of 6.4-km, nucleating around the small city of Tepoztlán are seven towns (1995 population range from 3,663 to 617) and nineteen *colonias*, housing developments. While 82 percent of Tepoztecans live in the five largest settlements, thirty-two *locales* contain only one or two dwellings. This socio-spatial totality constitutes the organizational system Tepoztecans continue to refer to and defend as "the pueblo."

Five distinct zones of vegetation harbor 700 species of plants and a grand diversity of birds, reptiles, small mammals, insects, and spiders (Cardona and others 1994). Official efforts to preserve the unique habitat began in 1937 when all but a few hectares fell within the National Park El Tepozteco. Another layer of protection came in 1986 when most of the area was included in a biological corridor.

The 4,134-hectare surface of the *cabecera*, administrative head town, is embedded in a rectangular sliver of the Valley of Tepoztlán. A moonscape of needle pointed turrets spiraling out of nearly vertical granite walls corrals it on three sides. To the southeast, cobbled roads slope steeply down into the Valley of Atongo, where in the 1950s a U.S. land speculator began to buy up plots coveted by campesino/homesteaders.

Not unlike a posh version of an offshore tax free-trade zone, on weekends Tepoztecans by the score migrate to the Atongo Valley to work as cleaners, cooks, nannies, and keepers of the verdant gardens of the holiday villas of Mexico's political, money market, industrial, intellectual, and criminal elite. Since the very existence of the 400 plus estates depends on access to ground water predicted for depletion by 2010, this zone of privilege is at the epicenter of the struggle for control of the empowering resource that is Tepoztlán: a struggle, a local journalist told me, "that at some level is always about water."

The town divides into eight *barrios*, neighborhoods, each with a chapel. In Lewis's time, citizens judged residents of the upper barrios "*pobres*." In contrast, most of the "*ricos*" lived in the lower barrios oriented to El Centro. Population growth and gentrification—villas, generally quoted in U.S. dollars, can sell in the millions—have now erased residential status distinctions.

Each technological revision has had profound implications for the organization of labor. For example, when the railroad arrived in 1897, it opened Tepoztlán to the forward options and backward tyrannies of the Porfiriato (1876–1910), the period of the dictatorship of Porfirio Díaz). Now a network of paved roads, highways, and freeways connect all the towns to regional centers. In 1967, Tepoztlán became an exit seventy-four kilometers off the state-of-the-art Mexico City-Cuernavaca-Oaxtepec superhighway. Evidencing its effect, only in the 1970s did the municipio regain its (estimated) pre-Conquest population of fifteen thousand (Gerhard 1972).

Between 1970 and 1990, the population surged at an average of two people per day with more than half in a head town that in an attempt to cope sprawls out of its valley-bed into illegal, quasi-legal, and legal settlements. Irregular settlements are invasions of ecologically sensitive spaces; the quasi-legal sites of villas have (at best) dubious titles to the plots they occupy. (Residents refer to the homes of privileged foreigners as "villas.") Legal settlements have also burgeoned. Kilómetro seventeen, one of ten new colonias, is the colonia located seventeen kilometers from Cuernavaca where I lived during the fieldwork that is the basis for this study. It is an island, as it were, bounded by streams of asphalt that converge on the northwest outskirts of the cabecera. The strong Olmec and Teotihuacan influences in artifacts ditch diggers still uncover suggest that it is the oldest settled area in the subregion.

Kilómetro 17

Four generic categories of Tepoztecans share this undulating plateau in the Sacred Valley of Tepoztlán. In 1995, fourteen homes belonged to *Tepoztecas/os*: stakeholders. One cannot become but must be born a Tepozteco/a. It is possible to acquire some privileges of the ranking through marriage; but marriage does not guarantee membership for a mate, though it does do so for children born to two members wherever they reside should they settle in the municipio.

Sharing the space are three categories of "foreigners," the name members assign to all "people from outside." *Tepoztios* is the name for the melting pot of resident foreigners: fictive Tepoztecans. Gables behind massive walls (which have several times inched upward) evidence a gated colony of *Weekenders* from Mexico City. Also not readily visible but there in modest dwellings are the *Swallows*, migrants, mostly from the impoverished south who began to arrive with agribusiness. Most still perform work members do not want or cannot afford to take.

Households of 1995 stakeholders represent a microcosm of the lifeways of end-of-the-millennium *auténticos*. The official adult population totals eighteen males and twenty-four females, but residential fluidity and seasonal migration means many temporary and some permanent householders go uncounted. Though all but one home (occupied by a recent widower) is family-based, none I visited was classically nuclear. On average, 4.17 family members share three jam-packed rooms, a kitchenette with a gas range, and a secluded *patio*, courtyard, in occupant-owned (self-financed or still paying-out), sturdily-constructed, tax-free homes. All have electricity and access to piped water (intermittent and not potable; only one has water piped inside the house). Everyone has a detached bath with a shower with hot water (hopefully) heated by a propane gas cylinder; and all have septic tanks. In the durable goods category, blenders, TVs, and radios are standard; and since most houses are empty during much of the day, at least one vigilant watchdog. All but one family has a refrigerator (two were out-of-order). Two cars and a pickup are put to commercial as well as personal use. In the bedroom of the ama de casa, votive candles usually flicker in front of images of the Virgin of Guadalupe.

Scattered about are small enterprises: a pizza parlor, a Frenchman's zoo of downcast African animals, convenience stores (the most recent is the "Mini Supermarket," a suburban branch of Don Roderic's El Centro "SuperTopzt," a grinding mill, and a museum of quartzes reputed to have life-extending powers. (I heard numerous testimonials to the restorative powers whiffing about the cerros, also reported to be landing fields for super terrestrials.)

In Km 17, it is possible to experience something of the endangered rurality. Pedestrians must remain alert for cattle and horses disoriented by the steady stream of trucks, taxis, vans, cars, buses, and the barking (sometimes biting) canine communities. (Despite an aggressive campaign, rabies remains a threat.) There is even the odd seasonal cultivation of a milpa that serves to remind older residents (several can still speak Nahua) of the time when the district was known, as it had been for countless generations, as Tekimilpa, "the place for making milpa." In 1975, the state requisitioned land fronting the Cuernavaca highway to construct Tepoztlán's only gasoline station. Giving directions, residents often compound Km 17 and its central place to reference it as the *gasolinera.* Here too a continent-spanning network of highways merge into a narrow road that twists blindly down to a late modern Plaza that despite all the things that have changed, Redfield and Lewis could still recognize.

El Centro

My primary fieldwork venue was the 51,850 square meters of El Centro, the downtown quadrant. In 1482, the last Aztec governor ordered citizens to construct the pyramid-temple of El Tepozteco (one version of the Nahua god of plentitude) that looms sentinel-like over El Centro (and is Morelos' second most visited archeological site). Other landmarks are the early sixteenth-century UN world heritage parish church and former monastery (now a national museum) and the 7,350 square meters Plaza containing the neoclassical Presidencia (City Hall), a public garden, and municipio market.

Commerce in El Centro is gendered female. In three surveys of twenty-five enterprises, the visible labor force was never less than 85 percent female. Moreover, task and function divisions make it rare for the 15 percent of mostly young adult men to work alongside women. Women and girls were mainstays of male and female-headed family enterprises. They were proprietors and clerks in market stalls, craft shops, and swimming-pool supply outlets. They staffed clinics for people and animals; unisex beauty shops; pharmacies; stationary shops; and financial institutions. Inside the City Hall, women carried out most administrative tasks, though none had ever held elective office. ("We women hold the jobs that require all day desk work," reported an administrative assistant. "The men here are too macho to elect a woman.")

They were teachers in the overflowing classrooms of three central district schools. On side streets, they kept *casa tiendas*, housefront stores, often harmonizing commerce with childcare. Where people congregated, women vended snacks and flowers, souvenirs and house wares, mushrooms from the forests. Others worked in eating establishments that ranged from classic Tepoztecan to Viennese and Gujarati. A considerable percentage of the labor force was still involved in some phase of Tepoztlán's oldest female industry, the production, elaboration, and distribution of *tortillas*, still the staff of Tepoztecan lives.

Most customers were working women, too, performing the economic tasks capital transfers to consumers as self-servicing (Glazer 1996): shopping, especially for food: to provision their enterprises, their households, or households where they were employed. At the parish church, laywomen and nuns committed labor to social cohesion, arranging flowers and candles, assisting at mass, teaching premarital courses for engaged couples, and conducting Saturday classes for throngs of children in the atrium. During the intense No to the Golf Club struggle, the Plaza functioned as a twenty-four-hour communication network, filled with women doing the risky—and in Morelos, sometimes fatal work—of social citizenship.

Civic Space and Land Use

Tepoztlán is one of thirty-three "free municipalities" in Morelos. "Free" means resident members possess the inalienable right of representation by a democratically elected administration. Councils composed of a president, or mayor, and council members elected for one three-year term, are limitedly empowered to make certain decisions: limited, because ultimately all decrees are contingent on the agreement of a consensus of members meeting in "free assembly."

In addition, the 1917 Constitution endows an entity deemed "indigenous" with administrative authority over "the development of its language, uses, customs, above-ground resources, and social organization." And though long (but never exclusively) organized as a mestizo (ethnically mixed) society, Tepoztlán continues to qualify politically as indigenous.

Accordingly, the term "pueblo" encompasses "us," our shared space, and those "entitlements" Amartya Sen (1999) specifies as essential to individual and collective development: political freedom, access to resources for gaining a just livelihood, transparency guarantees, social opportunities, and protective security. Moreover, citizens consider "our customs" and common law as legally binding as formal laws on residents and nonresidents. Each entitlement is an individual right, a collective responsibility, and to Claudio Lomnitz, a bond of dependency (2001:337).

This complex of privileges, obligations, dependencies, and struggles are the unified framework of Tepoztlán's collective identity that at the end of the twentieth century was still legally apart from and greater than that of any member or the sum of all individuals. Thus, Eric Wolf's (1957) idiomatic "corporate" structure that has enabled the pueblo to reach and enforce consensuses can also justify uneven distribution of entitlements.

Trying to find out more about how Mexico's reputed "corporativism" actually works in a society in which norms and laws that purport to be power-blind have different contractual implications for men and women and for specific men and specific women, I asked Doña Judith, age 80, "Do you think the pueblo will still be united in the years to come?" She replied, "*Cada cabeza* es *un mundo*": Every head is a world. So though I collectivize "the pueblo," every consensus is divisible into ways that individuals integrate into the corporation.

Use Rights

"Communal property" is property regulated by a community. Though predominantly communal since Prehispanic times, a wide range of power holders has controlled land allocation. Soon after the Revolution, the government restored land that had come under the control of plantation owners and *caciques*, local power brokers, a process completed much earlier in Tepoztlán than in most of Mexico. In 1929, the Mexican president decreed the return of 23,000 hectares in order to "guarantee" Tepoztlán's status as a "free" and "indigenous" entity.

There are three categories of land-use rights. First, there is communal land, comprising anything from land that is suitable for farming to space in the public market. In theory, any resident member has the right to use communal property to gain a livelihood. The council sets use rights and fees. Second, is the category known as the *ejido*. The state assigns the right to exploit ejido plots to "household heads" (a provision that long had the effect of excluding women). Until the 1992 alteration of Article 27 (the agrarian reform clause), a single heir could inherit a plot but it could not be sold, subdivided, rented, or mortgaged. The 1995 classification was 92.5 percent communal and 7.5 percent ejido. Only 5.4 percent falls into the third and intensely disputed category of privately controlled property.

The way a land parcel is used must conform to limits set by the municipio and to federal, state, and now international restrictions written into NAFTA and other multilateral trade agreements. A stipulation that turns out to be intensely gendered is titleholders must use plots continuously and as zoned. Unoccupied houses, uncultivated fields, and commercial sites not open for business at stipulated times are in jeopardy of invasion by insiders.

In practice, developed sites seem always to have been treated as private property with land, homes, and businesses rented, sold, or passed to relatives through various arrangements. The reality is that citizens have routinely manipulated restrictions in order to survive turbulence, profit from soaring land prices, and defend the commons from big commerce, international industry, and public and private developers.

Clearly, Tepoztlán's pluralistic organization means that small producers who use the commons as capital have a large stake in the politics of defending it against incursions and in adjustments that open it to international capital. The following very brief sketch of Tepoztlán's economic history shows why many of these small producer-defenders are working women.

THE ECONOMIC TRAJECTORY OF TEPOZTECAS

The Mexican pueblo is "inextricably related to the forms of organized labor" (Esteva 1983:156). This section imbricates generations of Tepoztecas into constraints and strategies dovetailing into the Decade of the New Economy. Situated modifications of the "smallholder/householder" (Netting 1992) institution continued well into the twentieth century depended on intensive cultivation of staples and continuous in-house fabrication and processing of products intended for consumption, local and distanced trading, male wage earning outside the municipio, and status. In the next coping era, the escalating pressure for cash restructured all modes and relations for gaining a family wage: except for the legal and social exclusion of homemakers from most employment. These organizing systems lead into a here and now when with all labor processes and social relations transitioning "with increased velocity" (Rothstein 2000:6), cash earning on a continuous basis is widely regarded as a natural extension of homemaking.

The Nahua World-System

"At the heart of the Nahua world, both before the Spaniards came and long after was the ethnic city-state, or *altepetl*" (Lockhart 1992:14). By 800 CE, the small *altepetl* of Tepoztlán was a fortified settlement in the orbit of Xochicalco, a civic-ceremonial hegemony that functioned, like other Prehispanic central places, as a "centrifugal force, to redistribute goods, values, and people outward" (D. Carrasco 1990:xviii). In contrast, according to James Lockhart (1992), constrained by terrain and lack of nonhuman transport, highland *altepetls* developed in an inward pattern. Thus early on Tepoztlán "imagined itself a radically separate, relatively equal [and] self-contained constituent part of the hegemonic whole" (15): an equilibrium of power" that had enormously "different consequences for each sex" (Clendinnen 1991:207).

Priests instructed men to go forth to produce or fight. A matron was to stoke the fire, instruct daughters, and fabricate a wide range of goods, especially cloth but only within her household and always within prescribed rules of decorum, down to the proper way of jumping a ditch. Paradoxically, her directives also included defending her household ritually and physically against all things evil and dangerous, including herself (de Sahagún 1950). In 1396, after a period of violent resistance, Tepoztlán became a conquered territory within the Aztec Empire. To Nash (1980), the "predatory economy" imposed by the Aztecs prepared the way for the profound changes in gender relations after the Conquest.

Countless centuries before the arrival of the Spanish, the region was "teeming with markets" (Hirth 1998). Besides tending nutritionally vital garden and keeping fowls, the contributions of Aztec period homemakers included trading in the well-organized market system (Berdan 1985). But above all, Tepoztecas engaged in weaving the cloth that was a major form of trade and self-provisioning, but primarily of tax/tribute, which under the Aztecs amounted to "a generalized form of enslavement" (Semo 1993).

Task-performance studies indicate women gain productivity by combining homework with domestic labor (thus making many forms of in-house production nonrational for men). Given the mountains of cotton and maguey fiber lengths women were charged with fabricating on a rigid delivery schedule, neither they nor their society could have considered cloth production "secondary" to other activities (Hicks 1994, Brumfiel 2006).

New Spain Tepoztlán

For Tepoztecans, the Conquest wave of globalization began in the spring of 1521 when Hernando Cortés led his Holy Band out of Tenochtitlán, the Valley of Mexico central place of the Aztec Empire. Preparing to launch the attack that obliterated "all those things never heard of, seen or dreamed of before," the objective was to close down key resource links with the present day state of Morelos (Díaz del Castillo 1965). The Conquistadors made a panzer-like swath across this "thriving and complex social landscape"

(M. E. Smith 1996). Alternately plundering, slaughtering, and lingering to delight in the hot springs, luxuriant gardens, and other fabled Morelos attractions, on their way to decimate the brilliant urban center of Cuernavaca, the Spanish came upon "one of the fairest views it has even been given mortal eyes to see" (Chase 1946:2): the town of Tepoztlán. Though admiring the fierce resistance mounted by its defenders—and taking due note of "the many pretty women and much loot" (Díaz del Castillo 1965)—the Spanish burned down the comfortable homes, palaces, workshops and factories, commercial and agricultural enterprises, markets, temples, and academies of its some 15,000 Nahuatl-speaking inhabitants (P. Carrasco 1982).

Within a few years, the Conquerors, now plundering, pillaging, and raping in search of personal fortunes, had returned to Morelos and Tepoztecans had integrated into the international economy. Tepoztecos were impressed into the many high tech industries Cortés, now Marquis of most of Central Mexico, initiated. Locked out of the production economy, in response to the "much coming and going" detected by William Taylor (1996) of unmoored men in need of indigenous women to make their tortillas, Tepoztecas created a frontline service sector.

By 1537, Cortés had built a palace-fortress in Cuernavaca and was making "vigorous, virtually uninterrupted use of his Morelos labor force," particularly the Tepoztecans, who were "only" a five-hour walk away (Riley 1973:49). Because the Spanish depended on tribute in the form of corn and numerous other staple consumables as well as labor, the "existence of community had to be protected" (Semo 1993:38). Cortés declared Tepoztlán a *Pueblo de Indios*, an arrangement under which Tepoztecans retained control of land not claimed by Spanish or Indian elites. In 1523, Cortés sent out the fateful order to plant sugarcane.

As the New Spain extractive economy flourished, entire communities were absorbed into sugar haciendas; but Tepoztlán gained territory and was almost unique in remaining highly indigenous (C. Martin 1985). By activating "inventions, borrowings, and irregularities" (Taylor 1996:320), its smallholder/householder framework endured as did the pueblo.

Men assigned to the many new industries earned scandalously low, irregularly paid wages. Few returned from the villainous silver mines that were the main funding source of several European industrial and artistic revolutions. At a time when women's commercial specializations were declining in importance, a growing number of widows, single women, and wives of conscripted husbands assumed the responsibilities of household heads, including fieldwork not only for subsistence but also as tribute. Ponderous machines men operated in factories replaced women's delicate backstrap loom. Soon all forms of women's home crafting fell into the impoverishing category of "artifactual anachronisms" (Cook 1993) where it has largely remained, except for the preparation of marketed foodstuffs. In 1535, Tepoztlán sued to pay tribute in currency, confirming that it had become more rational to pay taxes in cash than in corn or other commodities, which were needed to keep citizens alive.

Tepoztecas continuously invented new ways of earning cash. Some were part of the labor force of twenty women Tepoztlán had to supply the palace each month, and it was one of the first communities to have resident Spanish in need of personal and public services; as well, a Nahua upper class hung on. Tepoztecas worked in Mexico City and mining towns (and perhaps in the mines), most in Cuernavaca's pulsating street economy. Many went into the illegal home *pulque* (an alcoholic drink) industry (Taylor 1979). Doubtlessly, they staffed the numerous shops surrounding the Plaza and the "lively" markets, "a Prehispanic holdover" that continued throughout the occupation (Haskett 1991:16).

Spanish Baggage

Still, mobility made Tepoztecas net losers even while it opened niches into the monetary economy. A lawless environment constrained their options; so did lack of capital and Spanish and official exclusion from the production sector. Accepted notions of masculinity and femininity also provided "a readily comprehensible model for all other contexts of subordination and domination" (C. Martin 1996:158). Then, too, the white male Church bound up women's sexuality with labor roles and the salvation of their souls in ways that validated convergences of public and private patriarchy (Lavrin 1992).

"Of all the Spanish cultural baggage that crossed the Atlantic between the sixteenth and the eighteenth centuries, patriarchy arguably changed least in transit," argues Cheryl Martin; and once transplanted, "it found enthusiastic adherence among males who had every other reason to question Spanish cultural and political hegemony" (1996:158). Transubstantiated into *machismo*—"a code of honor and degradation" (Stern 1995:1)—the technology/ideology was imposed on old entanglements of complementarity and domination. Laws, sacred rituals, abuse, and new contexts of dependencies enforced patriarchy at home. Noting that women did not compete with men for jobs, Marjorie Becker holds that "this behavior not only subsidized capitalism, it also afforded men respite from the daily abuses they experienced" (1994:253). Yet we know Tepoztecas forcefully claimed their rights as economic agents and even dared to be at the centers of rebellions. Indeed, court documents describe the women as "worse than the men" and record incidents involving named Tepoztecas (Taylor 1996: 511–12).

Behaving Badly

Led by Big Mary, Tepoztecas were at the forefront in the riot of 17 October 1777, over an attempt by the grasping parish priest to ship to another church eighty loads of lime that citizens had laboriously produced to whitewash their own church. As the mule train arrived to transport the booty, men ran to the market to alert the women, who vigorously declaimed their grievances, threw stones, invaded sacred precincts, roughed up Father Gamboa, and attacked local men likely in on the scheme. When Gamboa called in troops, citizens fled to the hills. After several days, the archbishop negotiated reconciliation. The pueblo would be pardoned providing everyone returned to work and riot leaders were handed over to Gamboa for "exemplary punishment" (Taylor 1996:512).

To carry out their obligation to defend the pueblo and "their own and their families' integrity" (Haskett 1997:148), Tepoztecas resorted to the gender defense, counting on their subaltern status to make them not worth the punishment that would have been handed out to males: exile or death. According to the code, women's ranking as the physically and mentally weaker sex should have protected them from violent retribution. And the defense worked, but only insofar as it protected them from the usual male punishments. As for the ringleaders, they were stripped naked and publicly whipped by Gamboa.

Tepoztlán after Mexican Independence

National independence (1821) did not liberate all Tepoztecans, as both Spanish and local power holders expropriated the land. Families now sharecropping communal land were mired in inextinguishable debts, and men were willing to work in the sugar industry for literally less than it took to feed a mule (Esteva 1983:141). International capitalism came in to stay (Gledhill 1994), and, later, a technocratic state aimed to compel men to become low-waged workers or US style farmers (Kearney 1996). New economic classes solidified—a landed peasantry, a male labor force, mestizo burghers, and the consumption specialist: the homemaker. In reality, although most women were still eternally engaged in subsistence tasks, privation required them to contrive ways to earn cash on a consistent and timely basis.

Yet the career that a dizzying succession of Liberal and Conservative governments alike consigned to homemakers was to whiten Indian (read backward) households. The linking of the science and concept of modernization—"the search for an entrepreneurial elite and the disdain for traditionalism" (Centeno 2001:291)—is in practice intensely male gendered.

The railroad brought several new livelihood resources; and, as is the pattern for technological advances, a masculinized forward made a feminized backward. Tepoztlán became an excursion destination; but since tourists passed only a few hours, tourism was a source for only a few jobs, and these for men. However, fees and wages paid by the railroad helped to sustain four stores and a sprinkling of carpenters, butchers, and so on (Lewis 1951:101). Women participated as "supplementary" workers in these enterprises and in the most non-socialized tasks of a family-based industry that developed around a fragile plum. A more lucrative export was the charcoal produced by men generally working alone in the forests.

Tepoztecans were among the first Mexicans to give active support to Zapata (well known from his nocturnal visits to his Tepoztecan "second wife"). In return, between 1911 and 1920, various armies visited an apocalypse of starvation, pillage, rape, and exile on the populace. Men and women experienced these horrors differently. All men were compelled to enlist or flee, but memoirs and interviews suggest that numerous women stayed on: some to care for those unable to withstand evacuation, others to protect property. Some women were sexual preys, others held hostage by federal troops to prevent them from making tortillas for the Zapatistas. (Apparently, they did have a supply of corn.)

By 1920, many citizens and all animals were dead, fields were striped barren, and most of Tepoztlán—at a population nadir of three thousand—lay in ruins. "Most feminists concur that patriarchy was retained, perhaps even strengthened by the Revolution" (M. Vaughan 2001:194). As it filled power system voids, patriarchal capitalism also strengthened. Women's lasting legacy was a new division of labor that required homemakers to invent new ways to harmonize backward and forward forms of domestic and market patriarchies.

The Modernization Stage of Globalization

The rupturing (but not dissolution) of the plantation system and, later, the Great Depression meant that after the Revolution there were few waged jobs for men and none for women in the region (L. Thompson 1992). Reconstruction began with the reclaiming of the commons under the new constitution; but how were the commons to be used and allocated? Most men returned to making milpa, in the same old impoverishing way (Womack 1976). With prices of goods rising and crop prices plummeting, the only readily salable commodity was the charcoal men produced by burning trees. The consequent looming environmental catastrophe generated disputes that sundered the pueblo.[1]

Into the 1930s, for most citizens conditions were as punishing as ever. There was no electricity, no motorized transport, or resident physician. Women going to trade in Cuernavaca had to walk at night across a bandit-infested forest. The first mechanized corn mill failed, Lewis (1951:108) was told, because husbands were alarmed at the prospect of leisure time for wives. Another male informant described the success of the next mill "as 'the revolution of the women against the authority of the men'."

Pedro Martínez told Lewis (1964a:260) that the chief constraints on modernization had been water shortage, the disintegration of the public market, and inadequate schools: "But above all we needed a road." On a 1935 "flying visit," President Cárdenas committed to the construction of a highway to Cuernavaca, which would connect the pueblo with a new set of problems that have proven to be gendered in ways unlike any experienced before.

As the Institutional Revolutionary Party, the PRI, consolidated its power, it shifted its agenda to two new development strategies: first the depeasantification of agriculture and later an industrialization program aimed at protecting domestic capitalists (almost by definition PRI insiders). Measures designed to degrade small farming both furthered the interests of big agriculture and created the reserve of cheap labor essential to industrial capitalism. Reform models that played out as a retreat from smallholding into householding soon made stakeholders eager to utilize "the possibilities of 'getting by' that are offered by diversification and relationships to national and international markets," reports Marilee Grindle (1991:149).

For over six decades, PRI politicos, alternating rewards and punishment through *altepetl*-like patronage networks were "instruments of impoverishment and tyranny" (Stevens 1974). Nevertheless, the survival of the authentic pueblo points to citizens' mastery of the ability of Mexicans "to coexist with the state and even to colonize state agencies, thus securing direct and indirect political access" (Knight 2001:1993).

The agricultural revolution began in 1942, when a Spaniard rented a field on Revolution Avenue and used chemicals to cultivate gladiola. Subsequently, some farmers utilized the science to grow tomatoes in commercial quantities. The resulting profits translated into tractors, direct trade with Mexico City markets, and commercial ventures. Soon, the "tomato tycoons" became the PRI's local power brokers (Lomnitz 1982). Into the 1960s agribusiness remained the primary productive sector because it became increasingly commercialized, a factor that drove many men out of it. Lewis (1960) reports that even choice plots went unplanted and laborers had to be imported.

Though wages were too low for most male breadwinners, agribusiness worked for some "unemployed" homemakers. Doña Anita went into the prospering gladiola industry. "We were so poor that I was grateful for any job but this one nearly killed me. I was up by 4:30 a.m. to get the kids off to school. My wage meant that all my children completed primary school and one daughter became a teacher."

Some men did take the bus to earn wages in Cuernavaca's new industrial park (known as CIVAC). Getting such jobs required connections (Arias and Bazán 1977). Most Tepoztecans also needed patronage to get an education that could open the door to decent jobs. The most lucrative option for men was contract agricultural labor "over there" (north of the Rio Grande). According to Lewis (1951:35), by 1956, 565 residents worked in thirty-three nonagricultural concerns; only twenty-five in this workforce were also farmers. Women predominated among teachers, corn merchants, and healers; they were also dressmakers and hairdressers, but were uncounted in their primary economic activity: unpaid worker in a family enterprise.

Starting in the 1960s, the Mexico City highway brought many tourists—and therefore female-gendered jobs—into the municipio. Doña Lupe, age fifty-five, homemaker and salad chef at a hotel, commented, "My generation was the first to plan their lives around going out to work. This is because of the highway and the prospect of getting a real job." Her some US$3 (top) daily salary, augmented by this and that, has financed a nursing degree for one daughter and a teaching career for another. But *real* jobs like Lupe's continued to be scarce. With a disabled husband and many children, Doña Josefa eagerly took a meagerly waged domestic job in Cuernavaca. "Each Friday I returned on the last bus, cared for my family, and left on the first bus out on Monday."

Formal jobs for women continued to be largely limited to teaching and nursing. There were far from enough of these or any other jobs to go around. The best (and often the only) option for many women was to create their own microscale self-employment. In 1962, Doña Julia, noting that there were now tourists every weekend, solicited a permit to set up a table near the bandstand. Selling "typical clothing" that she and her sisters made, she describes herself as the first Tepozteca entrepreneur vending on a regular basis to the tourist market. Now for her daily market operation ("going well" in 2006) she buys her stock of finely crafted clothes from indigenous women, "the only women poor enough to be willing to sell such skill and labor at these low prices."

As the weekend floating population began to exceed twenty thousand, the policy of excluding outsiders and encouraging "popular tourism" (described by one Tepoztecan as "tourism by and for ordinary Mexicans") did add "junk" jobs for women. Elite tourism promoted seasonal jobs for men in villa construction and domestic jobs for women working in them. However, many citizens complained that high living costs in a tourist area offset gains. Still, according to Grindle (1991:139), compared to many Mexicans, Tepoztlán did make significant gains—until the Debt Crisis "brought to a near halt" a prospering local economy. "Tepoztecans set their eyes on jobs in Cuernavaca, Mexico City, and the U.S. They complained bitterly about the futility of looking for jobs in the *municipio*, and of the need to look far and wide for sources of income." Throughout the 1990s, if the quality of the job declined, it often went to migrants or students who could be paid even less than adult women; if comparatively well paying, the job masculinized.

Roseberry (1995:151) argues that if are to pose the "right" questions, we need to know more about "the manifold ways" ordinary people have contrived to resist the "orders of domination that press upon them." Thus in the next section I narrate the antidisciplines of the Tepoztecan homemaker who was US anthropology's first transitional economic woman of the Mexican countryside.

ADDENDUM: ENCOUNTERING ESPERANZA

My short cut from Km 17 to El Centro passed the site that once held a two-room adobe house sheltering nine members of the family of Esperanza (1891–1956) and Pedro Martínez ethnographically immortalized by Lewis. To Lewis, the basic unit appeared to be collapsing under the trauma Marxists refer to as a change in the mode of production. The failure of the backward, patriarchy as usual, to meet newly entrained wants was, on one side, pushing the family to cooperate, and, on the other pulling them apart.

The "traditional village family," with its "authoritarian male," "submissive woman," and hard-working, obedient children (Lewis 1959:25), had been legitimated by dependency on a "benevolent" patriarch. Lewis takes us inside a household churning with resistance to the backward. And, into a time when, as they contrived adaptations to the nascent forward, stakeholders were bringing into existence new modes and relations in and of production-reproduction that could serve as a base for establishing themselves within a radically new variant of patriarchal capitalism: Tepoztlán's New Economy.

Without a private farming plot, Don Pedro did not have control over the means of gaining even a dependable impoverishing livelihood: land. Generational class formation spoke to the fact that both parents had been bereft of the human capital and decision-making freedoms now within their children's reach. Taking the household as the locus of struggle, Lewis showed how transactions in the caregiving sphere could subsidize shortfalls in breadwinner incomes if only from meal to meal; but shows too that Esperanza's caring labor could not shelter her from "the tender violence of Pedro Martínez" (Lewis 1964b).

Likely, there were no jobs for women with Esperanza's disadvantages. Yet she, not Pedro, came closer to making the ironic adaptation Sol Tax (1953) lauded as "penny capitalism." But like Marx, Lewis never did go the next logical step and people with real Tepoztecans the kind of economy that is created when inequitable institutions are also the institutions that people have to work with.

A destitute, malnourished, and pregnant teenage mother of a dying enfant when Pedro went off with Zapata, she contrived to keep the family alive and even hang on to a few assets. Though suffering from a chronic, eventually fatal illness, throughout the hardscrabble years ahead, she worked continuously in the seasonal plum business, the family's only regular source of cash; marketed fowls and produce, and maintained networks continually undermined by Pedro's neurotically antisocial behavior. In short, when push came to shove as it routinely (and sometimes literally) did at meal times, Esperanza managed to manage crosscutting systems of subordination within the dominant economy.

"What could she borrow now? What small thing could she sell? These questions faced her every day" (Lewis 1959:43). Lewis's account of one day in her provisioning life demonstrated how her own and her female trading partners' need for cash complicated the local exchange of just-in-time foodstuffs. He also shows us how female subservience in the face of male abuse (which Lewis thought Esperanza willfully perpetuated), together with "archaic" labor patterns (which Lewis thought Esperanza deliberately clung to) made the household—at least when tortillas, beans, and rice were on the table—different from any other regulatory institution, instilling an "allegiance beyond coercion (without neglecting coercion)" (Taylor 1996:6).

Esperanza's New Economy Sisters

By the last decade of the twentieth century, new livelihood options, urbanization, and education had brought dramatic changes to the Martínez family. None of the sons became farmers. An imposing concrete dwelling with indoor plumbing has replaced the adobe homestead. The owner is one of the eight granddaughters Esperanza never knew. Members have sold off portions of the plot to educate themselves for professions and start businesses. What remains is worth an amount inconceivable to Pedro and Esperanza; yet the surviving son (a retired professor) will "never" request a permit to sell his share of the plot (or at least his share of the small portion the family has not already sold). Like all citizens I queried, he continues to valorize membership.

Lifestyles and aspirations of the women of this family are widely shared among Tepoztecas. By Mexican standards, they are well educated: 22 percent (versus 25 percent of men) complete basic education, 33 percent of generation now age groups get some technical or superior education. They marry, likely another Tepoztecan, a decade or so later than Esperanza and give birth to 9.54 fewer children. Unlike Esperanza, they can expect to live long enough—84 percent of them in Tepoztlán—to know the children of their children, who have a 90 percent chance of becoming adults.

The surviving daughter (she of the especially tasty tortillas) still lives in an adobe house—albeit one with a TV dish—just behind the site of the old homestead. She and a married daughter operate a corn mill. They stay in touch by cell phones. Of five other granddaughters, two are teachers, one owns a taxi, one heads a highway maintenance crew, and another operates a concession stand at a busy toll station. Two great-granddaughters attend school in Cuernavaca. Both have high career hopes: one to teach English to primary school students, the other to be a computer programmer with a transnational corporation. All are decidedly career-oriented.

Nevertheless, none of Esperanza's female descendants is likely to engage in work that is not comprehensively gendered. They will almost certainly work in occupations either exclusively or mainly female sex-typed. They are unlikely to be on a career track or have managerial status. They will continuously mesh reproductive and productive tasks, making costly—to themselves and the pueblo—adaptations of education and employment patterns to long-term obligations and family income shortfalls. Whether employed in the formal or informal economy, whether full- or part-time, their labor will be valued at less than men's, even though in 1995 male salaries were below pre-1982 levels.

As in "the traditional village," to a great extent, to themselves and their society, their prestige will depend on performing gratis tasks men seldom undertake unless for decent wages. They often find their economic options limited by the inability to control their own fertility decisions; and by harassment and violence as well as spousal desertion, abuses against which they still have scant legal protection. (In Morelos, rape is less heavily punished than castle rustling.)

The names for these forms of subordination at work are *gender segregation*—the relative sex compositions of different occupations—and *gender segmentation*—status differences within an occupation. At both the labor supply-side (workers decide) and the labor demand-side (management decides), in all aspects of all realms of all labor-capital relationships, in late Tepoztlán, as across Mexico, gender remains the primary variable that correlates with but does not explain women's inequalities at work.

"Our capacity to think and act on the world is dependent on other people who are themselves also both subjects and objects of history" (Gramsci

1971:346). Was Esperanza a subject or an object of history, an actor or an acted upon? Abandoned by her father, abused by her mother and a controlling, dysfunctional husband, denied education, suffering the privation-linked deaths of six of her twelve children, impoverished by a society that marginalized her economic class are ideal conditions for objectification. With options so constrained, the labor processes she created could not but rationalize her dependency status. At the same time, though, her activities give no indication of an acceptance of public or private subordination. Esperanza turned herself into a value-creating subject.

On the one hand, as a feminist, I must think about Esperanza as a talented user of technical ways of making-do. On the other hand (again quoting de Certeau 1984), while I deeply admire her "makeshift creativity"—her "everyday practices that produce without capitalizing"—as a working woman, I know "clever tricks" are no substitute for tradables. Not Esperanza the tragic heroine, then, but Esperanza the Tepoztecan homemaker making the transition work became my guide into the worlds of work of her New Economy sisters.

Chapter Five

Counting and Measuring Gendering, 1990–2000

> Few people realize how critical statistics are to the allocation of resources, policy formation and legislation. Phenomena—and people—that are not counted or measured are quite easily ignored.
>
> —Martha Loutfi, 2001

Silver jewelry from Taxco, blouses embroidered in the Yucatan, tarot cards, swimming pool supplies, domestic labor in villas, *quesadillas*, gladiolas, and above all, authentic Tepoztlán—its legends and fiestas, its architectural and miraculously still pristine cerros: By the end of the 1970s were "staple crops" in a Tepoztlán that had completed the transition from Redfield's prototypical folk village to Scott Lash and John Urry's prototypical "postindustrial space." Such economies depend on the delivery of commodities described by Lash and Urry (1994:193, 200) as "increasingly design-intensive and/or semiotic." In these spaces, all commodities are "infused" with the particular social characteristics of "first line" traders as "consumption stuff" transits across "the conventional circuits of capitalism." This chapter counts and measures gendering as it infuses into what Arjun Appadurai (1992:13) calls the "*commodity situation*"—the "*exchangeability (past, present and future)*" of the stuff of postindustrial Tepoztlán.

In the virtual economy of the economists, a *labor population* consists of all potential sellers and buyers of labor power. But real time/space convergences are never configured outside "the matrix of gender relations" (Elson 1995:1852). Focusing on the 1990 to 2000 matrix, this chapter utilizes qualitative and quantitative information to record and detect gendering trends. The topics include occupation, task, and sector divisions, working conditions, ways of obtaining credit, and household economies. In the final section, I turn statistics and participant observations into issues that tie together the next chapters.

TEPOZTLÁN'S TECHNOCRATIC REVOLUTION

The Debt Crisis that erupted in 1982 signaled the start of Mexico's first top-down revolution (Centeno 1994) and for Tepoztecans, the end of three decades of economic growth. Today's economy evidences the increasingly unequal income and asset distribution that "were not inevitable; they were the result of policy choices made in the context of the trade liberalization strategy" (Griffin and Ickowitz 2003:585). But for Tepoztlán, as José Tavara asserts for Latin American communities in general, the emergence of "new forms of production organization and social institutions" warn against thinking that "nothing substantial was happening" (1993:391).

Evidencing its capacity to accommodate even the "poisonous mixture" (Salas and Zepeda 2003:554) of the technocratic revolution and levels of ineptitude, corruption, and criminality astounding even for the PRI, by the summer of 1993, Tepoztlán was experiencing a tourism led mini-recovery. Then came the 1994 "December Mistake Crisis" heard round the world's currency markets (Edwards and Naim 1997) launching Mexico worst economic depression. The collapse of Mexico's financial system compounded with the No to the Golf Club events to devastate the local economy. In many households, savings had already been depleted; now assets were sold off in mostly futile attempts to overcome the budget-decimating effects of the removal of government subsidies on two hundred commodities; an inflation rate that in five years rose from 30 to 52 percent and a contraction in state budgeting for social programs from an already low 29 percent to an unevenly distributed 16 percent. Merchants said business was off "80 percent or more on most days." A municipio official estimated male unemployment as "exceeding 33 percent and *much* higher among young men." Underemployment reached new dimensions as income and buying power declined to modern lows. "In Tepoztlán, you don't have to be out of work to be poor," was the matter-of-fact comment of restaurant owner Don Arturo.

Out-migration—still mainly male but increasingly female—skyrocketed and became more open ended. Many households activated the "traditional survival strategy" of "sending" "unemployed" homemakers into the ravaged labor market (Torrado 1978). Families risked (and often lost) emergency savings to start up small business. Many homemakers employed themselves at the lowest levels of a service sector flooded by students and workers from regions even more direly affected. As coping increased competition, the inevitable unintended consequence was to depress earnings further.

For profoundly child-centered parents, the overarching issue was finding the means to educate children to fill jobs in the promised "knowledge society." Though post-basic credentials were now essential for any (nominally) middleclass job, even if such a job became available, it was unlikely to pay a socially and increasingly even materially acceptable wage. The lived contradiction marking the decade is then that this cherished goal in tandem with catastrophes led many mothers into a degraded labor market and sent fathers abroad. In short, as in globalization waves past, women used a feminized "forward" to *make* a feminized "backward": "what market actors actually do when they find that rational calculation will not serve" (Carrier 1995).

Arts of Using a Technocratic Everyday

"Do you favor NAFTA?" I asked bus driver Don Pablo. "I have to, don't I? What other hope is there for poor México?" In these hard times, many citizens clung to Don Pablo's deeply skeptical optimism. With strong indications that the Mexican economy might be going down for the last time, stakeholders had only NAFTA to look to as a way out of Tepoztlán's persistent principal structural and everyday obstacle of underemployment. By 2000, Tepoztecans had achieved a precarious stabilization underwritten not by power-free trade but in large part by the overused and under compensated labor of women of Tepoztlán.

In 1997, another dollar remittance and tourism led mini-recovery was gaining momentum. Officials estimated a 40 percent increase in tourists, mainly day excursionists heavily concentrated on Sundays. In 1997, there were 38,585 visitors to El Tepozteco's Casa (the restored Aztec period pyramid) and 79,823 to the sixteenth-century convent now a national museum. Around 10 percent were not Mexicans, a good sign since non-nationals are assumed to spend more. Population increases continued, augmented by even harder times elsewhere and people with means anxious to escape the criminal and environmental dangers of Mexico City, thereby intensifying the disequilibrating effects of the simultaneous growth of producers and users of consumption stuff.

Most jobs created were suitable only for "unemployed" homemakers and students desperate to cover substantial tuition increases. (The government defines "employment" as a person 12 years or more active at least one hour in the census reference week for a salary in cash or other type of remuneration.) Of course, cash inflows, called *remittances*, from householders exercising

Hirschman's (1970) "exit option" were a huge factor; however, only when operationalized effectively by citizens exercising the "voice," the staying-on option, supporting Hirschman's premise that exit gives scope to voice when voice rationalizes exit.

The accelerating demand for consumption stuff made staying on possible and reasonable despite the deterioration in job quality. Reflecting ever-wider openings of the local market was a torrent of much coveted products. Many were priced at or sometimes even above U.S. levels but often below lower quality goods produced by formerly protected domestic industries. Like Don Eduardo, some once prospering merchants turned shops over to family members and went to harvest apples in Oregon or blow leaves off lawns in Dallas, thus draining the pueblo of its primary wage earners. Rampant capital flight and the region's chronic dependency on external financing led to a full-scale invasion of consumption stuff of scope-seeking firms and investors with huge comparative advantages, further undermining local commerce. Yet however mini, recovery signifies the historic resolve of Tepoztecans to not only survive but also turn to their advantage the technocratic revolution.

In 1994, a number of homemakers reported needing "at least" ten dollars per person per week to provision their households with a "*sana*" (wholesome) lifestyle. Others shook their heads at this sum; and, like Doña América, said they needed perhaps twice this amount. With good wages barely one-fourth of the salaries of U.S. workers, even the ten dollar goal (which by 1998 had escalated by some accounts to "at least twenty dollars) was out of the reach of many families. Yet, in general, Tepoztecans agreed with Doña Carla who told me "We are poor, but we are not poor like many Mexicans." And the 2000 census verifies that during the 1990s many households, and not just those most well-fixed to cope, were not only meeting basic nutritional and other everyday human needs but even contriving material advances.

Then how were users of the neoliberal project making do? Explaining "the comparatively rapid (but notably uneven) recovery of the macroeconomy" from the cosmic 1995 recession, Kevin Middlebrook and Ednardo Zepeda (2003:20) point out that sporadic gains were based on utilizing successes achieved in the decades of the protected ("import-substitution") economy. Tepoztecans too made-do largely by converting the on-hand into new production-reproduction technologies. Since Tepoztecans were among Cook's (2004:243) "vast multitude" of "petty Mexican producers" contriving to insert proven means of gaining a livelihood into "international commodity circuits," the pueblo constitutes a veritable proving ground for his finding that they do so "in ways fully compatible with culturally pluralistic household and community reproduction."

Indexing Gendering

Mexico's *Instituto Nacional de Estadística, Geografía e Informátic* (INEGI) is the primary quantitative source for statistical information on the *economic population* (EP): inhabitants ages twelve to sixty-four residing in Tepoztlán during a census reference period. (See the bibliography for specific sources. In the interests of space, some primary data is summarized.) *Economic activity* (EA) is "the condition of producing goods and services destined for the market." The *economically active population* (EAP) includes the currently employed (EA) and the involuntarily or temporarily *unoccupied*. Characterized as *economically inactive* (EI) are members of the EP voluntarily not engaged in EA. These data sets frame the three indexes I use to count and evaluate economic gendering: an *Index of Female Segregation* (I-FS), an *Index of Female Demographic Equality* (I-FDE), and an *Index of Working Conditions*. Box 5.1 details the methodology.

Workforce Distribution

Officially, a *labor market* consists of all potential employees and employers. In reality, labor markets—a barrio fiesta, a border factory, a Chicago Taco Bell—involve specific population segments. Tables 5.1, 5.2, and 5.3 present and compare activity differences among demographically specific *resident population* (RP) segments: people residing in the municipio during the 1990 and 2000 census reference periods.

BOX 5.1

1) An *Index of Female Segregation* (I-FS) estimates the number and percent of women who would have to leave or enter a unit of analysis to achieve a sex-balanced work force. The baseline is activity at the time of the counting. For example, since in 2000, women were 33% of the Economically Active (EA) labor force, the index for occupational segregation is 33%. Positive signs (+) designate the surplus of women in the category, negative signs (-), the missing women. (2) The baseline for the *Index of Female Demographic Equality* (I-FDE) is an INEGI census-determined population segment. For example, in 2000, women were 52% of the resident Economic Population (EP). Therefore, when the entire Economic Population (EP) is the unit, the baseline is plus or minus 52%. (3) To calculate degrees of gender asymmetry, I focus on working conditions (i.e., salaries, authority positions, hours worked) to establish relative status of a worker and an activity.

Table 5.1. Population Segments Residing in Tepoztlán during INEGI 1990, 2000 Census Reference Periods

Population Segments	*1990 RP*	*2000 RP*	*1990, 2000 %Female*	*%Population Change*
Resident Population* [RP]	27,646	32,921	1990, 50% 2000, 51%	RP Growth rate^ 1980–1990, 3.8% 1990–2000,1.8%
Economic Population [EP]	19,511	23,166	1990, 71%/RP 2000, 70%	–1%/EP
Female [F]-EP	9,902	11,953	1990, 51%/EP 2000, 52%	+1%/F-EP
Male [M]-EP	9,609	11,213	1990, 49%/EP 2000, 48%	–1%/M-EP
Economically Active Population [EAP]	8,064	12,115	1990, 41%/EP 2000, 52%	+11%/EAP
Fs in EAP	1,886	4,014	1990, 23% 2000, 33%	+10%/F-EAP
Economically Active [EA]+	7,831	11,960	1990, 40%/EP 2000, 52%/EP	+12%/EA
Females EA	1,850	3,981	1990, 23%/EAP 2000, 33%	+10%/F-EA
Males EA	5,981	7,997	1990, 75%/EAP 2000, 67%	–8%/M-EA
%F-EA w/%EP	19%	33%	1990, 9%/EP 2000, 17%	+8%/F-EP
%M-EA w/%EP	62%	71%	1990, 31%/EP 2000, 85%	+4%/M-EA
Economically Inactive [EI]	11,053	10,970	1990, 57%/EP 2000, 47%	–10%/EP
F-EI#	7,797 71%/EIP	7,900 72%/EIP	1990 79%/F-EP 2000 66%	–13%/F-EI
M-EI	3,256 29%/EIP	3,070 28%/EIP	1990, 34%/M-EP 2000, 27%	–1%/M-EI

*Population growth, 1995–2000: 4.5%M, 5.6%F

^ Age groups 2000: 1–14 yrs, 33%; 15–64, 58%; 65+, 6%; 1990–2000 growth rate: <15, 31%; >15-64, 6%

+1990 and 2000, unemployment rates, less than 1%: in 2000, 33Fs, 122Ms

#F-EI as % of F-EP: Homemakers -1990, 59%; 2000, 47%; Students - 1990, 17%; 14%

Table 5.2. 1990 and 2000 Principal Occupations (O_i); with number (n) and percent all Economically Active (EA) and F-EA in occupation (F_i/O_i) and percent chang

Principal Occupation (O_i)	*1990 n in O_i w/% all EA n = 7,831*	*1990 n & % F_i in O_i*	*2000 n in O_i w%/all EA n = 11,960*	*2000 n; %F_i/O_i; w/%Change*
Professional	O_i = 249 3%/EA	F_i = 58 23% F_i/O_i	O_i = 438 4%/EA	F_i = 198 45% F_i/O_i; +22%
Technician	O_i = 206 3%	F_i = 117 57%	O_i = 310 3%	F_i = 161 52%; –5%
Education Worker	O_i = 657 8%	F_i = 397 60%	O_i = 743 6%	F_i = 454 61%; +1%
Arts Worker	O_i = 92 1%	F_i = 22 24%	O_i = 143 1%	F_i = 46 32%; +8%
Bureaucrat, Director	O_i = 149 2%	F_i = 28 19%	O_i = 194 2%	F_i = 58 30%; +11%
Agricultural Worker	O_i = 2,007 26%	F_i = 39 2%	O_i = 2,057 17%	F_i = 81 4%; +2%
Inspector, Supervisor	O_i = 108 1%	F_i = 6 6%	O_i = 109 1%	F_i = 8 7%; +1%
Artisan, Worker*	O_i = 1,131 15%	F_i = 130 11%	O_i = 1,888 16%	F_i = 348 18%; +7%
Machinist	O_i = 224 3%	F_i = 49 22%	O_i = 237 2%	F_i = 58 6%; +4%
Aide, *Peón*, Day Laborer	O_i = 598 8%	F_i = 25 4%	O_i = 903 8%	F_i = 85 9%; +5%
Transport Worker	O_i = 280 4%	F_i = 4 1%	O_i = 518 4%	F_i = 2 .4%; –.6%
Office Worker	O_i = 412 5%	F_i = 214 52%	O_i = 556 5%	F_i = 362 65%; +13%
Commerce Merchant, Staff	O_i = 613 8%	F_i = 303 49%	O_i = 1,209 10%	F_i = 694 57%; +8%
Non-fixed Trader	O_i = 73 1%	F_i = 29 40%	O_i = 351 3%	F_i = 272 77%; +37%
Domestic Employee	O_i = 268 3%	F_i = 253 94%	O_i = 1,211 10%	F_i = 759 63%; –31%
Security	O_i = 133 2%	F_i = 9 7%	O_i = 150 1%	F_i = 17 11%; +4%

*Includes construction labor

Table 5.3. Indexes of Female Segregation by Occupation (I-FS) and Female Demographic Equality (I-FDE)*

Principal Occupation [O_i]	*1990 I-FS w/n F_i/O_i Base:23%/F-EA*	*1990 I-F DE Base:51%/ F-EP*	*2000 I-FS Base:33%/F-EA*	*2000 I-FDE Base:52%/ F-EP*
Professional	F_i = 58; I = 0	F-IDE = –69	F_i = 198; I = +53	I = –30
Technician	F_i = 117; I = +70	I = +12	F_i = 161; I = +59	I = 0
Education	F_i = 397; I = 240	I = +62	F_i = 454; I = +209	I = +68
Arts	F_i = 22; I = +1	I = –25	F_i = 46; I = –1	I = –28
Bureaucrat, Director	F_i = 28; I = –8	I = –48	F_i = 58; I = –6	I = –43
Agriculture	F_i = 39; I = –422	I = –985	F_i = 81; I = –598	I = –989
Supervisor	F_i = 6; I = –19	I = –49	F_i = 8; I = –28	I = –49
Artisan	F_i = 130; I = –130	I = –447	F_i = 348; I = –275	I = –634
Machinist	F_i = 49; I = –3	I = –65	F_i = 58; I = –20	I = –65
Aide, Laborer+	F_i = 25; I = –113	I = –280	F_i = 85; I = –213	I = –385
Transport++	F_i = 4; I = –60	I = –139	F_i = 2; I = –169	I = –267
Office Work	F_i = 214; I = +119	I = –4	F_i = 362; I = +179	I = +64
Commerce#	F_i = 303; I = +162	I = –10	F_i =694; I = +295	I = +65
Non-fixed Trader	F_i = 29; I = +12	I = –8	F_i = 272; I = +156	I = +89
Domestic employee	F_i = 253; I = +191	I = +116	F_i = 759; I = +359	I = +129
Security	F_i = 9; I = –22;	I = –59	F_i = 17; I = –33	I = –61

*See Box 5.1
+Day laborer, peón
++No women drivers
#Owners and staff

Gendering Trends

The outstanding fact is that across the decade, women's activity increased by a historically dramatic ten points, rising above the national average of 29 percent and nearly on a par with Cuernavaca and several other more industrialized cities. As the male/female (M/F) EA gap contracted from 52 to 34 percent, though remaining highly gendered, by 2000, Tepoztlán's labor force was one of the most sex-integrated in central Mexico. Numerical increases came in every age group, indicating life cycles did not predict women's employment decisions as independently as long hypothesized. Other indicators suggest that the shape of all changes correlates not only with revisions in family relations but also growth in certain types of jobs, new priorities, and longstanding segregation and segmentation patterns.

A cross-decade comparison shows that from ages twelve to sixty-four, each female segment increased its presence by more than the ten-point (23–

33 percent) aggregate increase. In 2000, each twenty to fifty-four age cohorts surpassed 33 percent. For the prime eight cohorts (ages twenty to fifty-nine), the F-EA ratio is 37 percent. For the peak years forty to forty-four, the figure is 49 percent. After the thirty-something segment, there is a gradual decline of increased entry rates; however, many in this group entered employment in the 1980s. Employment for women in the sixty-five and over group is three times more likely than for the twelve to fourteen groups. Still, aging is more a factor for women than for men who are twice as likely to remain in the labor force. Perhaps most provocative, though, is that during the decade, the F-EA ratio of the total EP rose from 9 to 17 percent of the entire economic population, versus an increase for men of 31 to 35 percent.

Table 5.2 (and a participation graph) shows the New Economy shape of women's work. Peak characteristics give no support to the U-shape hypothesis long relied upon to correlate women's employment rates to economic transitions. Historically, some chartings indicate that at first women's employment rates decline. Participation rises with human capital advances and industrialization. To the contrary, this U-shape tends toward inversion, the standard pattern for male participation, an inversion that becomes more pronounced.

The 1990 graph has a double peak. To Patricia Roos (1985:42–48), this pattern indicates a surge in participation before marriage and first child-bearing years; then a drop off, followed by a return while children are still quite young. The 2000 graph has a single peak. Roos states that this pattern reflects the fact that from their late teens into their forties, age group decisions to enter the labor force remain substantially consistent. She speculates that the two patterns respond to the increase in part-time jobs. In addition, the single peak form suggests that when male out-migration rates are "excessively high," married women fill family-wage voids. The Gross Domestic Product (GDP)—the market value of all final commodities produced in the municipio in a single year—for 1990 and 2000 verifies the intensification of the Roos pattern, which explains household-level infrastructural gains in a time of financial crises. The 2000 pattern suggests a heightened degree of extradomestic labor, facilitated by the flexibility of available jobs. Doubtlessly, the existence of male exit options heavily influenced women's staying on decisions and their ability to accept low quality jobs, a factor that capped all salaries.

Regarding economic inactivity, as the EA percent was rising ten points, the ratio of EI women was dropping 79 to 66 percent, a decline sustained during early child rearing years. The twelve years and above female student population also decreased, from 17 to 13 percent of the F-EP. (Teachers report they left to go to work or because parents were unable to pay school fees. Some students said their education had become irrelevant to the jobs available.) Together, these factors show an increased tendency for women of all ages, and thus at different life cycle periods, to privilege the type of employment locally available. Still, demographically, the total F-EI population dropped a mere one point. Underexamined is the option many, likely most, women choose: opportunistically overlapping domestic and extra-domestic labor. The EI rate calls attention to the intensifying need for unpaid caregiving, the inevitable result of socially regressive policies. However, even this frontline need did not diminish sex typing; of the 5,161 declaring "homemaking" their principal occupation, 99 percent were female, a decade increase of 1 percent.

Table 5.3 displays occupational and demographic integration/segregation by sex/gender remained intense. Significantly, there were distributional changes, responding to a complex of changes in the conditions of male employment specified in later chapters. It seems then that a statistically important surge of woman into paid labor has multiple, often contradictory origins. Patterns suggest women were responding not to impressive human capital gains but to crisis driven factors like increases in men's migration; the vanishing family wage; and in large part, to the creation of female-typed jobs.

Replicated in Tepoztlán were a number of reversionary changes at the national level that had a strongly gender differentiated impact on labor market formation. Increasingly, rural and metropolitan workers pursued jobs in mid-size cities with world market-oriented comparative advantages, such as free-trade zones or a tourism industry. Population growth created female-typed front line jobs while intensifying competition for them. In sum, Table 5.3 leaves no doubt that tenaciously in Tepoztlán occupations have gender. Of course, the key issue is whether this is a symptom or the disease of inequality itself.

Besides agriculture, only three other occupations decreased in ratios of actively employed, and these from just two to one percent. All but three occupations (technician, transport, domestic worker) absorbed the same or a larger percent of women. Yet allowing for the increase of Fs-EA, the results are quite different: only in the professional, office worker, non-fixed trader, and bureaucratic categories did expansion take place. At a general level, the indexes of segregation and demographic equality confirm that whether expanding or contracting, whether in the formal or shadow economy, occupations continue to be sex-typed along pre-existing lines. As earlier pointed out, women did not fill the most male-identified jobs vacated by outsourcing men. On the other hand, as tourism became more technocratic, I detected a trend for men with access to capital to increase their presence in certain female-typed jobs, notably as own account workers in the high growth industries of restaurants and hotels and paid domestic labor.

Summarized, 44 percent of women were in occupations that were all but exclusively or mainly female. They continued to be overrepresented in already female-typed slots. With a 39 percent increase, numerical feminization was highest in the non-fixed trading category. In ten occupations, to achieve gender equality, there would have to be 2,550 more women. Gender also structures jobs and tasks within occupations. For example, 50 percent of professionals and technicians were in health and social services and 25 percent of office workers in government despite decreased funding. Women made up 75 percent of the personal services and 68 percent of health and social services. Not surprisingly since new jobs were predominantly in this sector, women were overrepresented in all but the two highest economic class categories, supervisor and business services. Up to this point, it can be stated that supply, numerical feminization, is primary to demand, occupation structures.

Activity Sector Transitions

Although Tepoztlán is within an officially marginal agricultural zone, historically, most male "household heads" engaged in small-scale farming primarily for self-consumption and local trading. Before the highway, women's main agricultural (and economic) activity had been marketing 'surpluses', so also a small-scale activity. A sharp decline in agricultural revenues that began in the 1940s intensified from 1950 to1990—a period when the municipio population increased from 7,264 to 27,646 and much of the most fertile land sold to developers. However, into the twenty-first century, agriculture has remained numerically the largest and most male-dominated sector.

Beginning in 1980, subsistence and commercial agriculture and related activities (including herding) fell from 83 to 26 percent of the municipio GDP. In 1995, the non-agricultural GDP was (an estimated) 102,947,000 pesos. Construction and manufacturing (at artisan levels) rose from 1to 13 percent while commerce expanded from 3 to 9 percent. A diversifying range of personal and public services constituted the major growth sector, spiraling from 6 to 36 percent. In 1970, women made up only 10 percent of the EAP, but even at this level evident were the gender dimensions of sector and job trends that intensified between 1980 and 1990. Significantly, the categories that expanded the most (25 percent) were service activities that in 1980 could not be "sufficiently specified."

While agriculture was the primary gainful occupation of 70 percent of EA men, 46 percent of women worked in the service sector: 18 percent in professions (mainly education); 11 percent were non-agricultural employees; and 7 percent in commerce. In addition, women in other sectors generally were also consumption stuff providers.

Calibrated in terms of the classic (but never uniformly agreed upon by economists) three-activity sector division, from 1980 to 1990, the primary (extractive) sector declined from 26 to 17 percent; the secondary (commercial) stayed the same at 27 percent; and the tertiary (services) increased from 54 to 57 percent. A cross-decade age-based comparison shows that from ages fifteen and up each cohort increased its labor force presence by more than the ten point overall rise (from 23 to 33 percent) in Fs-EA. And in 2000, each segment ages twenty to fifty-four surpassed 33 percent. If the prime eight working age segments (twenty to fifty-nine) were isolated, the 2000 F-EA increases to 37 percent. For the peak years of forty to forty-four, the figure is 49 percent.

Gendering Trends

By 1990, there were four distinct activity divisions. (1) The extractive sector includes agriculture, ranching, forestry, floral culture, and animal husbandry for local and global exchange. Though continuing to fall, and still mainly for self-consumption and local trading, agriculture remained (by a margin of 2,573 workers) the major employment sector. Primary cash crops were red tomatoes, gladiolas, and cactus (*nopal*). (2) Construction, utilities and manufacturing, a category that primarily involves artisan and processing activities, make up a transformation sector. (3) The distributive sector includes transportation, communication, warehousing, and wholesale commerce. (4) The service sector has the following divisions: services to businesses and other producers (financial, and some professionals, such as lawyers); technicians; direct services to consumers: maintenance, hotels and restaurants, and personal services; real estate; and retail commerce. Public services include education, health (including sports) and welfare services, and governmental and (increasingly after the Golf Club) NGO activities. Sex typing of each sector—and gendering is most pronounced at divisions within sectors—confirm that men and women operate in labor markets that expand and contract in response to different market signals. Moreover, at salary level, gender trumps activity sector and job growth patterns.

A dialectical connection between growth and decline in a sector correlates with systematic job gendering. For example, as small farming and the ratio of men earning a daily wage decline pueblo policies encourage the expansion of female typed jobs. Thus between 1990 and 2000, as the percentage of men in agriculture declined, the percent of women economically active in the sector went from 2 to 4 percent. Moreover, dedication of wages also differs. All significant sector increases for women were in services. Notable is that the ratio of women in Restaurant, Hotel, and Maintenance services dropped and that of men increased.

The perception is that women's earnings flow directly into the practices of everyday life while the money men earn (particularly when earned abroad) goes toward longer terms investments, including home and neighborhood improvements. Perhaps, this perception is a function of the absence of women in the highest status male occupations.

Returning to Tables 5.2 and 5.3, using the Index of Female Segregation—based on the number of women needed to achieve sex balancing (see Box 5.1)—in 2000, in all categories, there were generally too few and occasionally too many women. For example, missing in agriculture were 598 women, 275 in construction, and 169 in transportation: all but excluded from these all but exclusively male occupations were 24 percent of all EA women. On the other side, overrepresentation totaled 664 workers in a combination of precarious services (by 26 percent of Fs-EA). The lower the I-FS, the lower the percent the job contributes to the GDP. When the issue is working conditions, what stands out is the uniformity across sectors of women's inequality.

Working Conditions

While women's wage share markedly increased, at an aggregate level whether under or over represented, they trailed men at low and high ends of pay scales. In all sectors, the 5,275 workers added mostly entered profoundly underpaid jobs that gave them little control over their own labor power. This section summarizes gendering trends in working conditions, including authority positions, hours worked, and salary levels. The finding is that within and across occupations and sectors, Tepoztecas were highly more likely than Tepoztecos to work part-time, in jobs that pay just above minimum and below minimum wages, and in positions that seldom give them supervisory status. Wages in services (in which an average of 56.5 percent of women participated) were low versus male dominated trades. But in all occupations—whether white, blue, or pink collar—women's representation—whether high, low, or relatively equitable, or in the formal, quasiformal and informal sector—had little overall effect on male/female status gaps. These conditions indicate the failure of meritocratic analyses to explain away gender at work and point to the overriding significance of the massive change in capital's interests and strategies.

Gendering Trends

Though to be sure municipio salaries are uniformly low versus living costs, even when compared to inadequate male salaries, on average, women's salaries were meager, a gender gap that did not lessen during the decade. In 2000, 1,249 workers (10 percent/EA) were making from 50 percent through 1 MS. Women were 61 percent of this group. The lowest waged part-time labor was highly feminized. As to this costly correlation, sometimes Tepoztecas were compelled to choose part-time jobs; but often they were responding to the macro-policy backed deregulation or supply siding of job creation.

In 2000, women (33 percent/EA) were 68 and 57 percent of the 2 salary levels below 1 MS. However, since around 50 percent of EA women working (at least) a full day were underpaid, and Mexico's definition of employment a charade, the part-time aspect cannot explain illegal pay levels. As to status, segmentation, the scale of the economy is a factor in the scarcity of managerial positions. However, even in the unionized education industry, only one woman had directorial status. Women primarily participated as employees and self-employed workers (rising from 21 to 25 percent), men also, but not nearly at the same ratio.

Women selecting self-employment often chose fixed and mobile (nonfixed) or home sited commerce, fields with a long history of female entrepreneurship and exploitation. The wage gap in the self-employed category indicates that there were significant quality differences in the terms of participation that structurally limited entrepreneurial women's earning power. Twenty percent of men but only 2 percent of women were manual laborers, mainly in the heavily male-dominated sectors of agriculture and construction. However, even when conditions closely resemble the "*peón*" category, women do not describe their work with a classification reserved for male workers. Clearly, multiple interacting factors drive the absence of women in sectors that provide many jobs for men, jobs that are no more consistently low paying or more likely to be perceived as necessarily man's work than many other options.

Across the decade, salaries for men and women fell far short of a family wage level. However, it is impossible to extrapolate from the data sets a range of significantly gendered factors. Take the hotel sector, which has grown considerably since 2000, as a number of people have converted their homes into lodgings. Of the five male owners I interviewed, each had at least one other primary income source. Their wives did not. Indeed, some who were very active in the business did not define themselves as employed. My observations suggest this may well be a function of the fact their often simultaneous occupation with private homemaking.

During the decade, there was little change in salaried hours worked, more decreases than increase in wages levels, and near stagnation in women's low status location in the labor force. Women's increased economic activity does not correlate to substantive gains. Though deeply disappointing, I argue the need to view feminization from another perspective, namely women's labor market creativity. Data sets leave no doubt that gender remains a profoundly significant but by no means fixed variable in all work process decisions. Combined with and interrogated by other information sources, statistics guide us toward detecting reasons why a great many Tepoztecas could not participate economically in ways that counted officially or lessened their economic dependency.

Observational Data

As Loutfi (2001:8) observes, the narrow definition of productive activity as commodities exchanged in the market system means people are "less confused than they ought to be" by statistics. The participant observation approach of Appendix A allows the inclusion of activities often obscured because they involve labor not performed in the municipio, nonstandard, and/or gratis labor. Validated as well is Standing's (1989:1080) argument that work status classifications are "grossly deficient" because work today compresses many different statuses, thus requiring multiple mechanisms of control.

Gendering Trends

Appendix A indicates the dimensions of the distortion of the systematic failure to give equal scientific importance to women's unremunerated labor and to forms of paid labor that are so low status they fall outside formal calculations. Essential as well is to correlate men's disempowerment to women's centrality to particular, often concealed engines of neoliberal capitalism. Therefore, we need to investigate at points where hidden and misunderstood activities interlock with postindustrial capitalism as it really is.

The House Economy

There is material evidence that, as in Redfield and Lewis' time, Tepoztecan households do not have to be unitary to operate effectively as cooperative units. Taking even dysfunctional households as "corporate, long-lived units that are organized for specific ends" (Gillespie 2000:468), this section focuses on house economies; particularly on the ways activities interlink to sustain structure. Highly important is that few families pay rent or, because of Tepoztlán's communal status, property taxes. On the other hand, they must self-provision services that in the U.S. that are public goods or when purchased, represent a much smaller percentage of total wages. (Of course, everyone pays value added taxes; and Mexico's inequitable income tax increases advantages of the wealthy.) To relate waged and unwaged labor to budgets, living costs, and consumption decisions, I begin with sketches of cooperative family labor forces.

- The Hernández Family of Barrio San Sebastian: Blanca, mother, age forty-two, sells shoes on commission, cleans the homes of foreigners three times each week, and tends the family's plant nursery. Father Claudio, age forty-five, a teacher at a middle school, sells the plants on market days. The six children, ages five to seventeen, devote considerable time to family projects. Three times each week, the oldest son works four hours as a helper at a villa. Daughter Anita works as a nanny for the same family when they come. Another son works at odd jobs, usually in the flower industry. All spend their "free time" constructing a new greenhouse.
- The Moreno Family of Barrio Los Reyes: Yanet, a homemaker age twenty-four, mother of two boys, sells Avon products. Her husband, age thirty, is a skilled carpenter; his sister and mother share the house; both are domestic workers and support themselves. Yanet prizes her Avon job because it has benefits. All others were seeking either better jobs or additional work.
- The Zavala Family of Barrio San Miguel: Lilia, age thirty-eight, mother of four, and her husband Daniel, age thirty-six, own a pick-up. He is a commercial transporter; she runs their housefront grocery, *casa tienda*. One daughter regularly helps her mother in the store.
- The Cardoso Family of the Central District: Magdalena, age seventy-one, mother of seven, goes to work six days each week in one of the family's numerous businesses, usually in the poultry shop. Husband Alberto, age eighty-five and no longer robust, has turned many of his ventures over to his children. All live in Tepoztlán, have university degrees, and pursue careers of their own as well as maintaining family firms. In the casa, there is a paid staff of four. Magdalena oversees and often participates in domestic duties.
- The Ramos Family of Barrio San Miguel: Several generations of this family have occupied the site where Rosa, age twenty-four, now operates a unisex beauty shop. Behind her shop are the family home and her father's metalworking business. Money she earned and loans from the family were the source of start up expenses, including two years of training at a Cuernavaca beauty school at a cost of 9,000 pesos. She paid 18,000 pesos for

rather rudimentary equipment plus various taxes and operating permit fees. She pays no rent. She is pleased with the volume but finds it increasingly difficult to make a profit.

Living Costs and Budgets

Here I highlight more than fifty shopping surveys in which I asked resident shoppers on their way home what they had spent that day and which items they generally bought. Amounts varied greatly, and many factors entered into buying patterns. Almost everyone reported adjusting spending to income and changes in prices. So for example, during the rainy season when the price of tomatoes is "even higher than usual," Doña Gina prepares more meatless meals. With four young children, Doña Luzmila cuts back 100 pesos per week by switching from fresh to subsidized powdered milk even though "the children despise it."

The erasure of subsidies on corn profoundly affects household economies. In an informal sample, the average tortilla consumption per day per man was twelve. Growing boys can eat at least double this amount. The buying patterns of many Tepoztecans depend on whether they have a private supply of corn. If a family grinds its own corn, the cost is around 1.50 per week; buying the same amount of *masa*, dough, costs 8 pesos. No unit reported having enough self-supplied corn to last through the year. Some goods are cheaper in cities; but savings can vanish with the addition of transport, lost time, and stress. A price increase of say 50 centavos on a bus ticket or earning a wage makes local shopping greatly more attractive. These shoppers mostly but not exclusively buy locally; they prefer to shop on special market days:

- Anita, age forty-four, spends 50 to 70 pesos weekly for her husband and herself "when I have it."
- Teresa, age thirty-five, family of four, spends 150 pesos every three days.
- Bette, age forty, family of five, spends 200 weekly, always adding "something a bit special."
- Elvira, age twenty-five, family of three, spends 40 to 70 pesos each visit always on staples.
- Delfina, age fifty-two, spends 450 pesos weekly for five adults.

Here is a 1997 budget for selected items for three families described to me by the wife/mother in each family. The families are related. Wives 2 and 3 are sisters and are the aunts of family 1-wife.

Table 5.4. Partial Household Budgets in Pesos

Annual Budget Items	*Family 1* *5 Occupants*	*Family 2* *4 Occupants*	*Family 3* *3 Occupants*
Food	11,000	22,550	9,125
Family fiestas	1,500	2,500	1,000
Alcohol	500	—	1,200
Household expenses	2–3,000	5,000	200
Taxes	—	400	—
Maintenance	1,000	2,000	—
Education	2,000	—	500
Health	1,000	5,400	3,000
Civic fiestas	3,000 (2)	3,000 (2)	3,000 (3)
Diversions	2,000	5,000	Very little
Total	24–25,000	49,500	22,525

Box 5.2
Partial Budgets for Three Family/households, 1997

Family 1: Five occupants of a small, modern home, recently married couple, husband's mother and two younger brothers. Husband, age twenty-four, holds several jobs and averages 100 pesos per day. His wife, twenty-four, is a nurse; pregnant and not employed at the interview time, but engaged in various ventures; did most chores and prepared meals for her family and often for the entire household. Home belongs to husband's mother; they do not pay rent but pay their share of daily expenses. Mother, divorced housekeeper of a villa, makes 60 pesos/ day and receives "some" child support. Dependency ratio: two regular earners, three non-regular earners.

Family 2: Mother, forty-eight, and father, fifty-seven, their daughter and son-in-law occupy a spacious home. The senior couple works in an El Centro candy store purchased with money she inherited. Husband also a tollbooth operator, makes 700/week with "generous" benefits, including private medical insurance. (The Japanese company that built the highw.ay also manages its operations.) Until she had a baby in 1996, daughter, twenty-one, taught at a private school. (She gave birth in a local private maternity hospital at a cost of 10,000.) Her husband, twenty-two, works as a baker's apprentice. (The next year, they opened a house bakery; all contribute labor.) Dependency ratio: four earners.

Family 3: Couple, both self-employed, and a son occupy a modest home. This couple has struggled financially. Wife, fifty-five, has a jewelry stall in the mercado, estimates profits "around" 40 per day, but there is great variability, usually on the down side. Husband, fifty-eight, combines construction and agriculture and makes "almost" enough to cover budgeted items. Son, twenty-one, is training to be a teacher. He is in a state program in which he works as a teacher's aide five hours per day, earning exactly what he pays in tuition at a Cuernavaca normal school (500/month). He does not contribute to expenses, but covers most personal expenses by working at various tasks on weekends. Parents financed high school in Cuernavaca (1,000+ pesos per year). Dependency ratio: two full-time, one part-time earner.

Gendering Trends

The overall impression of house economy data is that Tepoztecan families do concertedly act as economic units. Allocation of funds indicates that despite economic class differences, the three families privilege the same "good society" markers. All the women are or aspire to be regular through not primary contributors to family budgets; at the same time, none regarded domestic obligations as secondary. For women with heavy domestic demand for their labor power, the quality of a job appears to be the deciding factor.

Moreover, the social construction of gender within a household appears to be of much less immediate importance than the availability of jobs that suit the women's skills, time constraints, and material needs. Though parents no longer rigidly enforce child labor, it remains important not only to the family but to the larger economy.

Because it is the cosmic difference between a strategy and a tactic, belonging to a unit formed around home ownership in a secure and beautiful environment conditions all aspects of the lives of the three families. Support systems and working conditions are embedded in forms of sociality, which can only be even minimally socially acceptable if, Sen (1999) argues, they make goods and services continuously available. One breadwinner per house could not keep up. I asked Family 3 while they spent as much on fiestas as much better off Family 2. The mother replied, "In Tepoztlán, you lose respect if you do not repay hospitality in kind. Also, it is my way of thanking my customers." In sum, capitalism does not stop at the door of the household, as some argue, even on a fiesta day.

Observations of house economies indicate that all social reproductive expenditures are recognized as critical to maintaining the basic cooperative structure. This includes Saturday house cleanings by daughters and young boys sweeping patios since overcrowded homes require the constant maintenance of hard won assets. Mothers must be astute about meals and fathers must have backup income sources. Of course, it is possible to purchase most consumables in the market; for many Tepoztecans, doing so requires making allocation decisions that have the potential to destabilize structures.

Financial Arrangements

There is wide agreement that the most constraining form of economic discrimination women experience is that they have too little access to and pay too much for credit. Because of usurious interest rates (that continues to spike; in 1995, borrowing rates of commercial banks were 40 percent; active rates, much higher) and often the inability to get a loan from a financial institution, Tepoztecans avoid borrowing from banks. Keep in mind, however, that even when not coming directly from the money market, the international money market conditions all financial arrangements.

Money earned away from the municipio is now likely the major source of women's investment funds—often come as dollar transfers. Moneychangers can now pay in foreign currency. To draw dollars, the charge is $4 per $100. A number of women said that loan programs sponsored by various development agencies seldom "fit" their needs. Some had borrowed from local saving and loan cooperatives; many had participated in a *tanda*, a rotating monetary system.

Savings and Loans

Cooperative Tlahuica limits clients to "pure Tepoztecans." Cooperative Integral does not. Cooperative Tepoztlán's 1,000 pesos minimum for opening an account was high by local standards. If loans are not serviced or repaid in a timely manner, cooperatives seize property. (This is no empty threat.) The financial institution most utilized is the *tanda*, a socially organized association that, though grounded in mutual trust, is rigidly cash based.

Tandas

Indebtedness is to the pueblo but far from being a backward approach to women's credit crunch, the plan closely corresponds to microloan programs endorsed by the World Bank. Tandas work like this. (1) Investor groups form voluntarily but not randomly, because through payouts are made to individuals, ultimately every investor is accountable. Consequently, information on members' social and material assets is vital to determining "trust." (2) Each investor commits to putting into the pot a uniform specified amount over a specified time period, say at two-week intervals for three months. (3) A drawing establishes the payout sequence; each person receives the same amount but at different times. (The highest amount I heard about was 1,000 pesos.) (4) After each payout, participants replenish the fund the original amount. Of course, payout placement makes a great difference, since the first to receive the fund is essentially getting an interest-free loan. On the other hand, investors may prefer postponed payouts since some reasons for enrolling were: "It forces me to save"; "I loan my salary to myself"; and "It is safer to have money in a tanda than hidden in the house" But barber Don Chucho feared that "I can lose my money and my friends." To the merchant being shaved, "Tandas are an excuse to be robbed. Anyway, I can lend my money out privately and get at the very least 30 percent interest in just a few days or hours."

It is possible to withdraw after a tanda has commenced. But the loss of *confianza* can have huge repercussions since financial reliability is one of the few ways individuals can achieve independent economic status: Not surprisingly then to Don Pedro "Women need them more than men." "Always," several people replied when asked when tandas began in Tepoztlán. According to Doña Mirabel, women did not "do" them until the late 1970s when "jobs became more plentiful." She also correlated doing them to the uncertainties of dependency on male remittances. "As wage earners, we were able to help each other out."

While urbanization was the source of most wages, it vastly increased the risk of cooperation. To most players, the critical issue was the ability of the initiator to make informed judgments about investors. Confidence-raising factors were membership in the pueblo, adulthood, and a steady and dependable income. Though never directly mentioned as a prerequisite, because of occupational sex typing, gender becomes important since coworkers form many investor groups. Tandas do have the advantage of not indebting women to a volatile, unforgiving credit market; but bear in mind credible studies suggesting that women fare worse in the absence of capital markets.

Overcoming "the Great Silence"

Miriama Williams (2003:19) asserts that "the great silence around the gender dimensions of trade liberalization" reflects the belief among officials that trade policies are "gender blind in orientation and gender neutral in its effects." Activated in this chapter and in Appendix A are specific procedural/ideological biases, each linked to the exclusionary definition of economic activity and to the failure to integrate the activities of the basic cooperative unit, the family/household.

Pattern analyses are limited by the narrow and changeable reference periods—because much employment is intermittent and seasonal (factors which are highly gender-sensitive)—and the routine undercounting and misreading of women's often (to economists) "nonstandard" ways of participating in production. Then, were patterns direct responses to men's migration; to the vanishing family wage; to revisions in gender conventions; to the creation of female-typed jobs? To what extent and at what point in work decisions did human capital factors kick in, factors such as more years in school, later marriage, and a falling birthrate? Clearly social capital has a huge impact, though whether favorable or not is another unanswered question. Were decisions conditioned by cultural priorities versus the failure of the state to provide or at least subsidize support systems, especially reliable childcare? Another impediment is the inability to differentiate between workers seeking jobs and the voluntarily inactive. Are the EI discouraged job seekers, laid-off workers, or vital but irregular contributors to family for-profit enterprises?

A major distortion in Tepoztlán's highly localized family-based economy is the failure to incorporate cross- and intra-household level exchanges in cash and kind and counterpoise them to the quality of available paid jobs. High among urgent need to-knows is part time work. Is the decision to work part time involuntary or driven by the privileging of reproductive obligations?

Evidently, women's near exclusion from a number of occupations pushes them into jobs. The fact that their primary employment sites are the major arenas of growth means they face ever-stiffer competition, not only from other women but also from male migrants and students. Already, new immigration restrictions are increasing direct competition with men. Limited access to affordable credit constrains women's ability to take advantage of new capital-intensive options even in the most feminized occupations. Skewed access to education, skill sets, and job training mean that women have insufficient control over the reproduction of their labor power.

As the GDP declined between 1993 and 1998 despite the expansion of the service sector, and as women surged into these jobs, for most Tepoztecas, structural adjustments were changing but not meeting their material needs. Nevertheless, in a severely depressed economy that dipped in an out of volatile recoveries, male and female stakeholders remained intent on integrating into the pueblo's New Economy. Hugely significant is that these gendered gaps also anchor neoliberal policies that slot even the most localized workers into phases of the globally interlinked economy. Many studies emphasize the importance of isolating transactions by means of which the macroeconomy incorporates specific supply siding inequities. Are jobs sex-typed at entry or substitution levels? Is gender integrated at or even before job creation levels? The stress by development agencies on entrepreneurship brings us up this increasingly central issue. Is the micro entrepreneurship now so strongly endorsed in the best interests of women or of firms that profit doubly: by excluding women from protected forms of employment while bringing them into the consumer culture?

The information in this chapter confirms that however fundamentally reorganized, gender continues to be a backward/forward dialectical contradiction in a production-reproduction system that is, in the words of Roger Barta, "the actual state of capitalist economic and social development in Mexico" (2001:13). The chapters ahead are situated explorations of problems of meanings and relationships raised up to this point.

Chapter Six

New Economy Housework

> Current labor market trends raise new question about the links between paid and unpaid work and about their distribution and boundaries. A transition is currently taking place in the ways in which this distribution is affecting individuals, household and communities.
>
> —Lourdes Benería, 2001

Quehaceres del hogar—the chores (*quehaceres*) a person performs to create goods, services, and information intended for immediate or delayed consumption by members of her own household (*hogar*)—is the work process interrogated in this chapter. I use the feminine reference "her" because it still can be taken for granted that in Tepoztlán, Tepoztecas undertake the lion's share of housework. However, as I soon discovered about the performance and the meanings of New Economy housework in all its stages—from determining the need for a particular consumable to creating and allocating the developed necessity—little else can be assumed.

Structural adjustments have both expanded the need for and made possible new combinations of *trabajo*, paid work, and the multitude of activities undertaken to reproduce individuals and societies. Conditioning all work women perform for the household is the requirement to stabilize two organizationally conflicting enterprises. Gender is the factor that makes linkages across the domestic and extradomestic domains at once more achievable, more essential, and more individually and collectively costly. Probing adaptations of chores Tepoztecas design to solve New Economy problems specific to a unit, this chapter revisits what has long been the central materialist feminist issue: "how women's work within the home is related to her subordination both within the home and outside it" (Mackintosh 1989:394).

A HYBRID WORKING CLASS

Earlier, I pointed out that when asked, "What is your occupation?" all but a few women replied "homemaker," *ama de casa*, including daughters as well as wives and mothers. In addition to "fulltime homemakers," even entrepreneurs prosperously engaged in trabajo reported allocating considerable "free" time to chores. The 1990s was a period when the for-profit and for-consumption tasks women performed came to more closely resemble each other and replicate each other. The hybridity of this working class alerted me to the fact that most were using the keyword "housework" in two senses. The reference could be to a complex of tasks done within the domestic domain, everything from making beds to shopping. Or housework could describe activities in which the produced commodity was school fees. Yet as the case studies ahead indicate, even though the organization of *trabajo*/work (economic activity) and *quehaceres*/chores (economic inactivity) interlock continuously, official discourse treats the two systems as incommensurable, thereby insuring that they are contradictory pairs.

Doña Rita's Diary

Conversations with homemakers suggest that like economists, they too differentiate the meanings of work and chores. So what do Tepoztecas who define themselves as "fulltime homemakers" explicitly identify as chores? The diary that is the basis of Table 6.1 is representative of the work processes many women perform under the rubric "housework."

As on this day, from her selling activities, Rita usually nets around two US$2.25 minimum salary, a significant contribution toward maintaining an acceptable lifestyle given the uncertainly of husband Memo's employment. As to hours, by the time she sleeps, Rita has put in seventeen hours of work. For a six-day workweek, this amounts to 102 hours (though of course, on the seventh day Rita does not rest). To give a context to her hours: 43 percent of teachers work twenty-five to thirty-two hours per week; 17 percent of women in commerce, 64 plus; and 39 percent of men in agriculture, forty-one to forty-eight hours.

Fragmentation, capital's key reorganizing strategy, is the outstanding feature of Rita's opened-ended workday. Her complex of roles overlaps the economic activity descriptions employee, day laborer, manager, self-employed, and unpaid worker in a family enterprise. As she produces, processes, and distributes a wide range of commodities, her tasks crosscut activity sectors. To economists, this piling-on of disparate activities scientifically explains the degraded status of the labor power she sells in the market, which, in turn,

Table 6.1. Work diary of Rita Padilla, 6 June 1996. The family: Rita (age 26), Memo (age 32), children Luz, Carlito, and Paco (ages 10, 5, and 28 months), and Rita's grandmother Doña Susana (age 90).

6:30	I wake up; go to my kitchen to fix snacks for the children and Memo. I set out bowls of Maizoro, their favorite cereal.
7:15	Memo walks Luz to school because it is still dark. Grandmother, Paco, and I have our cereal. I clear up.
8:00	I make the beds and start to prepare my dinner, clean, and put Memo's work clothes to soak. A cousin who also has a son in kindergarten picks up Paco.
9:30	For a neighbor [an elderly widower], I prepare a dozen tortillas. I deliver them, he pays me, and I return home.
10:00	I finish the snacks I sell at two schools. My grandmother fills plastic bags with these and treats Memo bought in Cuernavaca. I prepare my hotcakes, then my fruits.
11:15	I put everything into 2 bags and hurry to the kindergarten. I get my small table (*mesita*) from inside the school where I'm allowed to store it. I arrange my things (*mis cosas*) and start selling as the children come outside for recess.
12:20	I rush to the primary. I get the *mesita* I leave in the house of a friend who lives near that school. I start selling. Luz comes out of the school and helps me.
1:40	Today we sold almost everything. I pack up. I return the *mesita.* I visit with the woman. She starts to cry when she tells me about how her husband beat her.
2:00	I count the money. The total is 33 pesos.
2:30	I finish the housework and prepare my tortillas. I nurse Paco.
4:00	We eat. Today I serve chicken, rice, radishes, squash, and fruit. Memo finishes quickly, gets Zorro [his horse] from the pasture, and goes to the milpa [they rent from his uncle].
5:00	Luz washes dishes. I clean, do my laundry, and rest.
6:00	The boys go out to play. I start filling bags for tomorrow. Luz finishes her homework and goes to visit her cousins.
7:00	I mend and watch *María del Barrio* [a hugely popular soap opera].
8:00	I boil water for lemon tea and put out a few leftovers.
9:00	It has stopped raining so the children and I walk to meet Memo and Zorro. We all drink tea and watch TV.
10:00	I prepare the clothes for everyone for tomorrow. I make sure the children have their supplies in their backpacks. I take my bath and wash my hair.
10:30	Now everyone sleeps.

rationalizes the overloading of reproductive activities (G. Becker 1991). They interpret the requirement to combine work processes as the trade-off wives and mothers willingly make to "have it all." Ingrid Palmer (1991) interprets it as a "reproductive tax" extracted from homemakers.

The bottom line is that Rita's labor complex underwrites the sub par wages and entitlements of others as well as chronic shortfalls in the local and national GDPs. Fusing paid and unpaid work deprives her of privatized forms of flexibility, optimizing choices such as taking the afternoon off to golf with other CEOs. It is however the form of fragmentation that to Nash masks the real economic value of women's unpaid labor but which also enables women to assess scientifically the "global development processes [that] have undermined social reproduction" (2005a:145). The next section updates the terms and impact of the separation myth that continues to feedback across domains as gender inequality at work: the myth of the systematic separation of the *casa*, the house, and the *calle*, street or market.

ADAPTATIONS OF THE CASA/CALLE MYTH

"Women here do not work. It's not our custom." The presence of two female secretaries and three businesswomen clients did not deter the male manager of a savings and loan cooperative from this pronouncement. Nor did the women react to his transparently incorrect assessment. This incident and many others confirmed that the venerable casa/calle division is still an active social fiction even in a pueblo that widely perceives cash earning as not only appropriate, but even obligatory for homemakers. The high rate of domestic and extra-domestic task and occupational segregation indicates that the terms and meanings of all variants of women's work continue to incorporate this fiction. Conversations with three resident foreigners provide insights into carriers of adaptations.

Lawyer/journalist Don Carlos, age sixty-two, the son of Tepoztecans who relocated to Mexico City in the 1930s had this to say:

> Many people say a regime of matriarchy prevails here. Tepoztecas do like to order things but they try to conceal their power. They respect only a man with whom they can share power. They taunt men who let women tell them what to do; they say, "He wears a dress, not pants." But even the most valiant and loud-mouthed want to be bossed because they think it inspires men to be aggressive and brave.

To Doña Elvia, age fifty-four, widow of a Tepoztecan, a labor and feminist activist:

> Women here are very traditional, many, I suspect, because they have no choice. Though not as pronounced as in some places, machismo is a powerful hindrance. I noticed changes in consciousness among Tepoztecas who went out to work for the first time. Feminism has had some effect on even the elite women who have good reasons to want to perpetuate tradition.

South American photographer/author Doña Eugenia aesthetically expresses her passion for Tepoztlán. In her view:

> Family, especially her children, is everything to women here. Family is her identity; homemaking makes her an esteemed person. Her special spaces are the kitchen and that most sacred of domestic sites, the sink [*la pila*] where she washes things belonging to her family. Her children seek her advice on many matters and she expects them to follow it. In turn, she seeks and is required to obey her husband's advice.

Each interviewee emphasized women's complicity as co-progenitors of the separation myth. Each assumed the privileging of mothering, a premise well supported by observations and by the many women who said providing upward mobility for their children did constitute their reason for being. Yet I found no Tepozteca who endorsed any of these models even when their labor processes seemed to be confirming it.

Are Partnerships Adapting?

In the "adaptive partnership" model, "'family' is a self-balancing system which adapts to structural changes and internal requirements" (Meissner et al. 1989:476). But so interwoven is family with our beings, to avoid ruptures too costly to absorb, balancing occurs exceedingly slowly. Applying this concept to my study brings up the question of what adaptations look like inside Tepoztecan households.

Between 1990 and 2000, Tepoztecas increased their economic activity by a ratio of 10 percent; their domestic labor rose by 1 percent. In 2000, 99 percent of all homemakers were female. As male activities fell by 8 percent, men did not take up chores; however, Tepoztecos began to move into growth sectors long dominated by Tepoztecas. Labor distribution patterns fell far short of validating the adaptive partnership premise, but interviews and observations reported in this section suggest that neither do they rule out the possibility of soft transitions.

Women continued to perform most conventional chores while integrating caregiving duties the state shifted to individuals, including such essentials as care for the sick, infirm, and disabled, mounting school expenses, and contriving to put on the table unsubsidized tortillas and other nutritional necessities. What factors stand behind the entrenchment of domestic labor norms at a time when gender divisions of waged labor are in a state of great flux as households struggle to cope with the deterioration of male incomes and other devastations?

From studies of labor divisions inside Mexican households—especially Brígida García and Orlandina de Oliveira (1994)—I expected younger, upwardly mobile men to be the partners most into chores. This pattern did surface, but it was far from the whole story: I encountered socially conservative farmers and day laborers who said they had no problem with taking on women's chores. However, in no instances did task reallocations appear to hinge on a conscious striving to gender balance work and chores.

While quite a few women repeated Doña Elena's assertion that "the men here are lazy"—yet another observably untrue myth—in regard to certain chores, the decisive allocation factor seemed to be the degree of a unit's reliance on the most reliable income sources. However performance continued to be strongly gender-differentiated even when homemakers were making substantial, regular monetary contributions and men did not hold steady jobs. The spending of money reiterates the homemaking status quo inequality. That is, husbands' incomes tended to be associated with expenditures that had the greatest potential for conversion into recoupable income (assets). Women's incomes went to purchase commodities intended for household consumption. But the next section emphasizes that the constancy of the casa/calle myth had significantly different results for different women that economic factors alone cannot explain.

Men Being Men

Don Silvano, age thirty-six, works in a Cuernavaca factory owned by a Japanese company. He spent five years in the U.S. In English, he told me he greatly enjoyed its "freer" lifestyle. In a questionnaire that itemized domestic tasks, he was one of only two men reporting no participation in female-typed chores. "Men in the *calle,* women in the *casa*: That's the way it should be and *is* in my household."

For ten years, Doña Inéz, age thirty-eight, has been in a consensual union with Silvano. She works "as many hours as possible" in a home laundry operation, experiencing more stress to earn less than in "regular" jobs she has held since age twelve. "When my children can help, I will make a big change, but right now, change would be too dangerous."

For Don Martín, age seventy-five, a "pure Morelos campesino," what is at stake is "what is in the best interest of the hogar. Now that women have smaller nests, they have time to go out to work. This is a good thing as long as the hogar always comes first." Doña Concha, Martín's wife, nodded agreement. Of her wide-ranging micro ventures, she said, "There was never a problem because I never neglected my household." There has never been a day when she leaves home without informing Martín of her mission. She does not perceive this as asking permission: "It's just good manners."

The four people in these contrasting unions have in common the belief that women must privilege the domestic. Silvano switched to Spanish to state a rationale seemingly valid across Tepoztlán that not only justifies asymmetrical commodity culture obligations but masks dissimilitude. Asked why chores are inappropriate for men, he replied, "*Porque un hombre es un hombre*" (Because a man is a man.)

Local women do not routinely engage in waged labor commonly considered "dangerous" or "heavy." I never saw a girl or woman digging a ditch, laying bricks, or driving a bus. They continued to be missing in the comparatively lucrative fields of construction and transport. On the other hand, their presence in lower-status male jobs tended to increase a few percentage points (for example, agricultural worker and day laborer). It is mainly as self-employed small entrepreneurs that they have begun to have an economic presence in some gender atypical jobs. I asked men how they felt about women undertaking jobs still widely deemed male appropriate. I also queried them about their participation in domestic chores.

Certain outside activities—notably construction—are categorically men's work (though I observed women carrying out such tasks). Rather than the actual heaviness of a task, what seemed most to gender a chore masculine was how closely it resembled the waged labor undertaken by the man. Only two men said no employment was inappropriate for women. To day laborer Don Ignacio, "No honest job is a bad job for campesino men or women." Don Fernando, the personable thirty-something lawyer son of a prosperous local family, stated, "For my part, all housework is appropriate for men and any work a woman wants to do is appropriate. After all, we are not now in the era of the cavemen." He, several other men, and some women objected to women holding jobs that necessitated dressing like men. On the other hand, he was one of only three men who said that it was "appropriate" for men to make tortillas. (Two male commercial tortilla producers were among those who found it "inappropriate.") Fernando had "tried my hand at it but failed." The politics of failure proved to be highly relevant to the allocation of domestic chores.

The performance context appears to be everything. I saw other men, like the tortilla manufacturers, performing tasks in public they almost certainly would not do at home. So, on most Saturday mornings Don Diego, age fifty-eight, joins other merchants to sweep the churchyard. Street sweeper Don Jacob, age fifty-two, earns 40 pesos per day. Neither of the men could recall sweeping at home. Flower arranging is also male appropriate when done in a church as an offering by members of the politically powerful all male association of flower cultivators. Contrarily, once standard female forms of home-based subsistence labor—such as keeping pigs and fowls—have all but vanished while long-stigmatized subsistence farming became at least acceptable as men left it.

Women do not perceive employment as replacing chores. While it may be necessary to leave family members to their own devices to, say, put a meal on the table, employed women usually make sure the means to do so are at hand. So, for example, when Doña Lupe was not present, her daughters did not have to settle for a sandwich on the run. Before going to work, Lupe soaked the beans and set them to cook, and chopped onions and other fresh ingredients. Most days, the sisters sat down together at the family table to share a proper if hasty *comida* (meal).

While exercise and other out-of-house activities have become important to a number of women, many women reported that watching TV with family was their only "leisure" activity. Generally, they concurrently did routinized chores, perhaps folding laundry. This contrasts to the pattern when men watched football. No one expected them to divert their attention from their leisure activity.

Like place and perceptions, time as duration matters. Men mostly performed a narrow range of visible, exceptional, and non-time-sensitive tasks that, however motivated by altruism, did not appear to go far toward giving women control over their labor power. The three elective tasks men performed with some regularity were caring for young children, shopping for certain types of goods, and hosting: activities that are technically quite different from making beds and other open ended and often solitary duties. This format suggests that the chore itself and the techniques of its enactment were interwoven as the outcomes that gendered the task.

Mostly caregiving meant taking spruced-up children some place, sharing a treat, or purchasing a specialty item. At a lavish third birthday party, male hosting entailed pouring brandy, handing plates of food to notables, and passing portions of a cake that cost five minimum salaries. At a Christmas Eve party, with male comrades, the host convivially supervised the prestigious task of barbecuing. Given the nature and irregularity of men's domestic labor, on balance, it is not clear that homemakers actually "save" time. Now, too, children's labor contributions though still important in many households have been drastically scaled back. Indeed, in utilizing children to help out, women face a New Economy dilemma. Child labor allows them to increase and diversify salaried work. Yet since equipping children with a proper education often motivates labor choices, it is counterproductive to interrupt study.

How do children think about casa/calle partnerships? Though all named father the person "responsible" for the family wage, they were sensitive to the imperative to aggregate wages and caregiving. No one deemed mother's chores less significant than father's work. And mother's trabajo tended to be thought of and honored as a sacrifice made in the family's interest (though of course not only as a sacrifice but also as an accomplishment).

Women Being Women

Fiestas are now often the only times when female kin groups gather. Besides the fifty-two local and national fiestas (Echeverría 1994) and imported holidays, as members of extended families, many Tepoztecans are inundated with private celebrations. ("Children's birthdays keep me poor," said Miriam.) As in the event described here, gender continues to naturalize prescriptive forms of preparing and enjoying fiestas. The occasion is a dinner dance staged by the bride's family the night before the wedding of Sara and Raúl. Some forty family and friends were "invited" to share in preparing the festivities attended by two hundred guests.

Twenty-two women began arriving at Sara's home at first light. Culinary masters were charged with cooking. ("My great aunt Matilde is the person to watch. Her vegetable rice is the best in Mexico.") Unobtrusively signing the cross, a senior woman rubricated each task. Under a lemon tree in the patio, the women spent eight hours preparing and rolling more than a thousand *tacos* (filled tortillas). Even in this daunting collective undertaking, each woman worked as an individual, completing the entire production process for each taco. There was no grading of contributions. Women casually added completed tacos to common stacks. The rejection of a Fordist assembly-line format often stood out in other shared work processes. (Why Tepoztecas of all ages made this technological choice never became clear to me. I assume it has to do with the likelihood that during much of their lives, each would be on her own.)

Around noon, the men began to trickle in; unlike the women, most came by private transport. After rather formal greetings all around, they began to build a bandstand. There was much coming and going, some horseplay, and suggestive joking with the women. They completed the platform, a construction marvel given what went into it, ahead of schedule. Whereupon the men rushed inside to drink beer and watch a riveting football match.

As multi-burden studies show, stretched-to-the-limit women devise solutions to systems crises—such as increased gratis caregiving, low paying part-time employment, piling on of incompatible tasks—that in turn raise new sets of material and consciousness issues with significant consequences to the quality of a life. In the next part, I consider new syntheses and the costs to homemakers of absorbing problems and possibilities specific to the forms in which neoliberal Mexico is unfolding for all members of a household. While I do not intend the ethnographic studies to be ideal types, patterns will emerge when groups "share common placement in hierarchical power relations" (P. Collins 1997:377).

DOMESTIC LABOR PATTERNS

I distinguished six New Economy problem-driven patterns: (1) the classic unemployed homemaker, (2) the domain integrator, (3) the monetary economy facilitator, (4) the social welfare substitute, (5) the homeworker, and (6) the subsistence farmer. The manifold of homemaking activities fit variously and therefore contradictorily into three distinct forms of Enzo Mingione's (1991) "fragmented societies": monetary pursuits, domestic activities, and extraordinary domestic activities. To begin, a shopping trip (Box 6.1) with Doña Rita places allocation decisions in the everyday consumption challenges of Tepoztecas.

In just over an hour, Rita spent around 70 percent of her weekly budget. Only two transactions were woman-to-woman: one with a non-salaried principal in a family business and the other with a mobile trader of local origin goods. The stock of the market woman was found wanting when compared to Woolworth's selection.

Pattern 1: The Unemployed Homemaker

Married pattern-1 women "prefer" unpaid labor for a complex of the following reasons: (1) the budget does not require them to earn wages, (2) husband strongly objects to outside employment; (3) the couple agrees that it is essential for her to be at home at this lifecycle point, and, (4) available acceptable jobs pay wages too low to purchase substitutes for self-produced goods and services. This classic type is now rare, though not because these constraints are not operative. Rather, they tend to be outweighed by the necessity and resolve Tepoztecas have to be contributing wage earners.

Rebecca Ortíz

"You won't be interested in me," Doña Rebecca said, "I do *not* have a job and I do *not* think it is a good idea for mothers to go out to work or be away from the house unless it is essential. Anyway, Don Roberto would never consent as long as he can support us; in this, we agree completely. I strongly believe the proper place for a mother is at the side of her children. Who besides me is going to take proper care of my family?" Her somewhat defensive tone reflected a sense that she was out of step even with matrons of her generation. Of her eleven sisters and sisters-in-law, all residing in Tepoztlán, only two others have never been regularly employed. And the new generations of females in this family are intensely career-minded.

Although the attitudes of Rebecca and Roberto, both ages fifty-four, are more conservative than those of many Tepoztecans, they have dedicated their lives to making it possible for their four children to enter modern sector employment. In many respects a classic benevolent patriarch, Roberto

BOX 6.1
A Provisioning Expedition

A scorching hot Sunday mid-morning, April 1996: I accompanied Rita on a provisioning expedition. Table 6.1 introduced members of this household. On this day, Rita bought more lavishly than usual because her mother and a friend were spending a fiesta weekend with them. Husband Memo's wages varied considerably from week to week, but at this time, she had around 300 pesos to cover weekly expenses. Rita mainly shops locally, although she assumed she was paying at least 10 to 15 percent more than she would pay in Cuernavaca. The saving would have justified the bus fare--another expense increasing so rapidly that fare tickets were more than a year out of date--but she rarely could clear the time. Although she referred to her list only at the end, her shopping confirmed a plan which included ingredients for *pozole*, a special occasion stew: she did no impulse buying. The only extras were a Coke for Luz and peanuts for her grandmother.

Stop 1: First stop was a well stocked family-run grocery. Total: 96.60 pesos. U.S. brand items: 2 bars of Dove, a packet of Tide, a box of 6 Tampax and one of 12 Pampers, a medium tube of Colgate, and a Coke. Mexican items: 100 grams of salt, a liter of oil, and a liter of vinegar.

Stop 2: Like many others, Rita assumed (falsely in most cases) that the stocks of many of the itinerant dealers who came twice weekly had been acquired early on the same morning in the Mexico City wholesale market and were therefore "more healthful." Although she could not afford temptations such as Georgia peaches, she did purchase staple produce from these stalls. At Vendor 1, she spent 24 pesos. Although prices were at a seasonal high, she bought 1 kg of red tomatoes, 8 pesos; 1 kg of green tomatoes, 7 pesos; 1 kg of peppers, 9 pesos. At Vendor 2, she bought onions and *epazote.* He was the only dealer to give her a "something extra" (a *pilón*), a small bunch of *cilantro.* Purchases at Vendor 3 were 1 kg of a cereal used to make *atole* (gruel), 6.50 pesos; and a half kg of rice, 4 pesos. Vendor 4 supplied a half kg of Mexican apples, 3 pesos, and bananas, 5 pesos. At Vendor 5 she spent 5 pesos for half a kg of hominy (needed for pozole). (Her mother had brought the pork in Mexico City.) She encountered several friends and a cousin or two, but she did not linger to chat.

Stop 3: The final purchases were from two rural women traders. She bought lime (*cal*) to soak corn, 3 pesos, and 12 cactus leaves (*nopales*), 5 pesos. Although avocados were at a seasonal high, she purchased two because they are an essential *pozole* garnish.

Stop 4: Rita and Luz foraged studiously for a white hair ornament for Luz's upcoming confirmation. In the accessory stall operated by a Tepozteca, Luz found one she liked but it was rather shoddy and overpriced. (Ultimately, they found a better quality and cheaper barrette in Cuernavaca's Woolworth's.) Pressed for time and loaded down, on this oppressively humid day, she spent 8 pesos on a taxi to her home perched atop the steepest hillside at the edge of the community: a special price because the driver was Memo's cousin.

is a technician in a Nissan factory. In fact, they were the only examples I encountered of the pair Claudia von Werlhof (1988) identifies as the prototypical "pillars of capitalist accumulation": the fulltime housewife and the proletarian (a member of the industrial working class). But in the last decade of declining wages and benefits and mounting consumption costs, the struggle this wage-dependent family has had to maintain a middle-class lifestyle explains why von Werlhof states that it is rare to find a society in which the dyad is likely to be more than an ideal pair.

Both were older children who left school early, Roberto to farm and Rebecca to care for siblings. A teacher recalled that into the 1950s, fathers often took nubile daughters out of school. An acquaintance of her father portrayed him as a "typical *macho mexicano*" who might well have wanted his pubescent daughter at home. "He was famous for having lost an eye in the last bullfight held in the Plaza. The men in that family were known as the murdering Tapias because they went around with pistols in their belts."

Roberto's father, who had a heart condition, sold a splendidly situated Atongo Valley homestead for around US$10,000 and a used Chevrolet and moved the family to a childless aunt's barrio Santo Domingo property. Here in a grove of majestic trees, he built a modest but modern home. As was customary, he divided some proceeds from the sale with all the children. When he inherited the plot, he gave one-half to Roberto. Everyone understood that preference was given to him in part as compensation for his willingness to sacrifice his education and thereby diminish his lifetime earning power.

Roberto continued to watch over Doña Juanita, his widowed mother, and remains a surrogate father to his siblings, though none relies on him (or each other) financially. Out of her portion, Juanita gave house plots to two other sons. Each unit has the privacy to live a separate lifestyle while gaining the protections of being part of a "clan." Until her death in 2003, the diminutive Juanita remained the commanding personage a daughter described thus: "Father was stern (*duro*) but not *macho*. Mother was very strict with us, more *macho* than father."

At first, Roberto, with no land to farm and scant education, could work only as a laborer. Connections landed him the Nissan job. Three of their four children still live at home. Low wages, later age of marriage, shortage of housing, and preferences for a family-centered life mean that Rebecca may never experience empty nest syndrome.

Although by local standards, Roberto has a good job, in the last decade Rebecca has had to struggle to maintain a middleclass lifestyle. By 1995, his wages and benefits had reached a low point in a long decline that began in the mid-1980s. To explain this loss of economic ground in a world-market sector, we must think of all wages as conditioning each other.

I asked Rebecca if she and Roberto had ever formulated an economic strategy to deal with the threefold problem of the vanishing wage, inflation, and more costly necessities. She replied:

> We know each other's minds so well we scarcely ever need to talk things over. Because a father has little time to spend at home, it is the wife who has the greater obligation in household matters. His duty is to support the family. Mine is to be at home to provide my family a secure, healthy life. This obligation continues so long as a child lives at home.

Rebecca is that now endangered essential person in every extended family that maintains ties, the person dedicated to kin work. Besides always being there in time of needs, she has been central to ever more rites of passage and celebrations for which she is often in charge of preparing vats of beans, rice, and *mole*. She seldom leaves the compound except to attend church, provision the household, accompany a friend to the cemetery, or discharge kin obligations. She no longer goes daily to El Centro to shop but often buys in one of the many neighborhood convenience stores. As far as I could tell, she has no real interests outside the family. Juanita participated with amazing vigor in the Golf Club even going on a protest march to Cuernavaca. Rebecca took no active role, explaining, "Of course, I was concerned, but Don Roberto does not want me to be away from home a lot, especially if it meant going out of town." As a skilled and dedicated mother and wife, she has high status with herself, the family, and the pueblo. Though she is very much her own woman, political feminism is a concept outside her idiom.

Roberto also has an engrained template of duties appropriate to a benevolent patriarch that he performs well. He wishes to make life as agreeable as possible for his family, but not at the cost of diminishing parental authority. Rebecca said that when they were "much younger, now and again he got drunk and abused me a little." She learned to avoid potentially divisive subjects or situations. "He was seldom *macho*. Our life together has been harmonious though not always easy." To their daughter Julia, "My mother is more intuitive than my father. I never take personal problems to him because Papa has another mode of thinking."

Elementary school teacher Julia has an active social life. She makes a point of discussing plans to go out with Rebecca. Many evenings end with coffee cozily shared at home with friends and family. Her notion of the obligations of homemaking does not differ fundamentally from her mother's, but she intends to enact the role very differently.

> I don't envision not working after I marry. I want two children but I will just take maternity leave. Today a family can't live decently on one salary. Besides,

> I don't want to be a fulltime housewife. And I would never tolerate abuse from my husband or his going out alone at night either. [Most nights, Roberto plays dominos in a café.]

Meanwhile, Julia's plan to marry her longtime fiancé has been shelved. Unable to find a family-wage level job, he now works illegally in New Mexico.

Clara Ortiz

Occupants of the compound's newest home are Jorge, age twenty-eight, and his wife Clara, age twenty-seven, two toddlers, and a newborn. A "mutual decision" for a tubal ligation means the family is complete. Clara, who describes herself as "temporarily unemployed," is a beautician, a technical skill she had turned into successful self-employment (the category preferred by many homemakers). Jorge's strong objection to her wish to continue working "at least a few hours each day" made it "too complicated just now." Like many women in her age group, though intense, her career ambition did not include being the primary wage earner. In part, this represents a pragmatic response to the fact that a male income is essential to maintaining the cooperative unit. Her determination may also be a response to the many cautionary examples of classic unemployed homemakers who find themselves alone and unable to earn enough to support themselves let alone a household.

Blandina Escobar

Doña Blandina, age seventy-nine, exemplifies the high cost of specializing in quehaceres. Left an all but unemployable widow with her home her only capital, she attempts to get sewing. ("She's not very good at it," a client informed me.) She also sells Pepsi Cola at fiestas and sporting events. But even if she has great success and sells two cases, she makes less than 10 pesos. She said, "I get by as best I can. I never worked so I have no know-how. When Don Pedro was alive, we had a bit of meat most days. Now, in this poor home, I never eat meat. But shoes are an even bigger worry." She "gets by" only because she pays no rent or taxes and friends supply her with corn, though "only enough for a few months. After that gives out, I mainly just live on hope, and usually something turns up and I can buy my tortillas and pay my electricity bill."

Pattern 2: Domain Integrators

Rita Padilla

While integrators are not new, tracing the work histories of four generations of Tepoztecas demonstrates that each form of integration has a history that is gendered in different ways. Three members of the unit have already been introduced: Rita, her mother Modesta, and grandmother Susana. Doña Susana, the only woman interviewed who said women were "better off with no or few children," began the narrative:

> My father, a good man, died in 1919 from the Spanish influenza. An uncle stole our land. Mother kept us alive by washing clothes. I had the misfortune of marrying a mean man. He beat me once each month to teach me obedience. It didn't! We had ten children and he spent most of our money on himself. So, I slipped away to sell tortillas in the Plaza even though I knew I would suffer for it.

Doña Modesta took up the story:

> Father took me out of school to work as a servant. At fifteen, I formed a union with a salesman. He left just before Rita's birth and has never assisted us. To earn enough to support my family, I had to get a job in Mexico City.

Though still earning the low wage of a manual worker, she has advanced. This has been her routine for twenty years. She works at her federal maintenance job from 7 p.m. to 2 a.m. Most days she cleans homes. She shares a tiny flat with a colleague; they rent a bed to a student. But if her life has been hard and often desolate, it has also brought her much satisfaction. Modesta said,

> I am proud that I have been able to take good care of my girls. They are fine women. Personally, I am content. I found a way to raise my lovely daughters in a safe and healthy environment and take care of my dear mother.

At age fifteen, Rita married the handsome, dignified Memo. In him, she found a "kind and faithful comrade." She is keenly aware of his fine qualities and values his "clear thinking." To Rita, he is "a person who helps his wife a great deal and likes nothing better than to spend his money on his family even if he doesn't have a decent pair of shoes himself." Memo is an independent thinker. He favors spending less public money on fiestas. He had a vasectomy. A skilled electrician, he is one of the first to be hired when projects come along. When employed as an electrician, he earns at least 400 pesos per week. At this season, he was also refereeing football matches and cultivating a rented field. But for all his expertise and hard work, they are far from being financially secure. Recently, there were two devastating emergencies. Memo broke his shoulder when he fell off a friend's motorcycle and could not work for three months, and a client was unable to pay. Inflation makes even basic nutrition a constant concern, but most pressing are the escalating school fees parents must pay.

Looking for a way to integrate cash earning into her domestic routine, she had just begun to participate in the street economy by selling snacks to schoolchildren. She confided that before starting the business "I was very stressed by money worries."

> My stomach was always upset. The doctor said I had an ulcer. Then I had this idea of selling snacks at schools. Memo said, "Yes, do that if you think it will make you feel better." He has supported me in my decision even though the children are still so young. Now I am a different person, content because I earn enough to be sure we can pay school fees, buy books, and uniforms.

Rita's diary allows us to compare her day to the synchronic activity record Lewis (1951:62–71) kept of a 1940s homemaker. On this market day, the Lewis mother spent four hours vending "surpluses," four on chores, and three-plus caring for fowls and horticulture. A crucial difference is a daughter who devoted much of her day to domestic labor, including most of the six hours invested in tortilla production for the household. (Little wonder that she suffered from chronic headaches.) Rita's far more mixed routine included six hours devoted to business and twelve hours to chores. For neither woman was there ever an activity point when their enterprise was a seamless whole.

Even though he was at home that day (he was a bit unwell), apparently the 1940s father did no chores. Memo was always willing to help out but seldom at hand; Rita takes it for granted that she will do the chores. There had been "little change" in her domestic duties since she started her business, except that she depends more on her grandmother to care for the toddler. Entrusting the children to the feeble Doña Susana concerns her. But they cannot afford outside child care and it is "distracting" to take him with her. (It is worth noting that by 2000 Rita had a relatively good fulltime job; and she and Memo have separated twice.)

Pattern 3: Monetary Economy Enablers

Barter is an exchange process that does not entail what Marxists refer to as the alienation of commodities from the producer because there is no "mutual turning-of-backs when the exchange is over" (Humphrey and Hugh-Jones 1992:13). Intrahousehold barter between women describes the work done by women in this category. They substitute their time and skills for scarce cash.

Estela Castillo

Doña Estela, a single mother, age fifty-one, lives with daughter Socorra, son-in-law Hernán, and three grandchildren. Hernán produces a local craft. Socorra assists him and operates a daily market stall. She estimates weekly profits at between 300 to 400 pesos; but the "Golf Club years were very bad." (Even so, she was a movement leader.) The couple reacted to turbulence by working as many hours as possible and incurring high-interest debts. Continuous family labor contributions are essential to this undercapitalized enterprise dependent on the volatile tourism sector. Estela supplies many reproductive services. Hiring an employee to substitute for Socorra would cost more than the wage Estela could earn; and she has the satisfaction of making a priceless contribution to her family. The market's undervaluation of caring services in tandem with the high quality of the women's labor makes the arrangement reciprocally rational.

Angeles Flores

Angeles, age twenty-six, and Néstor, age twenty-five, and their two babies live with his divorced mother Norma and three younger brothers. Both firmly believe couples should not differentiate duties. Angeles, a nurse, is the only person in the household with professional qualifications. However she has been unable to find a post: "There are no jobs for nurses in Morelos."

Doña Norma, on the other hand, has a comparatively good job in an upscale restaurant. However, in this case it is rational (to everyone except Angeles) for her to do a goodly share of the housework. Three attempts to establish a home-based business failed and she has no savings left. Her dissatisfaction has begun to have an adverse effect on her relationship to Néstor. Twice she took the children and went to live with her mother.

Pattern 4: Social Welfare Providers

As previously noted, in accord with neoliberal fundamentals, the state has massively withdrawn from its responsibility to fund social welfare services. In Morelos, the most vulnerable are all but legally abandoned. Female kin are expected to care for those in need of care. Deserted mothers cannot even go to court until a husband has failed to support his family for two years. Routinely, the institutionalized are egregiously abused. In short, most people with special needs receive gratis care from female kin or not at all.

Yolanda Vargas

All support systems having failed her, Mexico City native Doña Yolanda, age forty-six, has no choice but to perform the conflicting roles of caregiver and financial supporter of Julio, age twenty-two, her severely autistic son. "My husband could not face that *he* had a less than perfect son. Of course, it was my fault and this justified leaving us. I never get a cent from him. Just par for a Mexican man, isn't it? I never considered putting him in one of those terrible hospitals." Though a certified secretary, because of Julio, she is unable to hold a full-time job. Here she describes the punishing costs of maximizing flexibility by minimizing job quality:

> I came here because it is a safer place for Julio; and seemed to offer the right part-time jobs. First, I worked as a maid for a local family, but the pay was much too low and the hours too long. Once I had a villa job. It paid pretty well but only when they came. Now I work weekends in a shop and do anything else that turns up. I pass out flyers, do Census polling, and Father Fili helps me a little. I must have more work, but Julio's care is more of a problem as he has gotten older. You know, the other day I was thinking it must have been ten years since I bought anything for myself except for enough used clothes and shampoo to keep me respectable.

Pattern 5: Homeworkers

Industrial homework and craft production are significant resources for many Mexican women but I could discover little such activity among Tepoztecas. Since the 1980s, a Catholic group has been trying to revive backstrap weaving. But sales are too slow and limited for women who, like Doña Hortencia, need "to put food on the table every day." On the other hand, factors that intensify dependency on family—such as continuous domestic obligations, old age, illness, failed and later marriages, single motherhood, and more years in school—are labor-supply sources that enable home-based family capitalist concerns to be competitive.

The Ayala Team

In one central section block, I counted ten *casa tiendas*, house-front shops. Besides food and drinks, products vended ranged from Dior sunglasses to plastic kitchenware. The comparative advantage of the ubiquitous casa tiendas is teamed labor, generally involving females. For example, on this block, women staffed all but two operations. (One staffed by a solitary male—a watch repair operation—opened only on weekends.)

The convenience store attached to the front of the Ayala home is an example of the flexibility gained by a female team approach. Doña Soledad, age fifty-seven, and her four young adult daughters staff the store. The girls are all completing their schooling. Since at least one is always on hand, Soledad can specialize in what she is best at, domestic chores, and the store can stay open longer hours than most.

The astutely stocked store is indeed a convenience for residents of this upper barrio. Besides mainstays of beer, soft drinks, and cigarettes, the store offers a selection of canned goods, packaged bakery goods, a cooler with luncheon meats and dairy products, and items too heavy for most shoppers to tote up the steep hill. The father, a plumber who mainly works in Cuernavaca, drives a pickup, so he takes care of some provisioning. Wholesalers deliver other products. The terms are cash on delivery, as they also are for their customers. No salaries are paid, but the parents pay school expenses and the girls get "pocket money." Daughter Lara, age nineteen, said she would prefer to have a salaried job "and be getting experience in business," but the part-time work available would not bring in enough to pay her expenses. Even though they enjoy working together and realize it is in their immediate monetary interests to participate in the family business, the daughters also see it as time lost in carving out the careers upon which their futures depend.

Pattern 6: The Farmers

As a family-wage resource, farming has greatly contracted with political changes designed to discourage small farming. The same reasons that account for its diminished importance to men makes it an appropriate use of a homemaker's unpaid labor time. One agriculturist told me he "regularly" sees more women than men in the fields. "They do everything, many things once seldom done by our women here. Maybe Tepoztecas are stronger than they used to be."

Inocencia Aguilar

The plot farmed by Doña Inocencia, age thirty-four, mother of four, is essential to her family and her household. Her tasks include weeding, planting, and harvesting, sometimes with her husband Don Marco but often alone. He works as a gardener and earns a wage that covers basic needs only when self-provisioning is incorporated. "The milpa makes a very big difference for us. Generally, I have to buy corn only for around two months. It makes sense for me to do these chores and for Marco to earn the cash we desperately need." She keeps "a few chickens but just for fun. Now it's cheaper to buy a chicken already cooked and with rice and salsa too." Her workday starts "by six," and except for an afternoon nap ("I sleep like the dead for half an hour or so"), she soldiers on until around eleven at night.

Chapter Gendering Trends

Maureen Mackintosh (1989:403) was among the first theorists to argue, "The social institution of the household should not be seen as defined in terms of domestic labor, but as derived from it"; therefore, ultimately also international capitalism as it really is. To preserve the structure of the basic cooperative institution, New Economy homemakers must greatly expand the market-direct dimensions of chores in order to supply three resources essential to sustainability: (1) goods and services that must be purchased and sometimes sold; (2) commodities that are at least acceptable, though perhaps not culturally optimal, when bought in the market; and (3) the labor she dedicates to creating consumables that embed qualities that cannot be purchased, such as empathy, guidance, and mutual respect. The "problem" of the *making* of family/households ascended to new heights as *makers* flooded into the global labor force. Since economic theory still cannot deal with commodity flows deriving from different domains (Bergmann 1995), "We encounter a glaring discrimination against the housewife" in the failure to recognize that "one cannot logically pose the social existence of (consumption) production without (production) consumption" (Chaudhury and Chakrabarti 2000:99–100).

"Production and reproduction are a unity," argues Nanneke Redclift (1989:44), "but of an often contradictory rather than a functional kind. . . . Nor is an explanation of one necessarily to be found in the other; rather their intersection shapes the form of the whole at any time." Thus in the next chapter, I move from the "contested domain" (Redclift) of housework to the "contested terrain" (Edwards 1979) of the labor market.

Chapter Seven

Three Primary Feminized Occupations

> Because needs are a bridge between 'is' and 'ought', disputes concerning other values can be settled empirically with reference to our need.
>
> —Garrett Thomson, 1987

Domestic employment, shopkeeping, and school teaching are "primary" occupations not only in regard to the representation of women in these labor forces, but also in terms of the capacity of a specific occupation to meet the New Economy needs of particular Tepoztecas and groups of Tepoztecas. Nancy Fraser recommends that we shift our angle of vision to focus inquiry away from *needs* understood as "the distribution of satisfactions" to a "*politics of need interpretations*" (1989:162–63).

In this chapter, I interface specific needs and ways of confronting them across three occupations. Each has a historically radiating as well as an emergent politics of structural adjustments to globalization scripts; thus, each also has a unique dialectic of gains and slippages.

With 1,211 domestic workers, in the 2000 census, the job category had increased by 7 percent since 1990. With 759 women, it was women's largest waged labor category. However, there was a dramatic shift in the sex composition, as women's dominance fell from 94 to 63 percent. With 694 women as owners and staff, women were 57 percent of the 2000 retail commerce sector, a decade increase of 8 percent. While commerce was already and remained comparatively gender-mixed, it became 8 percent more numerically womanized. Education workers, 61 percent (454) women, were 11 percent of all economically active women, a decade decline of 10 percent, and now the fourth largest employment category for Tepoztecas.

Based on a number of economic class typologies, historically teachers are members of the formal economy. For the most part, management and staff in retail commerce belong to the self-employed, an informal but regulated sector. Domestic workers constitute a distinct subclass of the informal economy. Today, the categories are useful as an indicator of economic class slippage as real wages plunged below 1970 levels and legal protections evaporated.

DOMESTIC EMPLOYMENT

Decades of research focused on salaried domestic work have produced different polemical traditions, all of which are relevant to the case of Tepoztlán. Many theorists position it as *the* paradigmatic case of exploitation through feminization. For example, Jayne Howell (2002) ties the occupation to Mexican women's lack of higher education and exclusion from and low status in the most lucrative forms of employment. To Shellee Colen and Roger Sanjek, for the worker, it "results in a measure of stigma," and for the society in which it exists, it reinforces "relations of power and inequality" (1990:1, 5). Stressing the alienation dimension, to Erving Goffman, a "servant [is] a classic type of nonperson, defined by both performance and audience as someone who isn't there" (1959:151). From a phenomenological perspective, "the defining feature" is the "psychological exploitation" that tends to occur in the fictive kin "relationship of employer and employee, both of whom are usually women" (Hondagneau-Sotelo 1996:44.) Inevitably, women have the "right stuff" for work that requires a worker to "display feeling states and/or to create feeling states in others" (Macdonald and Sirianni 1996:3). Having long predicted the demise of an occupation destined to be made obsolete by such technological advances as vacuum cleaners, economists must now confront the reality that the make up of the sector is part-and-parcel of free market-driven employment trends.

A notoriously underreported occupation, though partial, census data confirm that many negative assertions held true for Tepoztlán. With 42 percent of women earning sub-minimum wages, the work tended to be low paying even in comparison to other miserably paying, insecure, and dead-end jobs. Often, too, it did require a convincing performance by a depersonalized deliverer of pseudo-mothering. Yet none of these attributes responded closely to what a strikingly diverse group of domestic workers had to say about *their* politics of needs. Encouraged by municipio economic policies and positive evaluations from many workers, since the 1950s, salaried domestic labor has been among the most steadily growing occupations for Tepoztecas. At 19 percent of economically active females, it has a higher proportion of domestic workers than the national 11.3 percent.

As to evaluations, though in no doubt that salaries were often at a level of deep exploitation, workers did not approach it as an inferior form of wage earning. Indeed, even women with choices sought villa posts. In some cases, the very factors that degraded the career were essential to gaining what for many workers was crucial: time flexibility. Women were not punished for going in and out of the labor process, since employers knew that job-specific skills likely improved during rotations out. Some placed a high value on empathetic interaction with host families. I never heard the work described as unchallenging or boring. Most tellingly, no one wanted to give up work she internalized as productive labor.

Tepoztecas have all but ignored Cuernavaca's Union of Domestic Workers despite the fact that employers routinely fail to abide by even the highly watered down labor laws. Although limited in effectiveness by being unorganized, workers and some employers were innovating in ways that were tending, albeit incrementally, to transform domestic work from a "junk job" into a needs-matching career.

Mystified in the 2000 census as "deliverers of personal services and maintenance," all but a few of the 452 men in the category were gardeners, guards, or maintainers of commercial facilities. Similarly, almost all women were deliverers of personal services to private households. However, sex was not always a reliable guide to tasks performed. For example, some women employed as housekeepers guarded and maintained properties, including gardens, pools, and pets, often enlisting unpaid family members. Recently, men have become contenders for the best of the inside domestic jobs. Because misrepresentation and underestimation is extreme, I used ethnographic methods to get a more complete idea of this labor force. In my economically and demographically mixed samples, about four of every ten women asked had at some time or other performed paid housework on a regular basis. What stood out was the pronounced enclave-like structuring of this labor market.

The community has three distinct domestic employment sectors with terms of citizenship the dividing line. Workers in the homes of stakeholders were mainly from somewhere else, perhaps Guerrero or more rural municipio communities. I found no examples of Tepoztecas whose families had "always" lived in the community working in non-kin local households. (A few did work for relatives or godparents; all were salaried.) They worked in resident foreign and weekend visitor households. Tasks performed were much the same across enclaves—cooking, cleaning, washing, processing, and caring for children and others in need of care. With more gadgets available, generally, work for foreigners was much less labor intensive. Even in the most affluent local homes, wages could be as much as 50 percent lower, and hours worked were longer. Rare in both strata was for workers to live-in, except for villa nannies, usually unmarried teenagers.

Domestic Work Patterns

The following testimonies expose patterns of interaction while alerting us to the fallacy of generalizing about domestic work in end-of-the-millennium Tepoztlán.

- What do I like about domestic work? I worked many years in a family business and for sure, it is far better to receive any salary instead of none (Alba, age forty-seven).
- The pay is miserable, but these days no work is bad work, and the situation I have is reasonably secure (Louisa, age thirty-one).
- It's a safe place to work (Elena, age fifty-two).
- My villa job keeps me from being bored. But what I like most is the money (Idalia, age twenty-five).
- I worked in a factory and had to take orders from a supervisor who harassed all the women. At least housework is better than that job (Carmen María, age thirty-eight).
- Housework is really the only work I'm good at (Asunción, age forty-three).
- My husband would never consent for me to work with men (Elsa, age thirty-four).
- Working for foreigners is fine but not for Tepoztecans. Anyway, no Tepozteca wants another one to know that much about what goes on inside her house (Ana, age forty-five).
- I do chores five days a week in the home of a foreign family. My husband still must go to Canada but my wages mean he does not have to stay away as long (Mirabel, age forty-one).
- For some ten years now, twice each week I clean for a foreign family and I make enough to pay my travel expenses to attend teacher's college in Cuernavaca (Miriam, age nineteen).

Petra Reynoso

Domestic worker Doña Petra, age forty-two, is among Tepoztlán's considerable number of single mothers as well as one of a rapidly increasing population of transplanted Mexicans. At age seven, she moved to Tepoztlán from a hamlet in the State of Mexico. She attended school for "several years." She shares a small house with her mother, widow of a Tepozteco, and her eleven-year-old son, the only one of four children from two unions still living with Petra.

For fifteen years, she has worked nearby her home for the owners of a hardware store. The *Señora* of the González family of six works several hours each day in the store. Monday through Saturday, Petra cleans, washes, irons, and cooks from 7 a.m. to 3 p.m. In 1994, her daily salary was less than three dollars with one meal, which she usually took home. A cousin described the *Señor* as "tight-fisted." Given her skill level, Petra did not envision a better option in the current labor market. She did not express animosity toward her employers, but neither did she have or seek a companionable relationship. I asked her how she managed on $18 per week. "With this and that, we get along, and though we don't have much to spend, I think we are a happy family."

Ramona Bocanegro

Ramona, age twenty-eight, works in a particularly lavish villa: but only when the Mexico City owners are in residence.

> For several months, they may come every weekend. Then they don't come and don't pay me. But that's the only bad thing about the job. I make 70 pesos for six hours of work. If I work extra, I get 5 pesos an hour. Often I get tips from guests. I clean, do a little washing and ironing, but no cooking. I have little personal contact with the family but when I do, they treat me respectfully.

She considers herself "very fortunate" to have inherited the post from a cousin. But with her children at an age when rearing costs skyrocket, she regrets not having technical skills like her sister, who has a home beauty salon and "control over her hours." When Ramona started working, her "very macho" husband vehemently objected, "but he soon got used to the extra money." Like many other domestic workers, Ramona was looking for "a better job," which in her case meant not a better paying but a full-time job.

Magdalena Cervantes

Doña Magda, age forty-nine and mother of three, was born in Cuernavaca. She married a local baker, and settled in his family's compound, which included the bakery and residences of his parents and a sister and a brother. Ten years ago, following some personal problems, she and her husband separated, as did her brother-in-law and his wife. Both men continue to work in the bakery and both have set up new households. Both wives (there were no divorces) with their respective children still live in the compound. The stem family and some other residents ostracize Magda, and to some extent, even her children. But she earns enough working for superrich foreigners that she does not have to rely on the pueblo or her husband's family, with the major exception of living rent-free. Unlike the other compound residents, no one in her family works in the bakery.

For six years, a media tycoon whose villa is within walking distance has employed her. She is in charge of a palatial property replete with precious art works. She puts in around five hours daily and earns 80 pesos per day. The family seldom comes. Two years ago, her son Claudio was able to marry because she got him a steady job as grounds keeper. Though holding a professional degree, his wife, now the mother of two, for pragmatic reasons, prefers to work part-time at the villa as a cleaner. Because they are on the tycoon's payroll, Magda and Claudio have formal labor standing, which includes medical insurance for both families.

Fidel Madrazo

Don Fidel, age thirty-one, stopped me to ask if I needed someone to work in my villa. (As a foreign matron, I was presumed to have one and to require a staff.) "I do everything, from making quiches to pool upkeep," he said in English learned during the years he lived in Los Angeles. Fidel came back after his father died to protect an inheritance. "If I don't occupy the house, I will almost certainly lose it." He told me he left because of hostility to gays. Now there is a sizable, somewhat out gay population and he feels more at ease. He knows of about fifteen other men ("not all gay") now doing domestic labor at villas. He said: "It's the best job around. I usually work every day at different jobs and often do evening parties. I make from 80 to 100 pesos for four to six hours. And tips are not unusual and usually generous for Mexico." A woman who often employs Fidel, a U.S. citizen who has lived many years in Mexico City, told me that she has never felt "comfortable" with the local women she employed. "Women here are hard to get to know. Standoffish. I never seem to have anything in common with them. I think they are only interested in how much they make."

Sector Gendering Trends

Tepoztlán's trifurcated domestic industry exemplifies the "new geography of centrality and marginality [that] partly reproduces existing inequalities but also is the outcome of certain forms of economic growth" (Sassen 1999:77). Local forms express the convergence of polarities within the working class with polarities that cut across the privileged class. As throughout the global economy, feminization patterns are responding to internal as well as external material imbalances. Reactive changes are evidenced by the pragmatic exchange-based approach of Tepoztlán's domestic workers.

Especially domestic workers employed by well-to-do foreigners expressed a sense of gaining scope. Some workers value reaching out to a "host" family perceived as humanly needy, such as employed mothers or the infirm. Advantages can accrue to the worker's family when employers take an interest in the welfare of other family members. Workers take pride and gain self-confidence in their job performance (sometimes more appreciated than at home).

At a time when workplace and domestic violence against women is increasing, as a work site, homes of strangers offer women certain protections. It is likely to be a safe environment from some prevalent forms of more public harassment and, since men are usually absent, from sexual suspicions that can provoke domestic violence. In some situations, the worker is pretty much her own boss. And almost universally, economically active women I queried greatly prefer earning even a meager wage to non-salaried work in family enterprises.

What I judged to be most significant, however, is that many workers and some employers are "careerizing" the occupation by expanding legal and, particularly, tacit contractual rights. On the other hand, in Mexico "pushing the agenda of social justice in new directions" all too often exhibits a "disheartening pattern" (Montéon 1995:56). As overtones in these case studies suggest, the pattern can be in the direction of solidifying while transforming structures of disadvantages.

SHOPKEEPING

Historically, women have been omnipresent in Tepoztlán's ancient shopkeeping sector: as sole or co-proprietors, in family operations, as clerks, and, of course, as shoppers and buyers. On a 1930 visit, what stood out from the "primitive profundities" Stuart Chase espied when he turned down dusty village lanes was an El Centro general store. Attracted first by its familiar aromas, shelves overflowing with familiar commodities might well have been in "Middletown, USA."

By now, there were five central district general stores; for like Middletowners, even the poorest Tepoztecans would have been lost without store-bought necessities. By 1944, twenty stores were scattered across the head town. In 1990, 310 men and 303 women were working as proprietors and clerks in municipio shops. In 2000, of the 1,211 commercial workers, 759 were women. By this time, too, a notable trend was for Tepoztecas to prefer self-employment. However, another was for households to dedicate remittances and the "surplus" labor of its members to shopkeeping. For a generation of intensely entrepreneurial Tepoztecas, the two trends cannot but conflict.

Always comparatively small in scale and scope, in this age of encroaching superstores, local shops face more productivity barriers than ever before. To overcome comparative disadvantages, shops are compelled to rely too heavily on "non-market transfers" that have transaction costs that "nudge agents toward self-interested behavior" (Stark 1992:7), which is seldom in the self-interests of entrepreneurial Tepoztecas. And dependency on localism and *familism*—the extension to the labor market of women's normative domestic roles—often correlates to distortions in market functions that result in the overuse and underpayment of women's labor. Like domestic work, many labor contributions to family enterprises do not figure in the statistics. Family allocation may entail direct labor contributions, the meshing of disparate labor forms, appropriation of assets, or contributions members obtain from outside sources. My plot-by-plot survey of properties surrounding the Plaza revealed that while at least one-third of the sites are now leased to outside interests, all are still (officially) owned by stakeholders. However, continuity cannot be interpreted out of hand as enhancing the solidarity of siblings or parent/child units. To the contrary, in some cases that I heard about, inheritance of these valuable properties has been a lastingly divisive issue.

The rationality of shopkeeping was once a function of the on-site integration of women's multiple labor processes; now only a few El Centro shopkeepers occupy the old Spanish-style residences adjacent to most shops. Doña Rosa runs a sewing shop in front of her widowed mother's large Revolution Avenue house. She explained that given present conditions—she was referring to globalizing changes in market conditions—"I could not keep going if I had to pay rent or a salary." As Rosa and her mother move back and forth between duties and domains, caring for four children and serving clients, they do not conceptualize their labor as a fixed cost.

Since the 1980s, there has been a trend among female entrepreneurs to sunder business and house premises. Domain separation has certain modernizing features. But the loss of "helping out" family labor means that few detached shops can grow from one-woman operations. Men still control most of the more complex retail operations, in part because they also control commercial real estate.

In 1995, resident foreigners who opened only on weekends operated all but one of the El Centro boutiques catering to tourists. Anxious to get out of Mexico City, Doña Marisol, for boutiques, invested most of her savings from an executive job with a transnational corporation in a Brazilian woman's failed home decor business. Struggling (ultimately unsuccessfully) to protect her investment as the economy turned progressively worse, she opened her shop daily and dismissed her two local women clerks. But in all economic climates, the most upscale tourist-oriented shops have a particularly high attrition rate, despite the fact that tourists can be expected to spend more on single purchases than locals.

Even though businesses catering mainly to resident buyers are protected from direct competition from big commerce by land use restrictions, these buyers too can go away to shop, and there is always the street economy. So shopkeepers seek to maximize the convenience of buying locally by inventorying low-priced items that must be stocked in some depth (assorted sizes, colors, and so on), goods that have special appeal to the local market (such as decaled items), or products that have disadvantages (such as a short shelf life) that make them unattractive to their competition. The inventory imperative is that they have in stock items that people need to be able to *know* for a certainty where to find in an emergency, such as flashlight batteries. (Tepoztecans were not surprised at the brevity of the lifespan of batteries I purchased locally.)

As in all businesses, though no guarantee of success in today's design-intensive market, niche-specific information is critical to profitability. With few goods produced locally, proprietors travel as often as possible to urban wholesalers, hoping to find items not yet sold on the street. Merchants strive to improve relations with these vendors. Male principals often have the negotiation advantage of a credit history and the time advantage of a staff to mind the store when they go away.

As sons, daughters, and wives go into professions, merchant-patriarchs and matriarchs replace family with low-waged workers, a seemingly infinitely disposable pool composed mostly of young single women, generally working for rarely-present male owners. Between 1996 and 1998, wages ranged between 30 and 40 pesos for an eight-hour workday that can segue into ten hours. As to benefits, this sector is only slightly more in accord with (weakened) labor laws than domestic service. Nevertheless, though salaries in households or market stall are seldom less and sometimes more, many young women perceive clerking as superior in status. With clerking in El Centro a much sought after job, when leaving, clerks try to pass the job on to a female relative or friend.

The employment structure reflects the assumption that a female clerk does not *need* to earn a family wage or even to socially reproduce herself. Salaries reflect the assumption that she will retire when she starts a family or remain at best a supplementary worker. Yet clerks I queried who lived at home were contributing in ways vital to maintaining family units. Nor did they expect marriage or motherhood to end their extradomestic working lives. Instead, they viewed wage earning as essential to establishing the thing they most desired: their own household. They would be overjoyed to have a career-track job. Some women do find ways to use the experience gained to start small businesses, which have as high a failure rate as those in the United States.

Shopkeeping Patterns

Teresa Navarrete

Doña Teresa, age sixty-two, is the widow of Don Luis and heir to a valuable Revolution Avenue property. In the rear of the complex is the Spanish style residence that she still occupies with her four unmarried sons. Daughter Vanessa and family live nearby in a large house belonging to her husband's family. Fronting the Plaza, the general store owned and managed by Teresa who began working there as a young bride alongside her mother-in-law. After the death of Luis's parents, Teresa took over daily management, leaving him to devote his time to other financial interests (real estate and agriculture). The shop has been a major component in the family's upward mobility. Teresa said, "Since I got married, I have rarely stopped working even for a day, except to have my children. For me, work is a necessity. I would not like to be a full-time homemaker even if that were possible.

In her business, family is the critical operational and organizational factor. Vanessa and her two teenage daughters frequently work alongside Teresa. The four sons have other full-time interests and rarely help-out. As is common in multiform "family capitalist" arrangements, each enterprise should achieve the degree of viability needed to survive as an independent unit. However, the flagship business recognizes the obligation to provide certain kinds of direct consumption and social income and associative supports so long as these out-of-profit expenditures do not too heavily burden the operation. Indignantly, Teresa informed me, "Of course I don't pay my family a salary!" Relations of interdependency assume many different and frequently disguised input/output forms that make it all but impossible for outsiders (and, perhaps, insiders as well) to distinguish between private wealth and the firm's capital.

Her customer base consists mainly of residents unable to travel outside the community to fill a specific need. "Tourists only buy in an emergency, things like film. And they always complain about the prices being higher than wherever they come from." Tepoztecans also mainly make very small purchases. "Most people here buy only what is needed at that moment." Reluctant to miss any sale no matter how small, her stock consists of one or two of every item with some likelihood of being requested.

A longtime leader of the influential Association of Merchants, Teresa is a complete professional, able to advise clients on hardware requirements and keep personalized exchanges on an impersonal basis. (As this conversation was going on, a child well known to Teresa came in and asked for three different colored balloons needed for a school project. Unaware of a recent price increase, the child announced, "I am 5 centavos short"; after carefully considering her alternatives, she gave back the red balloon and Teresa returned it to stock. Later in the day, the child returned with the 5 centavos.)

> In 1995, I asked Doña Teresa to describe the impact of recent political and economic upheavals. After the 1994 devaluation, the first thing I did was to walk across to the bank and cancel the new credit card my sons urged on me. Sales have gone up and down but not as much as for some, probably because we deal mainly in small essentials. Inflation is the major impact. Savings are impossible; I do well to open the doors and very likely could not do so if I had to pay rent.

Conversations suggest that she engages family, shop, and pueblo interests as conceptually different but converging issues. She directs the shop as a productive and political activity with definite capitalist aims. On the one hand, Teresa seems keenly aware that for a family firm, success implies harmonizing reproductive and productive processes; and that it is not possible to avoid some collateral damage to each process. On the other side, she perceives her cluster of obligations as owner, manager, mother, and activist as minimizing the impact of social disruptions and threats to local control to commerce.

Elena Salinas

Shop owner Doña Elena exemplifies the new generation of keenly entrepreneurial wives and mothers. Nothing in her background suggests she is the kind of savvy risk taker reputedly the dynamos of free enterprise. Much of her confidence and motivation came from the goal of making sure a daughter could realize her dream to become a lawyer.

Born in Cuernavaca, Elena did not complete elementary school. As the oldest of twelve, she was always "needed" at home. At sixteen, she married a local agriculturalist. They have three children, including the gifted Alicia, now an attorney with a Cuernavaca law firm. She was "always keen about business; fashion is my love as well as my business. I started with a home business and did well enough to think a shop could be successful. Start-up capital came from my mother and husband, but mostly it came out of profits from my home operation."

In 1985, she rented a tiny space in a row of shops owned by members of her husband's family. Her monthly rent is 500 pesos. This sum is not lower than non-kin renters would pay, but it is unlikely the property owner would have taken the chance of leasing the choice space to such a high-risk tenet if she had not been family. Her hours are 10 a.m. to 3 p.m. and 6 to 8 p.m.

"or as long as there is someone interested in buying or something that needs to be done."

Elena contrives to stock a large amount of clothing in her cubbyhole, an estimated inventory of "not less than 6,000 pesos." Children's, women's, and some men's apparel included "too many items too long in stock." But sales from inventory are not what sustain the business. Each week ("when I have money to spend"), she travels to Mexico City to make the rounds of vendors where she often fills special orders: a gown for a fifteenth birthday or a suit for a teacher attending a conference. Her strenuous, perfectly plotted expeditions reflect considerable understanding of the industry's highly diversified market channels.

On one such trip, her routine was as follows. She arrived in Mexico City at ten and immediately embarked on a nine-hour odyssey that took her across the vast wholesale district. Wholesalers that require cash offer the best prices. Others extend credit, usually for fifteen days, at a high rate but still less than a bank rate. In most cases, she also has the option of making timely exchanges. She buys inventory and to fill special orders. On this buying trip, her purchases included several baby gifts, shoes for a boy taking part in a dance recital, and a dress for a mother of a bride. To add to her stock for the critical Christmas season, she bought frilly underwear, two pairs of dress pants for boys, and assorted sleepwear. At one high-fashion resource, she selected three blouses with prices higher than usual. "I love these blouses," she exclaimed when the saleswoman brought out the samples; "they look like my customers." Eventually, she turned out to be right. Studious browsing in a high-fashion department store for both the shop and Alicia's wardrobe was the last thing on her schedule.

To compete with large out-of-town stores, she takes a relatively (to U.S. mark-ups) small profit of from 15 to 20 percent, although "I try to do a bit better." She reports her net as around 500 pesos per month, almost the same amount her husband clears each month. Since this is what she pays in rent, she can make money only by having at least several much better than average months. Like stores in the U.S., she depends heavily on peak buying periods, such as Christmas, graduation, and mother's days, and on the windfall of a "big buyer." Even on these high-demand occasions, trade depends on maintaining a certain look even in slow times.

Niche-market-specific knowledge is essential. Her success ultimately depends on customer confidence in her buying skills, a reservoir of knowledge she has acquired through years of listening to customers and dealing with a range of suppliers, and on personal relationships with clients. The perennial problem is credit risks. Elena knows very well that granting questionable lines of credit can be disastrous, and she has the close-at-hand information to estimate risk. Yet cash shortage and the conditions of interpersonal exchange oblige her to extend credit to most of her customers and make it all but impossible to deal effectively with overdue accounts. Sometimes she even must make new sales to people with accounts long outstanding. "They always say, 'I'll pay you when I can.' If I refuse credit, they just take longer to pay the first bill and shop elsewhere. At this point I can't afford to lose even bad customers."

In contrast to formally salaried workers, who pay in 5 percent of their salary, to receive social security small businesses and the self-employed, must pay in 14 percent. Few can afford such benefits for themselves or an employee. Because of this and other hazards, the tendency in Tepoztlán, as across the global society, is for entrepreneurial ventures to be highly risky for women, especially women in single breadwinner households.

Regina Conde

Regina, age twenty-three, inherited her job five years ago from a cousin. It is in one of five nearly identical El Centro stationary stores. Besides school and office supplies, the store does a brisk copying business (3 centavos per copy) despite the fact that many copies are all but illegible. Regina lives at home harmoniously with her parents and three siblings. Her father is a construction worker. She described her mother as "a full-time housewife," although the mother often works a few hours in a cousin's laundry. She had "no problems" with her studies; she left school at age fifteen "due to lack of money." She gives her mother "about half" of her salary. Her goal is to be a wife and mother, but she expects to continue paid labor. Since she does not yet have a boyfriend, she cannot predict the attitude her husband will bring to the issue. "But these days, it is natural for everyone to work and earn as much as they can."

Strategically situated to two schools, the shop is in a row of eight other businesses owned by a Tepozteco who inherited a swath of downtown real estate. In many visits to this shop, I saw him only once. Regina was always the only person working; a sister replaced her on her day off. Steady streams of mostly small and micro transactions in the seldom-closed shop necessitate an inventory completely out of proportion to sales volume. Regina needs no printouts listing the highly eclectic shopkeeping units (SKUs). If an item is in stock, she goes immediately and unerringly to it. If the SKU is out of stock, she explains why and then when it will be available. She has infinite patience with children, even when they spend ten minutes or so deciding on the color of a single sheet of construction paper. She does not wait on other customers during the decision period. The shop layout makes it possible for one person to monitor shoppers. Regina performs this function diligently, and in a way that leaves no doubt shoplifters can expect no mercy, however tender their age.

Regina reported being "quite content" with her job though she does find it "a little boring." Indeed, her body language and general attitude conveyed a boredom bordering on the surly. She filled orders efficiently. But I seldom detected unnecessary interaction with customers or enthusiasm. With only one pay increase since she began—in 1996 she made 37 pesos per day and a few fringe benefits—she had good reason not to approach her position as a career track job.

Sector Gendering Trends

Women in diverse structural positions consider work in shops as a progressive occupation at least compared to many other local options. Since aptitude and attitude can partly substitute for investment capital, though to an increasingly ineffective extent, self-employed women value it as career opening. Women in family firms may value the ability to interweave reproductive and productive assets; and those who head successful family concerns gain high public status. Especially younger clerks see the work as an opportunity to participate in modern commerce and as a potential base for starting a business.

Inheritance customs that do not exclude women frame Teresa's prestigious career. Still gender norms burden her management with a number of contradictions. Privileging both daily and generational family goals, she uses the business to minimize conflicts and enhance unit solidarity, an outcome achievable only by both preserving and distributing assets and liabilities of the enterprise. Though Elena was intent on domain separation, credit policies forced her to count on family, especially at the start; and she has had to use profits to finance family projects. Because localism and a strong sense of family obligations make her labor less effective, though an economistic thinker, she cannot adhere to the capitalist imperative to keep capital working.

Though employed in the modern sector, as gendered daughter, wife, or mother Tepoztecas cannot make full use of opened markets to gain economic autonomy. Rather than classic patriarchy, the relationship that gives a pattern to the case studies is paternalism, a control system achieved by manipulating personal obligations. Before the technocratic revolution, compulsory social welfare liberated many workers from the paternalism long so marked a feature of the Mexican economy. Contradicting Weber's idea of *paternalism* as a noncapitalist relationship destined to be institutionalized in modern economies, neoliberal capitalism intensifies privatized dependencies. Moreover, even one-person operations are never a purely individualized matter. In lieu of cash, social entitlements are fringe benefits granted to cooperating units.

In sum, in late Tepoztlán, neoliberal forms of paternalism constrain women's empowerment options.

SCHOOL TEACHING

From the eminent professor emeritus Filiberto Martínez I learned that "nothing is more important to Tepoztecans than sending children to school, and educating girls has been almost as important as educating boys. Teaching has always been the occupation with the greatest prestige for a daughter."

Teaching was one of the first nonfamily employment options open to Tepoztecans with sufficient monetary and/or political resources to attend a teacher's college. It seems still to be the only local economic venue with no nonsalaried workers. By the 1950s, women had begun to "over-crowd" the profession, a phenomenon construed by neoclassical economists as self- rather than market-driven victimization. From 1980 to 1990, the population of *maestras* (female teachers) expanded by almost 50 percent. In the last decade, Morelos women had one of the highest rates of participation in the occupation in Mexico; and municipio women had the highest rate among Morelos women. Nevertheless, there is an urgent need for more teachers in more municipio classrooms. Since 1982, the educational sector has not fared well in the competition for limited government funding. Fees have skyrocketed as salaries plummeted. Moreover, gender-structured disadvantages long characteristic of teaching include the scarcity of jobs, not enough hours of paid work, and stagnation in the lowest status posts. Over the decades, few Tepoztecan maestras have climbed out of the lowest professional levels, which are downgraded not only in pay and benefits but also in power inside the system. Segregation and segmentation evidence classic sex-typing patterns far more attributable to the rationality of the market than to the irrationality of teachers. Even in the areas most dominated by women, supervisory personnel tend to be males. Statewide, salaries averaged around four pesos/hour. In an internal poll conducted by the local branch of the international teachers' union (known as SNTE), 86 percent of teachers reported spending a "great deal" of time on other wage earning. Teachers see this as profoundly damaging because not only is it impoverishing, but also because it limits the time they can devote to teaching and lowers the social status of what was once the most highly respected profession.

The long entrenched, uxorious leader of SNTE was an infamously co-opted PRI operative. Passing as a benevolent patriarch, his stranglehold resulted in a status quo that made SNTE an instrument for protecting the weaknesses of the national education system and repressed women's mobility, first as students and later as teachers. But with SNTE as almost the only channel for making gains, teachers often have to defend these very status quo politics.

Despite these systemic disadvantages, teaching's status as a formally organized profession is important to maestras at a number of levels. There are still significant material benefits for individuals and family members not obtainable in most other jobs. The prestigious occupation brings honor and political influence to the household as well as to the individual achiever. And in Tepoztlán, no capital is more fungible than political influence, especially when it entails having the means to advance the prospects of students, especially at time when only the wages of those competing high school or some higher education increased. These features go far to explain why teaching continues to be a profession of rational choice for many of Tepoztlán's most outstanding and most underpaid women. The lavish floral offering presented to teachers on Teacher's Day suggests the high esteem still accorded teachers. One young teacher received a splendid bouquet delivered to her home by an exclusive Cuernavaca florist. It cost the student who sent it three months of a salary he earns in a weekend job.

In a survey of fifty students, ages eleven to eighteen, I asked them to rate their degree of admiration for a list of important people in their lives. I gave them a choice of *A Lot*, *Somewhat*, and *Not at All*. In my sample, 80 percent placed teachers in the *Somewhat* (*Algo/Poco*) category, far behind *Mother*, a few degrees behind *Friend*, but comfortably ahead of *Father*, *Religious Practitioner*, and the most denigrated category, *Politician*. Many judged the primary motivation of teachers to be personal ambition rather than improving education or selfless service to the community. One female student, an aspiring teacher, commented: "I don't say this approach is wrong; in fact I think women are smart to look out for themselves. But I also don't think about teachers as being particularly noble." Less than 10 percent of boys but some 60 percent of girls sampled were "seriously considering" going into teaching despite known drawbacks. There was general agreement about the importance to future careers of establishing good relations with teachers, and critical when education was the prospective career. Gifting—regularly including sacrificing time to support the teachers' political activism—is a frequent way of going about this. (On the other hand, some parents denounce the union when teachers go out on strike and shut down the schools.) Of course, gestures of support can also come out of affection and respect for mentors.

Students as well as teachers and parents expressed concern about the quality of local schools. "Basics are not at a high enough level to equip us for modern professions," commented one engineering student struggling with classes even at the generally low rated University of Cuernavaca. Nevertheless, education remains associated with the middle-class status that citizens are fiercely resolved to provide for children competing for "knowledge society" jobs.

School Teaching Patterns

Rosario Navarette

A sixty-four-year-old widow, Doña Rosario has combined a distinguished teaching career with political prominence and intense social activism. Her father, also a teacher, served a term as municipio mayor. His reputation survived the office, and in the years that followed, he often served as an advocate for the community. He encouraged his six daughters to qualify for professions. "My father wanted his daughters to have more freedom to fulfill ourselves than women customarily had during the period. I am thankful to my father, for he encouraged me to lead a life of service to the pueblo."

Work and social ethic were strongly developed in her mother. Besides admirably bringing up nine children, she kept pigs and turkeys—"We almost never had to buy meat"—and had a thriving business as a seamstress—"She was one of the first women to own a sewing machine." Yet she found time to be actively involved in civic matters. "Mother was a leader of the sisterhood of Catholic women. Women and men often asked her advice; it generally proved to be sound." Rosario specialized in teaching Spanish to children from households where an Indian language was the primary language. "There were no openings here for my specialty, so I became one of the first women to go away to teach. It was my father who urged me to have the courage to leave home, but mother also supported me." Eventually Rosario got a local posting and went on to become a school director, a distinction women still only rarely attain.

Rosario married into a merchant family. Don Pepe, her late husband, was one of three siblings who inherited a choice El Centro plot. Two generations of his family had operated a bakery in a wing of their home. "My mother-in-law saw to the sales and most business matters." When the father died, the children divided the property. "Don Pepe trained in technical design, so he decided to open a paint store." He was not a keen businessperson, and with six children to educate, she took an active hand. When Pepe died, she retired to devote herself to the store. Because of economic trends, she was grooming only one of her ten grandchildren to go into the business. (In 1998, she leased the space to an Italian restaurant.)

Besides being active in SNTE, Rosario was one of the women "with power" who founded a political action group. She played a prominent role in the Golf

Club. At a tense meeting with the governor's representatives, as a designated spokesperson, she rose, spoke confidently and firmly, but chose her words carefully. Here I condense remarks from various conversations we had.

> I always encouraged students to be involved in protecting our patrimony, and I advised them never to stop studying. I urged girls to prepare for careers. I told them, work is good for you and women should make an economic contribution to their family. But I also told them to respect *our* customs. The tourists are important, but Tepoztlán is rich without them, rich because it is campesino, so we can always find a way to feed ourselves.

Miriam Díaz

A member of an intensely career-oriented generation, after several career changes, at age twenty-four, Miriam earned certification to teach English to primary students. She undertook years of financially and physically draining struggle because "I want to be important." "Important," I discovered, meant being looked up to by her family and the pueblo as a creator of social and material value. Despite this strong attachment to Tepoztlán, she was intensely non- and even anti-political. ("Politicians disgust me," she told me.) She did participate in union activities, mostly because it was required, though she was also sensitive to the importance of forging political connections with the education establishment.

Between 1988 and 1997, she commuted to Cuernavaca to attend first a high school, then an English language school, and a normal superior school that specializes in graduating English teachers. All family members made sacrifices to advance her dream. Since her father had deserted the family many years ago (and formed a second household), it was her hardworking, resourceful mother who made possible the years of schooling. Three years of high school cost more than 10,000 pesos in tuition. (Her mother's daily earnings never exceeded 40 pesos.) Miriam worked weekends as a waitress; an older sister working in Mexico City also made contributions. Miriam internalized these sacrifices as an obligation to succeed materially and as a considerable emotional burden.

During her final year at college, she enrolled in a government program. She worked part-time as a teacher's assistant and made 500 pesos a month, the exact cost of the tuition at that time. (In 2000, it exceeded 1,500 pesos.) She rarely slept more than six hours, and often less. She taught from 7:50 a.m. until 11:45 a.m. At 1 p.m., she took a bus to Cuernavaca for five hours of classes. Rarely returning before nine, she then did homework, prepared her clothes for the next day, and talked for at least thirty minutes on the phone to Alejandro, her boyfriend. (Because of his job in a restaurant, they could meet only on Sunday or very late at night. He insisted on paying the phone bill.) Generally, her day ended with a hot drink, a sweet roll, and TV shared with the family.

After graduation, she first taught at the assistant level. Soon she got a contract to teach Spanish in an English school. During her year in Manchester, she traveled several times to the continent. When she returned, a highly eligible young Englishman followed her to Tepoztlán to propose to her, but she refused him. During the summer, she passed an exam that qualified her to earn a salary of 1,050 pesos a month, less taxes and union dues. Most new teachers do not even aspire to a local posting but because of her specialty in the idiom of the global market, she secured one. Within a year, she passed two more exams that led to a contract to teach in Chicago. Her starting salary was $1,600 monthly (plus generous benefits) for fewer hours of work than in Mexico. With seniority, a position in a top private school would pay her not more than 1,600 pesos a month.

In Tepoztlán, she sometimes felt enveloped by all the people who cared about her and about whom she cared a great deal. She even carved out a private place in her home. But in Chicago she grew increasingly lonely. She went home at Christmas and married Alejandro, who returned with her to Chicago. Though his salary at Taco Bell was near the minimum, it was some three times his salary in an upscale Cuernavaca restaurant. At first, they intended to go "home" at the end of the school year. (Of 50 students interviewed, all but one intended to stay in school as long as possible, explore the world, make money, and return to make a life as a contributing member of the pueblo.) Then Alejandro found a career-track job, Miriam got a raise and the assurance of the superintendent that she could have the post for as long as she wanted it. They even adjusted to Chicago winters. They bought a house and an SUV, and had a baby girl they took home to christen her with the name of a Nahua princess. Though it is still as a Tepozteca that Miriam plots herself into a future of being important, right now, it is a luxury she cannot afford. It remains a dream postponed but paradoxically, one that becomes more out of reach as they build up equity not in the Morelos highlands but on the Illinois prairie.

Sector Gendering Trends

Rather than an effective bargaining agent, the union has enforced sexism. Though still prestigious, teaching can pay less than day labor. Getting a local posting often requires influence based on accumulated power. Most employed women found it advantageous to bracket the discrimination they were well aware of, but not teachers. Perhaps the disappointment of great expectations coming after years of sacrifice explains why they seemed more intent than did others on communicating workplace injustices. They have not conspired with oppressors to accept injustice on the grounds that teachers are a public good; but they are politically much weaker than male teachers since all needs and resistance mechanisms are corrupted by gender politics.

As I learned at a Mexico City seminar addressing the problems of the profession, certain flaws are deeply configured into the education system that have seriously weakened the potential for education or a career in education to serve as a force for women's liberation. Little wonder that increasing numbers of Morelos' most educated women are choosing Miriam's "exit option" rather than Rosario's staying on or "voice option": Hirschman's (1981) "two forms of activist reactions to discontent with organizations," which turn out to be a profoundly gendered matrix.

Chapter Gendering Trends

Considering the objective conditions of three primary feminized occupations, this chapter focused on the gender politics at the core of "needs talk" in late Tepoztlán. Much of the discourse has been occupation, task, and economic class specific. But at the most inexorable level, all sets of needs are "constructed as significant" because to construct a commodity culture *within* the dominant economy people must enter into "some form of labor/capital relations *and* because of capital's necessity to construct an ideology of fragmentation" (Narotzky 1997:218). Consequently, all too often seeming advances have turned out to be a figment of Mexico's illusionary development model: illusionary because gains for economic women are balanced by slippages for economic men.

Employed women's testimonies support the materialist premise: wage earning does tend to afford women more control over the allocation of their labor power and the direction of their lives. However, structural adjustments are diminishing the empowering potential of salaried employment, even as Tepoztecas discover it; and global feminization through flexible labor is diminishing the direct emancipatory potential of such capital as education, fertility reduction, and entrepreneurial goals. As women's multifaceted tasks are increasingly demanded and undervalued in the market, it is difficult to see how working women can bridge the increasingly contested domain of reproduction and the increasingly contested terrain of the labor market.

Chapter Eight

Making the Market System Work, 1990–2000

> [Conceptualizing globalization] requires examining at close range but in rich contextual detail the specific historical and contemporary conditions by which "global conditions" are made meaningful in particular places in particular times.
>
> —Michael Peter Smith, 2001

For as long as there has been a historical Tepoztlán, a market has been *working*: just not in the localizing way Redfield seems to have had in mind when in 1930 he wrote, "the village is a market." Instead, transformation has been in the globalizing pattern Sidney Mintz suggests when he wrote that the function of markets is to integrate "particular groups with differing stakes, within the same community, region or nation" (1976:xiv). What stands out in the time of the neoliberal project is that stakeholders continue to redevelop the system to interconnect individuals and populations with increasingly asymmetrical access to the assets that make markets work for particular individuals while maintaining strategic control over organizational arrangements.

Centuries of the struggle for control of the resource of rural Mexico have been both a technological and social conflict (Esteva 1983:11). At every transition stage, feminization and marketization have been of that order of struggle Keith Hart calls "a dialectical pair": "a contradiction that can be resolved only by the invention of a new idea" (1990:139). Arguing that a new synthesis must be based on women's experiences, with this chapter, I begin a four-chapter investigation of the venerable municipio resource. I counterpoise two questions. First, how does a *real* world market work for Tepoztecas in the time of global feminization through flexible labor? Second, how do Tepoztecas make a market system structured from the outside in and the inside out by gender equilibrate for them as economic agents-and-social actors?

THE LONG DECADE OF MARKETIZATION AND FEMINIZATION

Evident by the 1970s was that small-scale farming could not serve as a primary take-off base for Tepoztecans intent on achieving a modern Mexican middleclass lifestyle. As the 1980s advanced, structural adjustments destabilized all means of gaining a livelihood, disempowering not only farmers but also homemakers, day laborers, professionals, merchants, and bureaucrats. With the steady erosion of the standard male family-wage package of combining seasonal farming and construction with salaried labor largely outside the municipio, the need to create jobs locally for unemployed and underemployed residents became ever more acute. However, the goal stakeholders had in mind was to create jobs that had both survival and transformative potential.

Though tourism had been increasing as a revenue source since the 1950s, mainly it involved individuals leasing or selling off the principal resource—land—essential to sustainable development. Linked now to a network of superhighways, a tourism industry presented itself as the most attainable and socially and environmentally acceptable growth model. Many surrounding examples alerted Tepoztecans to the seismic effects on community of overdevelopment by predatory outsiders. Thus according to various consultants, local politics essentially became an often-acrimonious debate about how to transform tourism into a technologically controllable and socially equitable resource.

Two issues dominated and continue to dominate debate. Can the pueblo commercialize its ambiance without destroying its touristic comparative advantages? And lacking funds for building the infrastructure necessary to support a sufficiently lucrative tourism industry, how are gains to be kept inside? A shaky consensus emerged. Restructuring would privilege the form of tourism widely endorsed as "popular tourism": tourism for and by ordinary people.

A decade of vigorous expansion of participation in the seemingly already oversaturated market by local space holders evidences the viability of this model. To begin to evaluate the implications for Tepoztecas, with municipio women making up some three-fourths of daily populations of sellers, today's market system confirms that just as at international and national levels, expansion correlates with two New Economy consequences. Growth came only in hands-on services. And capital, the state, and the community "directly cultivated" the conditions that feminized the jobs, the process Ruth Pearson (1989) deconstructed as "the greening" of women's labor. As Florence Babb's 1989 study of a market in Peru made clear, to integrate marketization and feminization requires paying close attention to the full range of women's activities, including sourcing, processing, pricing, and allocating.

A Gendering Timeline

Biweekly sessions of the market continued (likely) from long before the Conquest up to the Revolution. And after this devastation, the market was the first commercial venue up and running, although, recollected Doña Emma:

> In those days there were more chickens and pigs than buyers. There was so little cash that my poor mother—a young widow with three little girls and no land to farm—traded the boys' belts she wove for the necessities that kept us alive. Click, click, click: I often heard her weaving [on her backstrap loom] through the night.

By 1926, Wednesday and Sunday market days were again held regularly. Redfield (1972:59) detected "a permanent pattern" in which vendors came and sat by [municipio] villages" to circulate "natural products"—sisal ropes, honey, wooden plows, plaited palm mats—that were "largely different" from village to village. Yet the 1930 session Chase attended was an impressively stocked nodal point on an integrated circuit of bustling regional markets. Though barter still obtained in satellite markets, in the head town, weighty bags of silver centavo pieces were required to purchase consumables, now including cans of pork and beans and proper attire for city-going men. From Redfield's photographs, we know that men predominated among the one hundred or so vendors gathered around the new market shed.

However, as modern consumer capitalism rampaged across the rapidly urbanizing region, expanded exit options made the market irrelevant to many buyers and sellers. Citizens had great hopes that the 1936 opening of the Cuernavaca highway would revitalize an institution deemed essential to development. To the contrary, at first getting connected strengthened out-of-town trade relations and further weakened an already entropic market (Lewis 1951:169). But with the 1965 opening of the Mexico City highway, new populations of resident consumers and excursionists enabled the repackaging of a drab, "shantytown" of a market (as it was described to Lewis) as a "spectacle": a central place where people "reproduce choices *already made* in production and its corollary consumption system" (Debord 1983) but—insists Henri Lefebvre (1991)—not passively.

Escalating demand for staples as well as for "postmodern goods" (Lash and Urry 1994)—goods with affective content—coalesced with a reservoir of women with the right mobility constraints to participate in the market as sellers and buyers. To municipio official Doña Mercedes, the need to compensate for hardships directly related to liberalization policies and catastrophes brought many women into the market during the 1990s. She added, however, that "we Tepoztecas" have always placed a high value on earning an independent income. "Most of us are very ambitious and given the shortage of jobs, for many women the market is the best and often enough, the only option." Thus, though still rather drab and mainly a makeshift sprawl, into the twenty-first century, the market system remains the largest, most demographically inclusive, and most flexible employment site for women of the pueblo.

Counting the Countable

Citing Malinowski's discipline-charting dictum that ethnography is first and foremost the "counting of the countable," anthropologist Martin Diskin counsels that to uncover the capacity of a Mexican market system to change through time, researchers must "carefully identify and count the constituent parts . . . [the] systemic quality of the system" (1976:50). But once systems are theorized as "gendered structures," gendering must be technologically evaluated as configuring "the functioning of the market from within" (Elson 1995:1852). And since gender as a structuring force tends to be buried in aggregate statistics, participant observation is required to assess the capacity of a "traditional" market to change by seeming to stay the same.

How New Economy Mangos Get Gender

My gender-focused counting began with a mango-tracking expedition. It was mango season and at a Sunday session early in my fieldwork I, a mangophile, found myself faced with the agreeable task of choosing among five mango options. Pondering variables, I noted substantive gender differences in vendor profiles. I also observed correlations between quality and sales techniques, likely driven by the critical distinction of who has control over particular stages of the marketing circuit. I decided to follow as best I could commodity chains from the mango trees to the point of consumption and compile a dossier of the ways a mango becomes a gendered commodity in Tepoztlán's restructured market system. All but one seller was female; to save space, I focus here on the highest and lowest quality mangos.

At the quality top were mangos sold from the comparatively commodious stall at the hub of market activities of Alfonso Vega, scion of a premier market family. With a wife and other family members to staff the stall during his absence, and as owner/driver of a late-model Nissan pickup, Don Alfonso, age 36, equipped with a Krups-brand thermos of strong coffee, drove through the night to make the challenging twenty-some-hour round trip (on one of Mexico's most high-risk highways) to the state of Veracruz where he acquired his prime quality mangos. The day he returned, after eating the hearty and hot repast his mother brought in, he had the well-deserved luxury of napping in a bed in a cozy alcove in the back of the stall while his efficient wife served customers and his sons and nephews unloaded the fruit, cartons of which was pre sold to a Cuernavaca dealer.

Alfonso acquired a stock of first-quality mangos in peak condition for selling, a rare and difficult feat given the fleeting shelf life of the fruit, from a connection he inherited from his father. In short, I had uncovered an old boys' club of mango traders.

At the lowest quality level is the operation of Adelita Orozco, a rural woman, age fifty-two "or thereabouts." Doña Adelita told me: "I make my own way in the world. I like it that way." When I asked her how she managed without having a family to share the burdens, she replied "I have had three husbands; all were lazy and expected me to serve and support them. As an orphan since age eight, making my own way is something I learned how to do by doing it."

The mangos, precisely arranged on a red vinyl swatch, she purchased from a third-tier dealer. Her journey from "around Toluca" was on broken-down buses that make many stops and travel poorly maintained roads to avoid tolls. Arriving well into the night, she wrapped herself in her coarse grey wool *serape*, cape, and slept in the microscopic space at a well-trafficked corner she rents for one peso "to make sure I'm not robbed of my spot."

Global commodity chains become the lived processes that gender a mango as it advances across circuits of capital. Each juncture differentially impacts men and women through the marketing processes traders mobilize to control such seemingly gender-neutral factors as the short shelf life of a mango and old buses and new pickups. Elson's (1995) "gender ascriptive" (the outcome of the patriarchal organization of society) and "gender bearing" (the outcome of the patriarchal organization of capitalism) social and technical changes coalesced to limit Adelita's and expand Alfonso's access to the high-yield resource of transacting equitably with other empowered men.

ORGANIZATION OF THE MARKET SYSTEM

Today's market rambles across most of El Centro, the downtown quadrant. The system consists of three historically, structurally, and functionally differentiated subsystems which, following local usage, I refer to as the *mercado*," the daily sessions; the *plaza*, bi-weekly sessions; and the *tianguis*, a weekend session designed to attract tourists and out-of-town vendors. All sites and channels through which commodities move are profoundly and not randomly but increasingly less straightforwardly gendered.

At most sessions, it is possible to acquire at least a version of most of the array of goods for sale across a region now inundated with the standard complex of big box retailers and maze of the self-employed. Now all but unfathomable are the transiting routes of commodities as ordinary as locally grown tomatoes and as extraordinary as cell phones assembled in Guilin. The trading population is as strikingly inauthentic as are the exotic origins and economic pathways of commodities that "appear and disappear before consumers' eyes as if by spontaneous generation" (Jhally 1990:49): "spontaneous" until commodity chains are tracked to points where commodities get gender.

Inevitably profoundly feminized is a market where demand tends to be irregular and cash hard to come by and profitability hinges on making many, mostly small sales to increasingly polarized categories of buyers. Routinely, sourcing and processing services that cannot be incorporated into selling prices are supply-siding strategies financed by women's time, which is treated as all but cost free.

The mercado and tianguis labor forces are numerically female-dominated. Women sellers (generally referred to in the literature as "vendors" although they tended to call themselves "merchants") are overrepresented in all sessions when measured demographically or by their representation in the economically active population. The overall predominance of women makes all the more significant the disparate dynamics of sex typing across and within subsystems.

The scope and scale of gendering means that all women experience the market in ways that differ qualitatively and quantitatively from the ways all men experiences its systems quality. While a certain amount of "gender scrambling" (Adkins 2001) is in evidence, when the focus narrows to the performance of the job, feminization remains intense and closely correlated to status and functional disadvantages, suggesting that even when free marketizing, gendering is not diminishing. Though mutually reinforcing, occupation sex typing (or segregation) and job quality discrimination (or segmentation) are organizationally distinct, and each process is a fundamental aspect of the production origins of the goods a woman trades in; the nature of the consumer services she is required to provide; her trading times and the sites she trades out of; the distances she travels and the conveyances she travels in; the financial agencies, suppliers, co-workers, and consumers she interacts with; her personal reasons for entry and departure; and the social and material evaluation of the value(s) she creates.

The Politics of Unruliness

Much of the vitality and ingenuity that sojourners from the time of the Conquistadors have written about as the quintessential ambiance of Mexican marketplaces has survived. But if continuities abound in its "color, sounds and smells, confusion and disorder" (Mintz 1962:12), survivals illuminate the ways that the traditional and the modern recursively recreate each other. Tracking the movement of goods, trading partners, and information across the 1990–2000 market system establishes that in a collectively organized municipio nothing turns out to be more rule-ordered than generalized forms of unruliness.

It is not only to gain advantages of scope and scale but also to guarantee property rights that traders aggregate in an organized marketplace. Permits to use the market floor for specified purposes establish the technical properties that reduce some uncertainties and risks of more open systems but at the cost of conforming to negotiated ways of operating that are always both power limiting and power conferring.

Like 85 percent of the surface of Tepoztlán, the market is a common property resource under the stewardship of local officials. In theory, every adult stakeholder has the right to use space in the market to gain a livelihood. In practice, getting and using space is both a bureaucratic and a political process. Space-holders negotiated in ways nuanced by personal and family influence, political affiliation, age, and sexual preferences, and all other ways that gender diffuses through chains of market mechanisms. Stratifying variables driven by both up-close and far-distant regulatory systems range from product diversity and origin points, price and wage instability, the stress on consumer services, differences in personal goals and family responsibilities, and access to financial, social, and human capital.

As with all of the increasingly valuable municipio real estate, there is rampant trafficking in market spaces outside legality, and the interpretation of legality is neither strict nor consistent in its inconsistencies. The intensity of competition means that these days neither entitlement nor prestige guarantees a space. Among the ways occupancy changes is for a person to inherit from a parent, other relative, or a godparent. Though technically illegal, purchasing and renting are commonplace. Nowadays, brokers may be involved in transfers. There are also resourceful traders who contrive to create a space almost out of thin air.

Flower merchant Doña Laura, age sixty-three, occupies such a space conjured into existence by its original occupant. She pays one peso daily for the right to sell from the middle step of a twisting flight of stairs that serve as a passageway into the mercado. Upon hearing of the death of her predecessor, an acquaintance, "I rushed to the City Hall to ask for her space." She recognized the potential of the space because she knew that her friend had supported herself out of daily sales. Having some expertise in the flower industry, Laura decided she could at least duplicate her operation. She persuaded two suppliers to extend (high-interest and short-term) credit while she nourished the business. Though she struggled for a time, eventually the middle-step enterprise became viable if only in terms of the very modest bottom-line expectations of Doña Laura.

The significant fact is that even a space as unpromising as this cement perch all but guarantees some daily sales. And if at closing time push is at shove, there is the possibility of bartering with other vendors with whom one has punctiliously maintained the proper degree of civility. However, to go beyond day-by-day subsistence requires resources sufficient to sustain continuous investments. The type of products vended and space occupied determine the investment scale. Getting a space, use restrictions, and profitability potential are components of a mosaic of political processes ultimately driven by the merchant's access to exchangeable resources.

Traders must secure a permit from the Hacienda, the municipio treasury, specifying the proposed commodities and sales techniques. Taking into consideration the size, location, and days of use of the space, and the financial condition of the occupant, the Hacienda sets a "floor tax." Most vendors occupy modest spaces with a daily rent of 1 to 3 pesos. In some cases, there may be an increase of 1 or 2 pesos for plaza and other special days. Only the largest mercado dealer ("our supermarket") and the largest bi-weekly operation pay the highest fee, raised to 10 pesos in 1998.

These two merchants pay by the year, four others by the month; the rest elect daily payments collected in the early afternoon by three uniformed female collectors who vary their routes. Twenty or so merchants (described to me as "needy") pay nothing. As far as I could determine, no space holders were paying into social security for themselves or their employees. Only a few were paying any tax other than the floor tax. (As communal space, the market is exempt from property or income tax.)

Doña Susana, the impoverished (self-described), still very energetic daughter-in-law of a Tepoztecan general in Zapata's army produced a cardboard box in which she had saved all the floor tax receipts from her five decades in the market. With pride, she told me "I never missed a payment"; so she never missed a vending day. Those who cannot make a payment are allowed short extensions but in theory, a member who does not pay "for some time" can lose the right to trade. (No one could remember enforcement of this regulation, though attrition rates tied to other factors were high.)

The average monthly income from floor taxes during the lean years of 1994 to 1997 was 10,000 pesos, a sum that during the Golf Club emergency (when

Tepoztlán was cut-off from outside government funding) became crucial to keeping basic services afloat, more or less. Despite the seemingly token floor tax, the low level of modern technology, and micro level of investment, market trading is not disguised unemployment or alms but a capital-driven form of market participation. Tepoztlán's market system is then an agreed upon governance arrangement that defines and enforces property rights and serves to set the direction of the integration of the local and the global into each other.

The Enclosure Debate

Starting with a 1950s national program, numerous municipio markets were enclosed. Except for a canvas covering, which tends to collapse in a downpour and keep the air from circulating, Tepoztlán's has not been. In theory, citizens favor formalizing operations by enclosing them in a building and partitioning trading spaces into cells. The issue has repeatedly figured prominently in high politics, but real politics have always intervened to block the project. (In 2000, the state turned down a request by the male dominated Merchant's Union to fund the installation of 850 semi-fixed stalls along Revolution Avenue.) Politically, the problem is that no one is sure who stands to gain and who will lose by upgrading and expanding the facilities. For one thing, enclosure would put central district shops and market stalls into even more direct competition. In addition, though merchants would surely rent spaces, enclosure produces outcast groups who congregate outside and start a new cycle of unruliness. While proper sanitation is frequently cited as a reason to enclose, vendors are scrupulous about keeping sites policed and stocks fresh. (I never heard of anyone getting sick from eating in the market.)

Another concern is that the apparent unruliness is the ambiance that draws tradition-seeking tourists, as well as buyers who perceive backward conditions as promising field-freshness and bargains from uninformed sellers. The fear of losing clients with other options recognizes the value created by the presence of the population likely to be the first "cleared," namely market women, the frontline bearers of authenticity and downsized profits.

Other Regulatory Mechanisms

Not infrequently, tourists complain about the prices of goods, many of which are on a par with urban markets. Since most dealers are small-lot purchasers, suppliers give them little room to negotiate. Though rarely overt, bargaining can take place through a *pilón*, an in-kind extra. Credit is rare except for the "supermarket," which extends credit to some restaurants. This stall is one of two dealers giving (very) short-term credit to mercado food service operations. Even kinship seems rarely to be reflected at the point of sale. Gifting is likely to be in the form of fiesta feasting in homes.

The most popular items are available across the market. A notable exception is sit-down food service, the major growth category limited to the mercado, though homemade snacks are a primary product of weekend roaming traders. Along Revolution Avenue and side streets, beer and liquor stalls have proliferated; on the mercado floor, beer but not liquor or wine is sold but only at sit-down eating operations. (The state prohibits selling alcoholic drinks in establishments that do not also sell food. In 2005, the municipio imposed a 10 p.m. curfew for selling liquor.)

Surveys I conducted established that c. 1995 vending populations were differentiated as follows. Members make up the population of mercado vendors. Numerically, women dominate this labor force at every session in roughly the same proportion that men dominate the economically active population. Since the purpose of the biweekly plaza days is to attract dealers in goods not routinely found locally, a majority of periodic sellers are not local. Women make up from 46 to 61 percent of this work force. Though the municipio intended limiting the tianguis to regional craft producer/traders, any craft that can be sold now meets a highly negotiable criteria; 74 percent of tianguis vendors were female, 46 percent resided in the head town.

Custom-driven customer preferences powerfully influence commodity specific gender stratification patterns (M. Scott 1994). In addition, when management is "decentralized and intermittent," shoppers can become surrogates for international chains of absentee landlords (Lopez 1996:51). In today's unbounded market, it is not always possible to disentangle cultural and material connections; however, targeted surveys detected distinct matchups of price givers (sellers) and price takers (buyers).

Except at eating and craft stalls, mercado shoppers are mainly area residents, primarily women. Many prefer to do their major shopping on plaza days, a preference that dilutes mercado sales of staple items. For most dealers, Sunday is the only session when tourists are a major factor. Shopping times accord with work schedules; homemakers like to get their routine chores out of the way. Purchases respond to budgets, access to other markets, jobs, seasonality, and household formations.

For tourists, the market is still a "happy hunting-ground" (Malinowski and de la Fuente 1982:61). But to homemakers whose major concern is the continuous quest for just-in-time affordable quality, marketing is serious business; and increasingly, product information is unobtainable even by the most astute shoppers. For their part, sellers have little choice but to define quality as whatever it is that makes clients come back. Homemakers have a competing definition. They conceptualize quality in terms of the obligation to provision a family with "*sana*," wholesome, products. It is far from clear that the two evaluation bases can ever be commensurate.

Gustavo Salazar, the merchant heading the Governing Council, described the Association of Vendors as a "semifixed arrangement designed to make the market run smoothly." To clarify relations, he drew five circles for the five trading categories—prepared food, crafts, butchers, fruit and vegetable dealers, and hard goods—floating around a core circle, which he labeled "the Governing Council." All were the same size. Don Gustavo said, "The council has no official power. Members sometimes ask us to arbitrate grievances and disputes. Frequently, they do not request or follow our advice." Others agree that the Association "is not important. To Don Pablo, "Gustavo's political ambitions are the reason why things no longer run smoothly." But as the Golf Club movement proved, most traders are intensely involved in pueblo politics, in part because they look to the political establishment to make infrastructural improvements and protect their use rights.

The Association's primary official activity is to join with other representatives of the commercial community to stage the major fiestas held from September 8 through 16. All dealers contribute according to their means. So using provisions donated by butchers and produce vendors, women in food services prepare a splendid (free) banquet for the large delegation of U.S. and Mexican clergymen attending a liturgical conference that always coincides with the "*Madre de Fiestas*." Reflecting the local cover-all-bases approach to rituals, equal homage is paid to the Virgin of the Nativity, the (voluntary) conversion of El Tepozteco, a bounteous harvest, the prosperity of merchants, and, with deafening shouts of *Viva México*, Mexican independence. (An ordinance now prohibits shooting off rifles.) Day and night throughout September, bells toll and fireworks are set off in the hills, often resulting in forest fires.

Trading Operations

The Hacienda distinguishes four categories of use permits: mobile, semifixed, fixed, and food services. The typology proved to be a reference point for uncovering gendered variations conditioned by the nature of the product, time-space constraints, and resource access.

Mobile vendors, *ambulantes*, move about inside the market precincts; the category is all but exclusively male. Semi-fixed traders operate out of assigned spaces. They sit on cartons, on campstools, or on the market floor (with their legs stretched out). Goods are displayed in pails, crates, or whatever. I never observed a man in this trading class selling perishable staples or sitting on the market floor.

Fixed vending is from a stall (*puesto*), kiosk (*caseta*), or shop (*tienda*). Stalls—really some number of tables or boards atop supports—are not enclosed. A *kiosk* is a room with a window opening. There are three groupings of *tienditas* (small shops); all are impressively stocked convenience stores. Structures on the margins of the marketplace can be on privately or communally controlled real estate.

Labor Management Variations

Cook (1986) stresses that in "petty" Mexican enterprises the "managerial function" is realized through the activation of a reserve of cheap, often family labor, usually female, that substitutes for monetary capital. I detected the following managerial patterns.

Self-employment

This worker is "the owner of his or her labor power and therefore takes upon him or herself reproduction costs" (Narotzky 1997:205). Since a distinguishing feature is retaining a degree of autonomous control over certain input/output decisions, self-employment is often the choice of people with investment capital, including their own labor power. It may be the most rational choice, but at very low levels of capitalization, self-employment in the informal sector can be the only option, in which case it is highly unlikely to be optimal. Reasons market women cited for choosing self-employment ranged from the desire to be independent, the opportunity to take advantage of an ongoing operation or a family tradition, the inability of the vendor or members of her household to find suitable salaried employment, availability of investment capital, to pressing needs. For men, self-employment may be voluntary or "forced entrepreneurship": that is, the deterioration of formal employment and/or loss of formal jobs can make self-employment the only option.

Collective Self-employment

Among the forms of this trading mode are wife/husband, mother/daughter, and sister teams. Though rare, male/male combinations exist, usually as full-time father and part-time unmarried son combinations, since most operations are too small to employ two or more heads of households. Collectives have many advantages (and some bottom-line disadvantages) over one-person operations.

Family Capitalism

Family-based enterprises operate in substantively different managerial styles. In one version, the family—couples, sons, daughters, grandchildren, cousins—coalesces around an agreed-upon authority figure. Sometimes members share a house or a compound. Workers who are at once family-wage consumers and producers pool their labor at different operational stages. Material, social, or political contributions often derive from nonmarket sources. The head may be a matriarch, a patriarch, or a son or daughter with proven managerial abilities. Often, gender roles in the late modern family condition women's insertions even at the managerial level. Though not formally contracted, many variants of family labor are counted on. The profits of one matriarch went first to sustain the enterprise and the homogenous unit; she distributed what remained in various ways to meet the needs of individuals.

Market Dynasties

Dynasties start when a founder ceases to be active in a family enterprise and distributes his/her interests among children. I identified five dynasties where members of a stem family have branched into independent market system enterprises. Each also has investments outside the market. Operations differ in size and profitability. Apparently, siblings operate as financially independent of each other, though none of the units competes directly. They cooperate in a number of productive ways but joint ventures I observed seemed to be opportunistic. Reciprocity in the form of achieving economies of scale and scope can be direct or delayed. For example, they may acquire goods for each other when on buying trips, lend a pickup, or share a family worker. The matriarch of one dynasty emphasized the importance of the joint family structure to each unit's ability to harmonize productive and reproductive activities. Doña Olivia said, "My mother brought me and my brothers and sister up in the stall, and I raised my ten children in the market." Now in their eighties, both parents continue actively assisting their children "in many ways." Four children now have their own stalls, and are also bringing up their children in the market, though not necessarily for market careers. The stall of one son (not the oldest) is considered the flagship operation. It seems likely that he rather than the oldest son will become the next official leader of the dynasty.

Formal Cooperative Arrangements

Tacitly formalized cooperative arrangements were actually understandings not to compete too directly. The setting of selling prices (detailed below) is by far the most significant—and amazingly uniformly observed—market-wide cooperative function.

Wage Labor

Salaried labor dates back to at least the colonial era. A good deal of modern market system labor for wages in cash and/or kind is irregular or spot contracts, but the uniformity of wage scales points to binding standards. Contract labor includes porters and watchmen. Part-time and full-time workers often had kin ties to employers. I found no workers defined as employees who did not expect to receive most of their wage in cash.

Though many of these labor arrangements do respond to social relationships, no matter how lowly, jobs in the market should not be analyzed as less than fully economically rational. For marketing work regularly performed, male and female Tepoztecans of all ages expect a cash wage scaled in accord with wages paid for nonmarket work. However, the vast amount of support labor done at home by family members seems to be formally unwaged.

Financial Issues

Regular accumulation of investment capital is all but ruled out for most market operations. However, all businesses no matter how hand-to-mouth require capital other than hard work. In chapter 5, I described women's access to financial capital. A few market women were borrowing from local cooperatives, but the purpose was to finance domestic projects. In this period of usurious interest rates and a wisely mistrusted financial industry, citizens neither desired nor could get a loan from a formal monetary institution. Market women viewed indebtedness to lending institutions in much the same negative light as allowing mates to have direct roles in the business. Many are also reluctant to stake their enterprises on government or NGO micro loans. One merchant anxious to expand her baking operation explained why she did not apply for a government-sponsored loan to finance a new oven: "These loans have to be paid back in a timely fashion, and my business is just too unpredictable." Numerous women participated in tandas (described in chapter 5) organized among market women. "We help each other out with tandas," explained Doña Milagros. However, the most successful operations were those that were able to draw continuously on family capital as a resource.

Chapter Gendering Trends

Foundational to the core neoliberal trickle-down premise—growth at the top *must* over time filter down to the bottom—is that unregulated markets *work* to solve the fundamental problem that, as classical economists Ricardo and Marx predicted, has proven to be deeply embedded at all levels of capitalist development: namely, increasingly asymmetrically differentiated and spatially distanced stakes. The validity of the trickle down neoliberal fundamental proposition rests on three assumptions (Epstein et al. 1993): (1) that markets efficiently allocate tradable resources; (2) that markets do not inherently favor one class of traders over others; and (3) that thereby markets eliminate abuses of power. Alternative theorists contest each assumption, insisting that markets are organized for the specific purpose of continuously expanding the power of the already empowered.

Transactions across Tepoztlán's redeveloped market system give a degree of support to both interpretations while also calling attention to the inadequacy of any late modern market paradigm that does not treat gender as a variable that interacts independently with all other variables. On the one hand, linkages to world trading systems have created and feminized slots for Tepoztecas. On the other side, M. P. Smith's "global conditions" (cited in the epigraph) become "meaningful" as particular patterns of the gender-based segregation and segmentation of the labor force. In the next three chapters, I explore the conflicting dynamics of marketization and feminization from the standpoint of market women's arts of using "new dimensions of inequality" to create "whole new sets of relations between activities in different places" (Massey 1995:3).

Chapter Nine

Embedded in the Market

> Economic institutions [are] constructed by individuals whose action is both facilitated and constrained by the structure and resources available in the social networks in which they are embedded.
>
> —Mark Granovetter, 1991

Daily mercado operations extend across 4,950m^2 of much coveted El Centro real estate. In ten surveys conducted between 1994 and 1998 during prime trading time and spaced to uncover daily and seasonal differences, the vending population ranged from a Tuesday low of 189 to a Sunday high of 497.

On most days, attendance peaks from 10 a.m. to 2 p.m. and since most nonfixed vendors trade in daily staples, as shoppers for that day's *comida* (main meal) thin out, they prepare to depart. Except on special market days, by 4:30, all but a few fixed vendors are shutting down. Around 5:30, a night shift of prepared food vendors starts to filter in. Heaviest traffic is for the daily-baked sweet rolls women sell on commission for local bakeries. By 9 p.m., on the fringes of the mercado, men predominate at food stalls concentrating on grilled meat.

Because sex typing has proven to be highly responsive to specific complexes of internal and external factors, I designed sampling to isolate gendering at occupation, task, working conditions, and sector levels. Table 9.1 indicates consistent distribution patterns.

Gendering Trends

Women dominated all sessions. For example, for four averaged 1996 surveys, 72 percent were female. If gender balanced in proportion to the economically

Table 9.1. Representative Market Labor Force Surveys by Number, Date, with Female/male Ratios

OPERATION	*MALE*	*FEMALE*
Wednesday 1-17-96, 11 A.M.–3 P.M. Labor force, 73% F, F/M ratio, 2.72 to 1		
Shops	08	08
Stalls	34	96
Kiosks	15	19
Food Services	07	45
Semifixed	02	19
Mobile	03	01
Total	69	188
Sunday 1-21-96. 11-00–4:30. Labor force, 68% F, F/M ratio, 2.09 to 1		
Shops	07	10
Stalls	70	149
Kiosks	35	44
Food Svs*	23	64
Semifixed	06	36
Mobile	07	06
Total	148	309
Tuesday 1-23-96, 11:00–2:00. Labor Force, 75% F, F/M Ratio, 3.03 to 1		
Shops	16	12
Stalls	08	42
Kiosks	12	20
Food Svs	07	27
Semifixed	02	39
Mobile	02	02
Total	47	142
Tuesday 5-28-96, 11:00–12:00. Labor Force, 73% F, F/M Ratio, 2.67 to 1		
Shops	06	13
Stalls	21	67
Kiosks	23	34
Food Svs	06	30
Semifixed	01	25
Mobile	01	—
Total	52	139

*Food service breakdown: Men in restaurants 6, small restaurants (*fondas*) 2, stalls 15. Of the 64 women, 51 worked in stalls.

active population, men would outnumber women by some three to one in each trading category. However, measured by the Index of Female Segregation (see Box 5.1), women were overrepresented in the four sessions by 39 percent, indicating an extremely high level of segregation. On the other hand, when the base line is demographic equality, women only exceeded their 51 percent of the economic population by 21 percent. Though numerically dominant, women are less dominant than in the activity categories of, for example, education and office work; men, on the other hand, never came near their level of participation even in the most mixed nonmarket occupations. The surveys confirm that the mercado is not a primary workplace for employed males, even at a time when male under and unemployment were at new highs. While during this period of loss of industrial jobs, many men were trying to set up small businesses, relatively few were going into the mercado. Disaggregated, segregation and segmentation patterns proved to be extreme and nonrandom but rarely straightforward. On the other hand, whatever the objective circumstances and regardless of other stratifying factors—such as education, age, skills, and prestige—sex typing consistently predicted inequalities in earnings and other job quality markers. Thus even when men were present, because of the high degree of job gendering, local women seldom competed head-to-head with local men, especially for the best slots; but diversely situated Tepoztecas competed intensely with each other.

What are the market-driven factors that predict the forms of the intensive gender division of the labor force? The day of a session and its limiting characteristics proved to be the most stable predicator of increased male participation. Yet even on Sundays and other prime market days when male participation is highest, men engage in a narrow range of male-identified specialties, most aimed at the most affluent and sporadic buyers. In fact, the presence of professional male traders predicted involvement of women at various labor-intensive stages of their operations.

To economists, men *prefer* to participate only in sessions when demand for male specializations is high and in the most investment-intensive jobs. In contrast, women *prefer* market work whether attendance is high or low; moreover, their rational choices generally coincide with factors downgrading the job.

As indicated by the food services breakdown, the narrower the unit of observation, the more sex-typed the category. Sector patterns confirm the importance of disaggregating data at the level of jobs and tasks within jobs. On Wednesday, 13 percent were male; on Sunday this rose to 26 percent. Of these sixteen men, thirteen were preparing and/or serving the Sunday delicacy of barbecue, a high-end male market specialty. Some male owners took orders. Rarely did they or high-period male temporaries serve. Space is also predictive. In restaurants, all wait personnel were male while the kitchen force was gender mixed.

Gender dividers include tipping practices. Though often serving the same fare, men in restaurants expected tips while women in stalls neither expected nor received tips. However, no divider was as certain and constant as tortillas: 100 percent of workers preparing tortillas (and 98 percent of servers) were women. Interested in the seasonality factor, I compared two Tuesdays (the slowest day). On January 23, 1996, the female to male ratio was 3.03 to 1; this was during the lowest volume period for sales to local consumers who had spent heavily in the holiday season. On May 28, 1996, during the cultivation and high construction season when locally earned cash had begun to flow in, the ratio dropped to 2.67 to 1.

For most enterprises, the sales volume and profit margins are so erratic extended calculations were meaningless. The daily wage tends to be less than the U.S. hourly wage for comparable activity. Rationalizing participation for women who do not have investment capital or who cannot risk their capital is the small scale of most enterprises that allows financing out of daily sales. For the most hand-to-mouth operations, it can be assumed that this market-driven imperative is being met if the vendor does not give up. With the flexibility to react to adversity or opportunity, more capitalized enterprises make profit-enhancing changes. It is even more critical for weak enterprises to adjust and because they do so within their limiting frameworks, adjustments are intensely challenging.

At a general level, all marketing processes and operations evidence the combined effects of smallness of scale, purchasing constraints, intensive and unfair competition, reliance on merchant capital and on unpaid family labor, limited access to profit-enhancing technologies, and the over-representation of homemakers as sellers and as buyers. However, significantly different ways of dealing with advantages and disadvantages did closely correlate to whether an operation was fixed or nonfixed. I look first at nonfixed market merchants for two reasons. First, because into the 1950s this was the only way independent women traded. Second, though seemingly the least economic way of participating, in fact it is the trading system most disciplined by the neoliberal strategies of advanced capitalist firms.

NONFIXED TRADING

My seat companion on my first bus ride to Tepoztlán was semifixed marketer Doña Luisa. On this sultry Sunday, she was returning to the municipio hamlet of San Juan to prepare comida for her husband Felipe and the three out of their seven children who are still living at home. She had arrived at the cavernous Cuernavaca market shortly after dawn to sell cactus leaves outside the south entrance. Under a white cloth, I glimpsed a few green leaves in the large basket she had placed on her lap (to avoid paying a freight fee). Even before we pulled out of the bus stop, she had dozed off. When the rattles of the non-express (and two peso cheaper) bus forced her awake, she spoke about a career fragmented by the reverberations in Mexican communities and households of the commodity-specific politics of agrarian capitalism. As Louisa's trading history tells us, policies designed to support agribusiness by undermining small farming gender exchanges long before they play out on the market floor.

San Juan is in a year-round farming area. The prickly leaves of the nopal cactus are the major dry-season crop, and its fruit, the wet-season crop. Village women expect to be actively present in the milpa as well as in the hogar. Another entrenched custom is for women to trade nopal in regional markets. Working alongside her mother, Luisa entered the three worlds of San Juan women's work: intensive homemaking, farming, and mobile trading. Especially since NAFTA, agrarian politics have dramatically transformed these work processes.

Unable to make a living ("I was working for the [agricultural] bank," Don Felipe told me), like many others, this family now rents out their ejido. Increasingly, large retailing channels control production and delivery times. Many men abandoned farming to go into other sectors; but since most women did not have other commercial options, they had to intensify market trading. As so-called surpluses vanished, they bought nopal in two non-municipio communities. And because their margin of return is best on consumer-direct sales, they specialized in the labor-intensive (and shelf life reducing) job of processing the sticky, prickly leaves. That this messy task is a precondition for sales to restaurants and busy homemakers explains why in the Tepoztecan market, San Juan women continue to have a dominant presence. Stall operators do not find it cost effective to compete with mobile women processors primarily because to be competitive with other women traders the women add nothing for their time, skill, and loss. It takes a highly skilled woman at least two and a half minutes to process a single leaf. If averaging 2.75 pesos per hour, the uncharged cost per twenty-four leaves is around 9 pesos. Not surprisingly other market women, too, have largely left the low paying trade to San Juan women. Their need for quick turnover means that like Doña Luisa they must travel to larger, more distant markets, sometimes trading at several in one day.

Nonfixed Traders Activity Studies

I observed four variations of the nonfixed vending mode: daily semifixed trading; fully mobile trading; periodic trading; and hybrid adaptations. In each variation, usually the operator is both management and labor. Table 9.2 profiles two trading groups.

Category 1: Daily Semifixed Traders

These mercado marketers are location-specific rent paying (1 to 3 pesos) tenants, but they do not have permanent facilities and must transport goods between sessions. Once set up in an assigned sliver of space they do not move around. On average, women were 86 percent of this category, making it the most female sex-typed category. In the two groups now described, women were 100 percent of the daily attending vending population.

This most micro and sex typed of enterprises has the longest continuous market history. As in earlier times, traders tend to be daily-attending matrons from satellite communities—most were in the thirty-five to sixty age group—dealing in perishable staples, often-homemade regional favorites. With highly limited access to investment capital and mobility constraints, no market group has been more substantively impacted by the contexts of the neoliberal project.

The defining attribute of semifixed trading is that vendors have a fixed location but no permanent stall; nevertheless, like fixed traders, to hold on to a space they must use it continuously. They must also establish themselves in a highly competitive market niche, a project that requires operational continuity.

Lourdes Aguilar, Produce Vendor

On this day as usual, Group 1 merchants were arrayed on stools, upturned cartons, or the cement floor, in spaces just large enough to accommodate a vendor and a micro-inventory. Stocks were in pails or set out on (usually red) plastic remnants. Doña Lourdes seemed to be the most successful of group 1 sellers of perishable staples. The consistency of her better than average results meant that her marketing—the family's only non-seasonal income source—could be as much as 70 percent of the family wage. Age twenty-nine, mother of two boys and wife of Ramon, a farmer and day laborer, Lourdes sells a seasonally varying selection of the traditional foods that are still staples at the tables of all classes of local consumers. A one-peso daily rent entitles her to a space some four feet long just in front of a bustling poultry shop and a bank of other shops. When not selling, she processes items to make them ready for the cooking pot or refreshes stocks with water hauled from the fountain.

Table 9.2. Profiles of Semifixed Trading Groups

Group 1: Wednesday, 1-24-1996, 8:00–8:30 A.M.
Location: a central walkway:

Number	*Origin*	*Commodity*	*Age*
1	Anatlahucan	Homemade peanut candy	68
2	Santiago	Black-skinned avocados	37, 44
2	Santo Domingo	Pine torches	50, 50
1	Tlacotenco	Boiled peanuts, pears	53
2	San Juan	Nopal	27
1	San Andreas	Pomegranates	35
1	Los Ocotes	Smoked and boiled corn ears	48
1	Santa Catarina	Squash, squash flowers, alpistre*	36
1	Santiago	Squash, corn	28
1	San Juan	*Nopal,* squash, squash flowers, corn, cilantro, huhuzontli**	33
1	Oacalco	Same mix except *nopal*	29
1	Amatlán	Fruit	82

Group 2: Friday, 5-31-1996, 11–11:30 A.M.
Location: in front of market shed.
All were tortilla sellers:

Number	*Origin*	*Product*	*Age*
3	Santa Catarina	Yellow maize tortillas	37, 42, 52
2	Santa Catarina	Flour tortillas and dough	44, 56
1	Santa Catarina	Flour and blue maize tortillas	35

**Alpistre* is a grass used as bird food.
***Huhuzontli,* a stalky green.

Many shoppers assume that the goods of Group 1 sellers came directly from fields. Instead, customarily, Lourdes and most other Group 1 traders purchase stocks at the early morning Cuernavaca wholesale market. She makes the three plus hour trips to Cuernavaca three or four time a week. Even on these days, she is at the market in Tepoztlán by 8 a.m. No later than 3 p.m., she has begun to pack up. Returning home (in overcrowded vans) occupies an additional hour or more.

Lourdes has the considerable range of skills needed to select and deliver on a daily basis good quality foods at the right prices—and in the right portions, since the low cost of doing business as a semimobile trader allows her to cater to consumers who generally buy only single-meal portions. Small-lot buyers can purchase a size-graded pile of five squash, a handful of cilantro, or a bunch of squash blossoms, and not be penalized. When she makes her purchases by the kilo, she has only a general idea of what the going rate will be across the market for a specific commodity. However, by the time she sets out her products, she is able to make adjustments. There is nothing random about the pricing, as I verified when I comparatively weighed products from various vendors. She "never" bargains, but a something extra is usual in some transactions. The *pilón* seems to hinge more on the amount and timing of purchases than on established trading relations.

She began trading six years ago, at first only part-time and out of a basket. The start-up investment of her current operation of around 150 pesos came from funds saved from various employment sources. She estimates average daily profits of some 40 pesos. She finances her fixed investment in goods and expenses out of daily sales. Lourdes has confidence in her skills and enjoys trading. She judges marketing to be the labor most "compatible" with other obligations, though she is concerned that business often compels her to "neglect" her family. At least while her boys are young, she would "probably" prefer being a full-time homemaker.

Lourdes told me she was "thankful" to have escaped the hard life common to rural Guerrero women. Unlike the men in her birth family, Ramón helps her with many household chores: "He is not macho like Guerrero men." Ramon made the following observations. "Nowadays wives must work, and when they work, it is the duty of the husband to help at home. But respect in a marriage is not based on money or on sharing chores. It's there or it's not there from the start. And, no matter what kind of work she does, the hogar must always come first for the wife."

Ximena Cuellar, Producer/vendor of Tortillas

Group 2 vendors numbering from six to twelve at prime selling times pay one peso for a designated space. Plastic and impeccably clean white cloths cover tortillas in pails and baskets. Most of the time, the vendors stand; often, they encroach a step or two into the passageway. Present on this day, as on most days in her twenty-two-year career selling tortillas in the mercado, is Doña Ximena, thirty-seven-year-old single mother and Santa Catarina resident.

Santa Catarina, considered the most Nahua municipio community, is unique for never having allowed an outsider to control even one of its 10,000 hectares (Hernandez Chapa 1995). For centuries, maize, the primary crop, has anchored the prevailing female trade: selling tortillas. I asked a veteran market woman to account for the specialization, given that producing and selling tortillas is seemingly the most accessible of all female occupations. After a moment to consider the matter, she replied, "I suppose it is the only thing they had to sell." Though there is now no comparative advantage to tortilla vending and there are other options, like Luz, some Santa Catarina women seem determined to hold on to their niche.

Ximena identifies herself as a "homemaker and full-time tortilla vendor." She and son David, age ten, share the home of her elderly parents. She left school at age ten "because I'm lazy." She went on to speak of a youth that included long hours of field- and housework. Each twelve- to thirteen-hour workday includes the following tasks:

- one hour to buy maize, husk it, and start soaking it in lime (*cal*) to soften it
- one hour to take soaked corn to the mill and have it ground into dough (*masa*)
- three hours to create fifteen dozen products by pressing the masa into a mold and cooking each tortilla individually on a grill (*comal*)
- one hour or more transportation time to the market
- five to six hours vending time and at least one hour to travel home

Until recently, by working the longest hours of any Group 2 sellers I observed, she somehow stretched the meager income. The removal of price subsidies has cut deeply into her already slim profit margin, as has the huge increase in competition not only from other semi-ambulant traders but also from national firms that entered the field with the elimination of the subsidy on corn tortillas. Two local tortilla factories also send women to sell in the mercado. Perhaps the greatest threat comes from local women who have set up neighborhood operations producing tortillas to order, a piping fresh dozen for 8 pesos. Ximena said there are now days when she nets "nothing." Even day-old stock is too stale to sell, so she feeds it to a pig, though this traditional way of putting unsold stock to work is no longer cost effective.

"*Tor-ti-llas, señores. Tor-ti-llas*": The cadence of this sales pitch announces the Santa Catarina origin of a vendor. Since sellers offer identical products at uniform prices, everything depends on attracting attention. By market standards, there is a high degree of pitching. Once a transaction is in progress, other sellers never approach and actual contact with buyers remains within market norms that discourage overly aggressive vending. Depending on the time of day, to a few "semi-regular" clients, Ximena might give a *pilón*; she sometimes extends credit but "only if I must."

Her son David travels with her to attend school because she believes that the one in the head town is better than their own local school. After school, he peddles candy consigned by another vendor. (Some fixed dealers employ children to "roam.") About being a single mother, Ximena told me: "It is good to have many children; but it is also good to have fewer children, especially in times like these." She approves of abortion "in some circumstances" that she would not specify. She acquired the jagged scar when she and David were beaten with a nightstick when the police attacked a community excursion to celebrate Zapata's birthday. "I only went on the trip because I wanted to give my son a little holiday and he wanted to see the Route of Zapata. Generally, I have no time for politics. Only for tortillas."

Laura Guzmán, Baker/merchant of Whole Wheat Breads

Doña Laura, age thirty-eight and one of the few nonmembers with a permit to trade, came to Tepoztlán hoping to tap into a niche market for whole wheat bread. Fashion-model thin and ramrod-straight, daily for five hours or longer, Laura stands demurely but attentively beside a large signature bakery basket atop an eye-level pedestal. It contains the five varieties of wheat breads she bakes. She exemplifies a new breed of trader attracted by a demand for exotic goods, but her trading life exemplifies the patterned ways that gender continues to condition semifixed trading.

A native of the adjacent state of Michoacán, Laura formed a consensual union with José, a manager of a vegetarian restaurant; during this period, she learned the art of baking wheat bread. Knowing that resident foreigners supported a health food market, this skill brought the couple and their three young children to Tepoztlán. (She also has two married daughters in Michoacán.) Within two years, the breads that she bakes in a small wood-burning oven in a house she rents across from the mercado were supporting the family.

In 1995, she organized her business thusly. She paid 1 peso for a standing space at the bustling west entrance and 3 pesos for a second space on special days. She had just added a weekend location on the heavily trafficked avenue to the pyramid. She also distributed through a health food store and a coffee bar. She baked in the morning and evening. In addition to stoking the fire, this type of baking requires seven hours: an hour and a half to prepare the dough and form the breads; four hours for the rising; then around an hour of baking. When they were available, the children undertook the final step of wiping the carbon off the bread. José, whom she described as "an alcoholic and an unreliable person," was doing little more than helping to fuel the oven and irregularly transporting supplies in the family's "barely running car." When she refused to give him money, they had "terrible rows." Like a number of children of daily vendors attending downtown schools, the children often took over the selling after school. On weekends, they cooperated in staffing the three spaces. When she first arrived, she had "a few problems" being accepted in a community she describes as "closed but not negative." By now, her hard work and her dedication to her children earned her the respect of other traders. (It is worth noting that her product did not threaten other vendors.)

In 1997 interviews, most clients were still from the foreign colony. (A number of local people savor the bread but cannot budget it as a staple.) With triple digit inflation on many production factors, her intensifying problem was not sales but finding a way to squeeze out a family wage. She and José had separated. His departure came as "a considerable relief." However, without him, she was unable to cope physically with the demands of the new location, and, even though it was "doing well," she had to give it up. She reported, "My gross increased but there was not enough profit to hire helpers." Her reliance on the labor of the children troubles her, but they are her only source of indispensable flexibility. A new threat has come from foreign-colony vendors and firms attracted to the product. Unlike white and corn flour, now monopolized by firms, with less demand, the price of wheat flour is more stable. In addition, by 1998, she had developed a market other foreigners began to exploit.

Category 2: Roaming Trading

The classic type of hawking inside the market is not an important category for women. When they do itinerate as fully mobile dealers, there are stylistic differences with men. For example, women tend to mass at a fixed base while men are more likely to be solitary and to roam. What seems most important, however, are the ways Category 2 traders use the feminization dimensions of footloose mercado trading to mediate the often-high transaction costs to women of mobility.

Juana Moreno, Producer/vendor of Gelatin and Flan

For a time, I rented a room in the Revolution Avenue Spanish-style bungalow of Doña Juana, age seventy-six. She exploited mobile trading to bring up her three children, though it is unlikely that anyone would identify her occupationally as an *ambulante*. With Juana, I learned that (reversing the usual U.S. order of things), in Tepoztlán often it is the quality of a worker that gives status to the job.

For almost half a century, Doña Juana vended the brightly colored gelatins and flan ubiquitous in Mexican market places. Her family returned from wartime exile shortly before her birth, a risky decision since her father was a member of a cacique (indigenous elite) family. Though most family assets were now in the hands of others, he was able to reclaim the heavily damaged family home. Juana was four when her father died. Though he did not leave the family destitute, she had a difficult youth. She recalled:

> My mother was the meanest woman around, spiteful and proud of it! Everyone left as soon as they could, but as the youngest, I was a prisoner. The first time I

> remember being happy was when I started school. But after a week my mother came to school and pulled me out, by my hair! I appealed to my kind godmother. She agreed to send me to Mexico City to live with her sister and attend school there. In secret, she took me to the station, but just as the train arrived, mother appeared and forced me to return. But in just one week I learned enough to read a bit. So I think I must have been a bright child.

Within a few years, her mother had taken to her bed. She promised to leave Juana, the youngest of eight siblings, the house in exchange for her care. "I did it, but not for the house, but because it was the right thing to do." When her mother died, she was recently married to a farmer; eight years later, age twenty-five, she was a widow and mother of three. "He was a kind and gentle man. I miss him still." (Hanging on the wall of the bedroom I occupied was his favorite straw hat.) The house was almost all she had. She began what would be a half-century of paid domestic work combined with trading in El Centro, a short but very steep trek above her home. "Working as a maid, I earned enough to keep us alive; marketing enabled me to keep the children in school." She prepared gelatin and flan, products she chose because she could integrate production into her routine. She rose before dawn to get the children off and start the main meal. She found domestic work two houses down with a leading family. Three times weekly, she devoted eight hours to cooking, stirring, filling glasses, and the final setting period. She said:

> I was able to sleep a bit in between. Now I generally only sell on some Sundays, but when the children were younger, I sold Wednesday and Sunday and other times as well depending on our needs. I always began with several tours around the market fringes; then, when business got slow, I moved into the streets if necessary. I always met friends and stopped to chat with them.

With her children settled, vending was no longer a survival and advancement strategy. However, it had become her way of life and she did not want to ask her children for money "though they are always giving me things, like the telephone they insisted I must have for safety." She continued in her domestic job and some Sundays and evenings, she still filled her glass case and went to sit on the steps of the City Hall and talk politics. She was keenly interested in the Golf Club, and people valued her opinions. In part, her interest in politics reflected the fear that she would lose her home to predatory realtors. She knew of several widows who had been "tricked out of their homes. They never even knew they had lost their homes until it was too late. These days, I dare not go away even overnight." She believed political contacts would help to protect her valuable property.

Several nights during my stay, she devoted to preparing her gelatins and custards. Having a gas stove and an electric refrigerator saved several hours of preparation time. TV was a treasured new companion, especially since she perused newspapers avidly but with difficulty.

Over the years, she tried her hand at selling "more up-to-date" items. On some Sundays, she shared a booth with a friend to display clothing purchased in Mexico City, a stock she stored in a tower of cartons in a corner of my bedroom. Early one Sunday morning, the cartons were loaded onto a dolly that she jauntily pushed up a nearly perpendicular block. But by the end of the day, her mood had turned to resignation. "I sold nothing. I had no luck today." She attributed this to "hard times" and to the competition from the recent proliferation of dealers selling used clothes from the U.S., an occupation that soon became overcrowded with men as well as women.

Teresa Torres, Producer/vendor of Designer Tamales

Tamales—a stuffed corn dough cylinder—are an important commercial resource for a number of women. In a joint weekend venture, teachers Sandra, age twenty-eight, and Joan, age twenty-six, collaborate to create and vend tamales just outside the mercado. Profits, estimated at 50 pesos, go toward family "extras." As is the local custom, the filling is a dab of shredded pork. The selling price is also standard (in 1995, 2 pesos each; 3 for 5.75) except for daily *tamalera* Doña Teresa. Using exotic fillings like anise and mushrooms and targeting the gentry, she ups the price a bit.

Teresa, age forty-five, first sold only out of her home. But when her husband lost his job, she started an enterprise that now consumes some ten hours daily. Each day, she makes two rounds in areas where foreigners congregate. Her metal pail contains two kinds of tamales filled with seasonal delicacies (never meat) that are popular with foreigners. She said, "It's my business and I do everything myself." She never wears an apron (as do almost all mercado women), and dresses like an office worker, as (perhaps) befitting a family breadwinner. One tour inside the market coincides with midday dining. She approaches people who are eating, particularly if they are former clients, a strategy discouraged by the food stall operator. In 1996, she charged 2.50 pesos per tamale or six for 10 pesos. In 1998, she boldly increased the price of single tamales to 3 pesos. She was not forthcoming on matters financial; but when I asked if she netted as much as 150 pesos per week she replied, "I always do better."

Category 3: Periodic Market Traders

Periodic markets refer to markets held regularly but only on certain designated days (called *plaza days*). William Skinner (1964) reports firms that are both producers and distributors find periodicity advantageous even when exploiting only one market. Long erased is the male dominated plaza day producer-dealer pattern of Redfield's time. Paradoxically, the reasons why homemaker-distributors are able to turn periodicity to their advantage are much the same as the technical changes that makes periodic trading in minor markets rational for transnational firms and not rational for small-scale male professional traders. Periodic markets are a cost-reducing way to enter problematic niche markets for women trading low cost goods.

Though the first impression is of a haphazard sprawl, the disposition of even a sliver of space is regulated and coveted. To get even the most unpromising space, it is necessary to submit a formal request to the Hacienda. Dividing the area into an L-shaped sector (2a) and an area (2b) inside and on the fringes of the 2,400-m^2 garden, M/F groupings were as follows:

Table 9.3. Plaza Day Groupings

Wednesday 10-18-1995 (2a/b) Time: 10:00–2:00	
102 M, 93 F	48% Female
Sunday 12-31-1995 (2a/b) Time: 11:00–1:30	
35 M, 22 F	39% Female
Wednesday 5-22-1996 Time 9:30–1:30	
2a 124 M, 108 F	47% Female
2b 12 M, 19 F	61% Female
Sunday 5-26-1996 (2a/b) Time 9:30–2:15	
115 M, 103 F	47% Female
Wednesday 8-6-1997 (2a/b) Time 10:00–2:00	
132 M, 113 F	46% Female

While more equitably distributed at the occupation level than the mercado, jobs were generally either all male or all female. I observed these activity patterns. Weaving in and out of crowds were matrons with baskets of local produce. Traders with permits tended to be younger and present irregularly. Foreign colony women outnumbered Tepoztecas. Both groups were non-professional traders, seemingly present because they could utilize outside connections or travel to the border to get products appropriate for the session or because they had a special short-term need for cash. Participation by older married couples was greater.

At these sessions, one finds comparatively large dealers of produce, dried foods, and bulky household wares. The larger the enterprise, the more likely they were to be gender mixed. And there is a good deal more pitching than is usual for Tepoztlán. On Wednesday, May 22, 1996, in area 2a there were male professionals selling watches, metal house wares, calculators and other high-tech gadgetry, fabric remnants, tire-rubber sandals, and reading glasses.

Local young people staff some stalls, but there was only one local independent woman selling baskets made in China.

As I moved into sector 2b, women and heterogeneous mixes of low-end items increased. Grouped together were rural women selling tomatoes, garlic, black avocados, and herbs and spices displayed on swatches of plastic. Present in her station just across from the City Hall was flower merchant Rosa Figueroa. Mostly older, municipio men and women were trading in peanuts. There were displays of Head and Shoulders shampoo (locally much in demand); the odd (often dented) canned good; and packets of Pampers. Today five foraging women were selling exotic specimens of wild mushrooms. (I purchased the yellow-speckled blue species but lacked the courage to consume them.) Inside and on the fringe of the garden—not a prime space—the vendor count was 61 percent female. Cement benches were selling slots for nineteen, non-head town women. Four women were selling dried foodstuffs. One brought a single gunnysack of beans that she sold in a few hours. A young girl attended her teacher mother's stock of five dresses (it was a school holiday because of a one-day teachers' strike). The scribe seated on a stone bench behind an ancient typewriter on a shaky table was a regular seasonal resident. Nearer the bandstand, a Tepozteca who sells shoes from a catalog was conducting business. Five foreign colony women were displaying assortments of clothes, jewelry, and toiletries arranged on a bank of stone benches and tree limbs.

Rosa Figueroa, Flower Vendor

I was especially anxious to hear Doña Rosa's story after seeing her bedded down late on a chilly night in her market space directly across from the City Hall. Engulfed in a wool cape, the resting place of the flower dealer, age "about eighty," was a stack of wooden crates. I later learned she often spent the night this way when she was to catch a ride with the flower growers who leave at 4 a.m. to deliver gladiolas to Mexico City. These days, Rosa lives in a rented room in Cuernavaca. Because she has been seriously ill, she comes to sell flowers in the Tepoztlán market only on days when she can count on brisk sales.

Her father, a railroad employee, was one of the many Spanish influenza casualties. She never attended school, but she did learn her letters from a half-sister. She taught herself to read "a little, but writing I never got the hang of it." At age fourteen, she went to work in a Cuernavaca market food stall "because my mother would not give me enough to eat."

Her first husband, a Tepozteco, was a long distance bus driver. After Don Hermilo "stopped turning up," she discovered that he had forty-five ("*Yes*, forty-five!") children scattered about his route. With Rosa, he had ten children;

only four are still living, and she "seldom" hears from them. She next married a retired local teacher, but soon separated from him. For a time, she worked as a laundress and later as a chicken merchant. Her flower business began when she was cleaning the villa of a "kind" Mexico City woman.

> She took me to a Mexico City flower market where she bought lovely white flowers for the church. Then she had the idea I should learn the trade. She helped me to set up a business. I thought that I could be independent but to my deep regret because of health problems, I sometimes have to ask for help. I have one friend who invites me to her home and takes care of me. It is now so hard to earn a living that I no longer enjoy my work.

As noted, Rosa sometimes travels to the flower market in a van belonging to a seller of gladiola, a major cash crop, and she can select choice stock from all over Mexico. These days, there is intense competition from new groups of local sellers. Regional growers now pay commission to women all over town to sell for them for a few hours. Especially keen on this work were mothers accompanied by young children. Rosa no longer finds it profitable to be in the Tepoztecan market except on selected days.

"You have had a hard life as a wife and as a laborer. Which has been the more difficult occupation?" I asked Doña Rosa. "If work, it depends on the work you do. If marriage, it depends on the husband. Though I count myself lucky with my profession, I was unlucky indeed with my husbands."

Category 4: New Economy Hybrids

Composing this recently emerging group are women who have contrived adaptations aimed at taking advantage of new consumer populations and distribution channels. Though they do not use mercado sites (so they do not pay a floor tax), Category 3 women are mercado-oriented, a factor that differentiates them from roaming street hawkers. Wisely made, a small and discontinuous investment in the right niche can result in immediate gains that some women use to enter full-time trading. Indeed, Tepoztlán's most successful female entrepreneur began her career as a restaurateur selling snacks at schools. She is a model for many of the women who target the three downtown schools adjacent to the central market. The combined enrollment of 1,559 represents an important market for snacks, almost certainly the most marketable and highest-profit food category in Tepoztlán. Mobile snack vendors ply the margins of the market at recess times and when classes let out.

In one survey of ten vendors waiting for children flooding out of the *kinder*, I noted that some were selling out of baskets; others used small carts or they set up tables. One seller took advantage of an ancient gated station wagon to set out an impressive commissary: candies, chips, ham sandwiches, pancakes, bottled juices, peanuts, popcorn, soup, carrots, and fruit salad. Each child seemed to have a definite preference for a particular snack. Many wanted them doused in complimentary hot sauce.

Sellers came from a broad cross-section of residents. Two mothers said they got the idea from observing other women when they came to pick up their children. They were "helping out" during "this difficult period." The profits of Doña Mai, age fifty-one, go to provide the nutritional needs of her family of five and "sometimes for birthdays." Also present was a villa resident. A year before, smartly dressed Doña Lidia, age twenty-eight, and her family settled permanently in their weekend home "to get away from the crime and smog in Mexico City." (Her husband commutes by car to Mexico City.) She said the orange juice concoction she sells from a shopping cart is "particularly healthy" for children. "It's diverting. Anyway, I come to pick up my child."

As trading slowed, some women literally dashed to the primary school Squadron 201, where students were just coming out and flooding into El Centro. New arrivals found other women and a few male vendors already waiting. The men, professional roaming traders, were selling ice cream from carts and packaged snacks. Women's products often had a homemade touch, and most were willing to sell any quantity a child wanted. Men dealt only in bulk goods, a time saver, though one that increased dependency on wholesalers.

The vendor proliferation creates another mobility option. Daily, a mother/daughter team made rounds selling sandwiches and yogurt to vendors who could not leave their stalls. Two sisters trundled a wheelbarrow of savory hot dishes. The wheelbarrow never entered the mercado; one sister went inside to solicit business and deliver orders while the other tended the commissary.

Nilda Aguilar, Vendor of Anything

Trading requires access to tradable resources; but when they have access to a market, even women whose only resource is resourcefulness and modest expectations can contrive ways to "get by." Doña Nilda is one of a growing number of senior women encountered in the streets selling dubious-quality products. To some, her trading mode may come close to being disguised begging but there is nothing in Nilda's spunky routine to suggest that she takes a negative view of her career. Fiercely determined, she rarely fails to spot anyone to whom she has ever made a sale. Her stock of generally overripe produce comes from other traders. Sometimes she sells on consignment; or near closing time, dealers may give her stock that could not be sufficiently "refreshed" for another trading day. Once or twice, I saw her successfully scavenging in discard piles. She always unabashedly asks the going price for perfect stock and, no matter how inferior the product, only reluctantly agrees to take a bit less. Moving about is her transaction asset. She attempts to trade wherever she detects a potential client: any person whose forward movement can be interrupted.

Sector Gendering Trends

Can we think about women's nonfixed trading strategies as productive in the economists' sense of "complex" production? Even on a very good day, it is "simple" production that at best yields but does not capitalize. Striking then is how closely the organization of the trading system mirrors late capitalist fundamentals. I noted many similarities to the just-in-time (JIT) approach of supply-siding capitalism: capitalism that focuses on factors affecting supply rather than demand. Clearly a stretch, or is it? Cook (2004) demonstrates that Mexican "petty" capitalists have a deep and present history of culturally particular but properly economic behavior: making optimizing use of scarce resources to achieve both continuity and flexibility within the dominant market system.

Perfected in postwar Japan, among the JIT tactics shared with nonfixed traders is to have commodities just in time to meet demand, in contrast to the old economy practice of just in case stockpiling. Matching characteristics include being continuous; reconverting a part of the means and relations of production into fresh production; and rapid reaction to market disturbances and decision defects. Producers must be able to move effectively among unlike tasks. Whether simple or complex, the chief benefits are the reduction of costs of inventory management, rapid detection of quality problems, abrupt changes in demand, and the ability to shift labor input, all of which are defining aspects of the nonfixed trading case studies. Though the JIT pattern is observable in all market system operations, I noted that it was particularly strong in the nonfixed group. I also observed their operational combinations mean that they have far more restricted options than do firms for protecting themselves from Cook's "dark side" market processes that "maldistribute economic value" (2004:84). Evidently, these traders do not measure productivity by the factors and outcomes that firms prioritize because the products they trade in and the way they trade them must respond to household-specific imperatives. And for them, an approach that calls for rapid turnover and product obsolescence intensifies the terms of their subordination in the capital market. The requirement of a high degree of time-space coordination discourages entrepreneurial innovation and degrades certain types of interactive skills that often are the only assets of the trading category.

In sum, the JIT tactics of nonfixed traders increase their sourcing dependency on global commodity chains, thereby indenturing their labor to the international financial establishment. Nevertheless, all categories of nonfixed traders were among the consensus of market women who view the redeveloped market as affording them empowering options otherwise not within their reach and sadly not there for the generations of nonfixed traders who preceded them.

Chapter Ten

Fixed Mercado Trading

> Technological innovation requires not the maintenance of existing regulation but a constant process of *reregulation*.
>
> —Anthony Smith, 1994

Clearly, the under representation of men in nonfixed trading can be explained by the fact that most operations are, like subsistence farming, all but structurally barred from producing a family wage. Though still under represented (compared to the 71 percent of economically active men), the productivity potential of fixed trading attracts more men. This chapter examines the marketing processes—the development, pricing, promotion, and distribution of commodities—that correlate to men's greater presence in this category. The objective is to clarify the ways these processes interface as advantages and disadvantages with specific variants of women's fixed mercado trading.

About *productivity*—the amount of output achieved per unit of input—a modernization fundamental is that by multiplying the effect of human labor, modern technologies translate into higher profits achieved with less physical input. In the mercado, technological innovations do show up as profit-enhancing efficiencies, but productivity is also independently associated with relations and conditions deemed "precapitalist." Enterprises activate these functions to get around a range of transaction costs in which gender is a recurrent reference.

VENUES

The types of fixed operations are shops, kiosks, and stalls. Women are 54 percent of the workforce in shops, 58 percent in kiosks, and 60 percent in stalls.

All traders confront many of the same local, national, and international problems. However, site-specific solutions to the organizational problems of fixed operations tend to require larger investments of social and financial capital. Often capital- and labor-intensive problems can only be solved by enlisting late modern (that is consented to) forms of familism: the syndrome in which the template for a woman's extradomestic labor is her gender-appropriate role in the domestic domain. Therefore, the dialectical pair of women's productive and reproductive roles must be analytically related to Narotzky's "picture of capitalism [as] based on diversified labor/capital relations (1997:212)

Stalls

Stalls, *puestos*, have the largest labor force of any vending mode and it is the fixed trading occupation in which women are the most overrepresented. In contrast to the 33 percent of economically active women, in the four surveys, this labor force is 54 percent female; unlike the nonfixed group, most are from the head town. (A market official estimated that head town members held "more than 90 percent" of the permits to operate out of stalls.)

A "snapshot" sample of twelve self-employed women stall-keepers gives an idea of the diversity of this economically important group. The sample age range was from twenty-six to eighty-five years, with forty-four years the mean, so twice the mean for the female population. Education levels varied, from no schooling to a degree in oceanography. Women younger than forty were five times more likely to have completed eight to ten years of basic education. Two had attended but not completed technical schools. All reported having some on-the-job training in Tepoztlán or another regional marketplace. Many had received this training while working under other market women, often kin who also helped them establish themselves. The mothers of three and the fathers of two women had had extended mercado careers.

Numbers of children ranged from none to ten. All but one woman, who began when her children were still quite young, mentioned household economic and/or marital difficulties as reasons why they became full-time merchants. The mates of five women had some limited financial involvement; one husband regularly participated in daily operations. Women who were not primary economic providers cited educating children and the high cost of homemaking necessities as their strongest financial motivation. Five women said they chose fixed trading because they wanted to be their own bosses. Ten agreed that it was preferable to have business premises away from home. Like several other dealers, Doña Gaby had lost her job in a state government office and invested her savings in the stall when she could not find a suitable salaried job. At one time or another, six had looked seriously, and fruitlessly, for adequately salaried formal employment. All said control over time and income were positive features of mercado self-employment but these advantages did not compensate for too much work for too little money.

All reported drawing out of revenues to meet domestic needs. Monthly profits varied greatly for individuals and across the group. Looking at the previous three months (not the same for each interview), Doña Cata said she had made no profit. Only six were readily forthcoming on the income question. The monthly range for these six was from 200 to 2,000 pesos. Accounting methods were a combination of "in my head" and recording certain nonfixed expenses. Doña Susana described her accounting as, "I have money to buy stock or I don't." Doña Silvia ruefully commented, "Bookkeeping is not important when you don't have any profits."

All but one trader participated "fairly regularly" in a tanda; at one time or another, three had borrowed from loan cooperatives, six from private moneylenders, and none from banks or government agencies. However, at least a portion of the start-up capital came from previous employment or assistance from a family member. The major problems identified were inflation, excessive competition in the community and the region, slow traffic during the week, and the small size of purchases. None had "leftover" funds to invest in growth and no one was paying into social security. All considered themselves very hard working, rarely getting more than six hours of sleep. All described themselves as "merchants."

All mothers except two said that they "regretted" being compelled to "shortchange" their children, adding however that they "never" put business ahead of emergencies. All said motherhood was their greatest personal satisfaction. For ten women, relations with mates were conflict-laden. Doña Raquel said that while marital problems had influenced her decision to go into the market, the work had become yet another source of tensions. Several commented, "Men here are lazy." All expressed confidence in their skills and though they did not expect the economy to improve, all but one intended to continue. None had plans to expand or change the format of the business. Each stated definite political opinions, though only two had ever been overtly politically active before the Golf Club. Several women commented that they had no time for "politics," by which they meant party politics as usual.

All were "glad" to be in Tepoztlán, and each considered tourism, urbanization, and work in the mercado as economically benefiting Tepoztecas. All said they had a "better life" and better relations with their children than their mothers and grandmothers. Perhaps the most important thing to mention is that they all said they enjoyed being a woman of the Tepoztecan market.

A Comparative Productivity Framework

At a general level, advantages and disadvantages were patterned enough to compare the (estimated) productivity achieved by some stalls. Input criteria for fruit/vegetable stalls included items stocked, access to transportation and labor power sufficient to attain a larger and/or more affluent clientele, and merchandising options. Labor and transport advantages strongly favored proprietorships that included men. These advantages coincided with other profitability indicators, such as product range, work force size, and a host of practical matters. For produce stalls, I awarded 1 point each for each of the following factors:

- every commodity stocked
- each non-proprietor worker
- each worker not a non-salaried family member
- private transport used for business
- each non-Mexican product
- vendor control over production of a commodity
- each service, such as credit and a *pilón* (a something extra for buyers)

I awarded two points for regular provisioning in Mexico City wholesale markets.

I compared these stalls because there is considerable uniformity in product, and in absolute numbers, produce vending is the largest and least sex typed category. Even so, because of operational diversity, I could directly compare only six male owned/operated stalls against six female operations. For this population, male stalls as a group had a 75 percent productivity advantage over female stalls as a group, or almost the same ratio in which EA men outnumber EA women. Since seemingly all enterprises use daily sales as operating capital, I evaluated the quality of the stock and found that as an indicator of liquidity, it coincided with other productivity observations. I also compared six stalls having female collective labor arrangements with six having a single female owner. In this case, collectively managed operations had a 52 percent advantage in productivity. I was unable to make other direct comparisons, but I could use the criteria as a heuristic aide.

Trappings are so spare that one's first impression is that primitive technology is universal. In fact, small differences can have big payoffs. I knew of no female vendor driving her own vehicle out of town. So great is the danger of being alone on the roads, men also did not feel safe when they traveled to Mexico City markets in the early morning darkness. With kidnapping occurring regularly in Morelos and not limited to wealthy victims, any journey has a certain amount of risk.

Stall Activity Studies

Silvia Gallo, Co-proprietor of a Produce Stall

"The market is my patrimony," Doña Silvia commented with considerable pride in our first interview. I returned often to this stall on one of the busiest mercado corners to observe and even participate in her marketing activities. Though characterizing the operation as a co-proprietorship with her husband, Silvia, age fifty-two, proved to be in all organizational respects self-employed.

Some fifty years ago, when her parents moved from Cuernavaca to start the market's first daily fruit and vegetable stall, what is now a prime interior space was on the market's outer rim. In 1972, Silvia married a Tepozteco. They have three children. Her father died and her mother retired and gave the space equally to her three children. Her sister did not want to work in the market, so Silvia and her brother Diego compensated the sister and took over the space. They divided it as equally as possible, and continue to operate back-to-back fruit and vegetable stalls. Diego's stall is just inside the market shed; Silvia's is on the portico of the stone building.

Separated by a canvas curtain, stall operations are also separate. Silvia's enterprise scored twelve, Diego's twenty. This difference reflected his larger and more exotic inventory (such as broccoli and iceberg lettuce), a son's frequent presence, and the Nissan pickup he owns and uses to provision regularly in Mexico City, Cuautla, and Cuernavaca.

There is a good deal of seemingly cordial cooperation, with either immediate or delayed advantages for both dealers: mechanisms of cooperation that are rare in the market. For example, when a customer asks for something one vendor does not have in stock, the other will provide it. Change making, a major headache in the market—largely because there are so many small sales—is a time-saving cooperative activity. Helping-out children sometimes moved between businesses.

Likely the major operational difference is that Diego's younger son had come into the business but none of Silvia's children wishes to have a market career, and they worked only randomly. In fact, Silvia seems decidedly apprehensive about delegating authority. Diego often entrusts operations to his son as he pursues other interests. He would not discuss finances, but another dealer told me that the stall could not net enough to support the family's middle-class lifestyle.

Silvia's stock, always less varied than Diego's, is sometimes also of a lower quality than might be expected in such a well-established enterprise. However, her stock of certain staples is usually of good, if not always prime, quality. Most mornings she travels at dawn to the Cuernavaca wholesale market, and two afternoons each week she attends the Cuautla wholesale market. Into the early afternoon, she makes numerous but often very small sales of such items as green tomatoes, limes, and seasonal fruits. Her clients tend to buy only what they expect to need for the day, or even for just one meal. One 10 a.m. until noon session, she made twelve sales amounting to some 80 pesos.

For the holidays when many people give gifts of fruit, Silvia invested in two cases of especially fine mandarins. She positioned them prominently and many people stopped to ask the price per kilo. However, she intended to sell them "like the supermarkets, by the case." She did sell one case, but toward the end of the next day broke up the other one.

I never encountered her co-proprietor husband. For many years, Silvia contributed "not less than 70 percent" of the family budget, because her husband's job as a driver for the local bus company paid "very little." This seemed strange since these jobs are highly coveted. A family friend explained, "Don Luis drives an old bus on a minor route." His main and important contribution to his family is his benefit package.

Silvia is acutely conscious of the high transaction costs of being a woman in business who is "almost always alone." She intensely resents having to hire porters to transport stock that many men can manage themselves. She feels greatly disadvantaged by not having her own transport and by lack of access to credit. Although she could borrow from a cooperative, she worries about not being able to meet repayment terms. ("I don't want to have my name posted as a delinquent.") So she operates the business almost exclusively out of daily profits. When funds run short, the stock starts to look tired and inventory, even of staples, shows gaps. Over the years, credit and labor problems have made her downwardly mobile. It is probably fair to say that only her expertise, skills, and grit have kept the business afloat. Now what with disappointments and a "touch of rheumatism," her supply of grit is diminishing.

Since starting in the market at age fourteen, she has worked steadily, taking a brief time out only for maternity. Her daily routine has remained much the same. She rises at 4:30 to catch the first bus to Cuernavaca's fast-paced wholesale yard, the only place where she can obtain market information in time to avoid daily losses. Dealing in perishables makes transaction cost information—such as knowing your competition and having a keen sense of quality and marketability—vital. Arriving at the yard, she goes immediately to her usual dealers to appraise what is right for her that day. One of several porters regularly assisting her (and with whom she exchanges somewhat racy banter) takes her purchases to a pickup point for delivery vehicles servicing Tepoztlán. She pays porters and dealers at the end.

The ride back shared with fellow vendors is a very important part of the business (and one that until this point I had not been able to pin down), for it is on these rides that prices per item are set for the day. This system both benefits larger dealers who may have negotiated better prices and gives smaller dealers time to avoid going directly up against larger buyers, before learning from a customer that their price is not right. As a rule, the prices set on these return trips prevail throughout El Centro, even for vendors who did not buy in Cuernavaca, and even among the rural direct sellers outside market entrances. However, there are several ways to sweeten a transaction. The common way is the pilón that goes to certain classes of buyers. Silvia seems to give this something extra, often quite generous, to two categories of buyers: sometimes to regulars even if their purchase is small; and always to larger buyers even if they are one-time shoppers. Since there is never a discussion of a pilón, it appears to be a dealer-client understanding. My own experience as a consumer is that it plays a more important role in the operations of small dealers than for the largest stalls. (Since small dealers are paying more in cash and credit for items, sweetening too costs them more.)

Always among the first to open and last to close, Silvia returns around 6:30 a.m. to prepare to open by 7:00 p.m. She closes at 7:00 p.m. or "when there are no buyers." Stocks get packed away in cartons or covered with cloths. She pays a communal watchman eight pesos each week, but she still loses stock to prowlers.

On Tuesday and Friday afternoons, she often travels on the 2:30 bus to Cuautla to buy items coming up from the south that she considers fresher than Cuernavaca stocks. One is the miniature banana (*dominica*). Since it is fragile, she buys a small stock, but one that fanciers declare the best in Tepoztlán. (Her brother never stocks this item.) Usually, her brother or his son or another family member fills in for her during this slow period. She returns around 5:00. Formerly, she went several times monthly to Mexico City, but at this time business was "too slow" to make it worthwhile. Diego was still making the trip at least twice each month.

Evenings she devotes an hour to doing "something" related to the business. She watches TV and chats with the family over coffee and rolls; bedtime is around eleven. When her children were young, she devoted one day each week to "serious housework," and her husband frequently replaced her. He no longer does this, and she reports, "I can't afford to shut down. Prices on everything I buy are now so high, profits have all but vanished but people cannot afford to pay more." In 1995, there had been a dramatic decline, more in quantities bought than in numbers of sales. (This means that her labor was costing her more.) She attributed the downturn to the hard times and proliferation of sellers. The fierce competition depresses her more than "the crisis," since even when conditions improve this trend can only intensify. She diagnoses her major problem as low profitability. "If I buy a banana for 1.50 pesos, I sell it for 2. From this, I must somehow cover business and living expenses. These days, that's too much to hope for."

She characterizes market work as "dignified and honest," and considers domestic, and market activities "important in the same way." She regrets having on occasion had to neglect the children, but "The most important thing is to sell because it is the basis of the life I make for the family." She speculates that her life would have been "better" if she had taken up a "regular profession." (The one she coveted was hairdressing.) "Now young women can find a job and take charge of their own lives. In my day, this was not possible." Although population growth and tourism give women options, they also bring "terrible inflation and damage our tranquil way of life" in a pueblo she remembers as "fresh and cool because there were trees and bushes where now there is only cement."

Piedad Ramírez, Proprietor of a Handicraft Stall

Doña Piedad, age forty-four, opened her craft stall fifteen years ago. She is well located for the streams of weekend tourists. Just across from her one-meter table is the one-meter table of her daughter Raquel, age twenty-four, also a craft vendor.

Piedad was born in San Andrés, where "women have always worked very hard. My mother went from the milpa to her comal. I never wanted my life to be as hard and isolated as hers." At age eleven, she left school to take a job in a cousin's vegetable stall. "Earning money has always pleased me." She credits the market with rescuing her from "my mother's hard life." At age nineteen, she married a farmer from Ixcatepec. They have five children. She contrived to set up her own business.

> I wanted to take advantage of the tourists but to get out of dealing in perishables. At first, I sold crafts from Michoacán, the ones you see all over town. Salesmen who work with us on a commission basis bring them here. With so much competition, markups were at best 20 percent, not enough on such low priced items. I realized that I had to find some new items and if possible buy directly from producers.

Now she and her daughter stock some items not seen in other stalls. Markups depend on a number of supply-and-demand factors that may change within a session. Their most upscale goods are intricate, very fragile terracotta miniatures from the city of Puebla that they must purchase. "We only make around 10 pesos per item, not really enough, but it gives us something others do not have and attracts lots of lookers."

Their most popular items were miniatures crafted from bread dough by Raquel and produced (without a contracted salary) by the entire family. Piedad said that "occasionally" family members worked in the stalls, "when they can. Right now I can't afford to pay them, so I buy them snacks." The two stalls are financially separate "but we cooperate whenever possible."

Originality is rare in the market, and on this day two California men (glad to "at last find gifts not available at home") spent over an hour selecting miniatures. They paid her with fifty U.S. dollars. Even locals are customers for the miniatures; the best-selling item is a 3-peso hair ornament. At first both businesses grew, but with the combination of a recession, inflation, and intense competition, now both women were hard pressed to finance their businesses out of sales.

At one Tuesday interview session, two tiny grandchildren were much in evidence and deeply resentful of the tetanus shots two public health nurses were administering to children in the market. The mother/daughter coping strategy gave me a chance to observe closely the on-site delicate balancing of mothering and marketing some women cited as the comparative advantage of market self-employment. Despite hands-on comforting, the children continued to express their dismay at the injections. At one point, the toddler managed to divest herself of every stitch of clothes to better enjoy a roll in a trash heap. Mother and toddler retreated to the public toilet for a thirty-minute cleanup while grandmother cheerfully took charge of a distraught infant and both tables. All was taken in stride. "The best thing about being your own boss," Piedad said "is that you can have your children with you." Raquel nodded her agreement.

Kiosks

In general, fixed trading operating costs are considerably higher than in nonfixed enterprises. Investments—in more costly goods, higher rent, labor, and municipal and other taxes—are highest for kiosks and shops, and commonly offset by extensive and varied use of a generally unpaid family labor. The kiosks tended to deal in the most time-sensitive inventories. I observed that they had a comparatively high ownership turnover, often accompanied by a shift in merchandise.

Kiosk Activity Studies

Asunción Ayala, Principal of a Pork Butchery

In 1995, six of the ten market kiosks were pork butchery operations. The reasons for this dominance become clear in the case study of Doña Asunción, the fifty-two-year-old statuesque widow who presides over the market's largest pork butchery. Located a few steps from the main market entrance, the kiosk is the nodal point of a cluster of structurally unlike operations that create employment for diverse family members.

During the day, it is the center of the butchery operation, including a lively trade in cracklings from an outside table. Another phase begins in the early evening, the selling of grilled pork tidbits from a *caseta comedor* operation, which can stay open into the early morning. Meanwhile, at all hours, the nearby family compound is a processing site as well as the headquarters for the reproduction of the labor force.

Ascunción carries on a community and family tradition. Tepoztlán's first recorded female-headed business was a pork butchery, and her mother, a pork butcher. At first operating from a small oilcloth-covered table, eventually her mother acquired a kiosk from a vendor who retired. This was technically illegal, but by no means an unusual exchange. Though the daily rent is only 5 pesos, she must also pay various taxes; buy a health card that costs 300 pesos annually; and a license to butcher pork.

She apprenticed with her mother for thirteen years. The custom then was to keep brood sows in the garden and fatten the shoats. The disadvantage was the long wait for a return on investment and the risk of diseases. Now she purchases piglets from local breeders or, more often, acquires mature animals on short-term credit from pig farmers. This arrangement affords her just-in-time inventory control. She pays the farmer after the slaughtering, a decision dictated by erratic daily and seasonal demand. She sometimes goes with her son to select pigs, a job formerly undertaken by her late husband, a state employee.

Farmers bring pigs to the family's large residential compound, where family members briefly care for them. (Not infrequently, a piglet attempting escape becomes a distressing traffic victim.) She pays two sons, a son-in-law, and a professional 12 pesos each for slaughtering each pig. (They dispatch the pigs by cutting their throats. Asunción told me this is the only step in the business she has never performed, "though of course I would do so if need be.") This distressingly noisy phase lasts from 3 a.m. until 9 a.m. the morning of the day they go on sale. Family members do the initial dressing in the compound and convey the carcasses to the kiosk. Most then go off to other jobs. Final dismembering takes place on the sidewalk near the kiosk, an event of surpassing interest to the market's half-starving canine population. For this task, she employs a male professional who also works for other butchers.

Dressed cuts hang from hooks inside the kiosk; smaller portions invite attention in the counter window. There is no refrigeration, but this is not a pressing concern because Tepoztecans insist on freshly killed pork (and local people are almost her only clients). Proof of freshness is the still-dripping head prominently mounted on the front of the kiosk. "I try to sell down each day, but pork meat can hold for several days. It does not go off as rapidly as beef or chicken."

Highly marketable is the crisped skin (*chicharrón*). Preparation requires four or five hours, done in the compound by several women, sometimes aided by adolescent males after school. Family members—there are eight adults and numerous children—also sell the product from a table to the side of the kiosk and from the compound, by-products not sold in the butchery.

So skilled at butchery is Asunción that she rarely needs to add or subtract from the portions that go on her scale. There is no bargaining and pricing is uniform, but in this operation, a pilón is an integral part of the exchange. One daughter failed to give an extra to a customer who had made a modest purchase. Chatting all the time with the daughter, a daughter-in-law attending to her new baby and her knitting, a granddaughter dropped off from school, and the client, Asunción deftly cut a choice morsel and nonchalantly dropped the tidbit into the client's shopping bag, already back on her arm.

Even in better times, for many people meat was a treat. During the recession, demand remained relatively steady but purchases were smaller. Still, she earns "a little" and distributes the profit among the family, in cash when possible but mostly as basic familial upkeep. (All adult males and two women have primary jobs.) In 1993, the family added a grilling operation that soon inspired five competitors now side by side.

Sara Gómez, Principal of a Beef Butchery

Doña Sara, age forty-eight, owns the market's only beef butchery. While beef requires a more high-tech support system than pork, she also must integrate the skills, ambitions, and time constraints of members of a family labor force. A retired schoolteacher—still *la Profesora* to most residents—she is Tepoztlán's only official female beef butcher. She too was born to her trade. Her grandfather was a rancher who expanded into beef retailing; her mother founded the present business, and Sara apprenticed under her. She also still occupies the spacious Spanish-style family home on Zaragoza Avenue, just across from the clinic. Sara earned a normal superior degree with a specialty in geography and taught for sixteen years while continuing to operate the butchery. She capitalized on proximity to the clinic across the street by opening a pharmacy as well.

She is married to a commercial farmer and they have two sons, ages twenty-three and ten. She characterized her husband's business as "bad." He sometimes works in the butchery. There are also several employees. Since her retirement with a full pension, her routine has been to spend the morning in the butchery and the afternoon in the pharmacy.

The handling costs of beef versus pork are considerably higher, partly because of the slaughtering, which must be in the abattoir and for which there is a tax. Sara purchases cattle directly from ranchers and always for cash. Refrigeration is necessary because there is much more meat and the higher cost of the meat slows turnover. Many of her customers are from the foreign community; she prefers doing business with "outsiders" because "people from here always try to bargain when they buy beef." She never bargains, but for larger quantities, she does give a pilón. (Several U.S. residents told me that they have little faith in local meat and buy only in supermarkets. For his annual Christmas gala, one expatriate arranges to have tenderloin sent in from the United States; though the cut was different, the quality was not superior.)

Although Sara intends the businesses to remain in the family—and expects it to grow with the foreign colony—she is allowing for uncertainty. (As is the case for the wholesale end of the chicken and pork markets, imports have sent the local beef trade into a drastic decline.) Her sons are being educated for professions; the older is qualifying as a pharmacist. In 1998, she added a grilling operation that she leased to a non-family-member. (By 2000, it was more profitable than the butchery and her husband had taken it over.)

Ricardo Sánchez, Principal in a Cheese-vending Kiosk

When the Cuernavaca factory where Don Ricardo, age forty-one, worked for fifteen years closed, he invested his severance pay in a market venture, a lifelong dream. He decided to sell cheeses because his wife's family is in the cheese business in Toluca. They assisted him to get started and supply him with the imported cheeses only he stocks locally. I was told that it was also family connections that persuaded the Hacienda to let him set up a kiosk that almost blocks a major entrance to the mercado.

The kiosk arrangement means that one person can easily handle the 8:00 a.m. until around 4:00 p.m. operating hours. When the couple's college student son is available to work, the kiosk stays open two hours longer. On Sunday mornings, clients come for a filled sweet roll the family cooperates to manufacture at home. Though reasonably successful, this enterprise requires that at least one member of the family have a job that guarantees a steady income and access to social income. In this case, the wife works full-time in Cuernavaca in the telephone industry.

Shops

Though located on the fringes of the marketplace, shops are the operations that are the most complexly integrated into the world market system. Thus gendering in each operation responds to a host of local and global factors. Trade pacts, time and space factors, buyers' preferences, skills required, and access to social and financial capital converge to drive the gender composition of each work force.

Shop Activity Studies

Enrique and Flor Villamil, Co-proprietors of Three Shops

Husband/wife co-proprietorship is a common way to organize shop keeping. Some Tepoztecans continue to deem even omnipresent wives "supplementary." The operation of Enrique, age fifty, and Flor, age forty-eight, demonstrates that such partnerships can be fully associative.

Both were born in Barrio San Miguel. Don Enrique completed high school and Doña Flor studied business for two years at the University of Cuernavaca. He went into trade because he had "no wish" to follow his father into the farming/construction/migration package. In 1996, the couple paid a monthly rent of 1,850 pesos for two adjacent shops inside the market shed (one a clothing enterprise and the other a grocery) and a second clothing shop on No Reelection Street, a heavy burden since 1995 and 1996 were their worst years since going into business.

Though adding greatly to operating costs, diversification in labor and goods is the key to sustainability. Flor, their two daughters, and a woman employee staff the shops. The daughters are in technical schools and work part time. They do not expect a regular salary, but "I pay their fees and when I can a small salary." Enrique's father is always to be found seated at a table in front of the grocery, continually occupied with such tedious but essential stock-keeping tasks as sorting beans. Flor also seems always to be present (and too busy for extended interviews). She spends most of her time in the boutique, which has a more high-fashion selection than the mercado shop. They travel together to Mexico City to buy clothing. Housework is also a shared family venture.

Enrique explained there are three peak selling periods for clothes: harvest time, Holy Week, and back-to-school. The worst periods are when it is time for school fees and some fiestas. "At carnival time, business drops as much as 60 percent. But this year has been nothing but bad." He said working with Flor has "never been a problem." Money is "no problem; we never disagree about how to spend it."

Armando Herrera, Grocery Store Proprietor

Even when women and men are equally active in a family business, there are considerable organizational differences in the way they experience market processes. Though unpretentious, Don Armando's cubbyhole grocery is a market landmark. For more than half a century his parents jointly ran the small shop. As family ventures prospered, his late father became politically powerful. Doña Carlotta, Armando's formidable mother, remains a person with considerable business and community influence in her own right. Family members still own the block of stores on the south rim of the mercado. Male and female relations operate several El Centro businesses, as well as many other commercial interests.

Until recently, Doña Carlotta worked many hours daily in family businesses. Still, "my father never officially approved of women working outside the home." Armando told me, "Tepoztlán is my mother's world. She has never spent a night away. She leaves here just twice each year. Once a year she goes to Mexico City to collect rents and returns on the first possible bus. And annually she goes with the same group of friends on a day trip to visit a shrine in Michoacán."

Thirty-six-year-old Armando well represents the worldliness of this generation of scions of families who prospered through commerce. Like many men and women from this more privileged class with options, he returned contentedly to settle down in Tepoztlán. After two years spent studying biology in a Mexico City University, he came back to teach high-school biology and work with his parents for eight years. He became the independent owner when his father died in the late 1980s. He still teaches classes "as [an unpaid] community service." He and his wife Tina have four children. One competitor said, "Armando is not nearly as tough in business as his parents were."

As is standard in Tepoztlán, the shop has a surprisingly wide selection. "I stock what my customers' request." Many clients are from the resident foreign community, and for them he stocks soy, granola, and wheat flour. In a refrigerated case are cheeses, bacon, and luncheon meats. His was the only shop where locally grown coffee was usually available. He described Tina, a member of a well-to-do Tabasco family, as "a housewife," but added that on most days, she works several hours in the shop.

Though his father "never" did household chores, Armando declared himself willing to "help out" with everything. "I cook and I take care of the children," he informed me. On the almost daily occasions when he leaves to conduct other business—his outside interests include a restaurant and a greenhouse—Tina usually tends the shop. Tina's sister who lives with the family works several unsalaried hours most days as well as helping-out domestically. One of the three is present during the ten to twelve hours that the shop is open every day. (There are also home and shop employees.)

Armando has various cooperative arrangements with family members. For example, he uses his mother's pickup to travel to wholesale markets and pays only for the gas. Many of the dealers with whom he works are longtime suppliers. He pays cash or gets credit for eight days: "I could have more credit, but I prefer to pay cash and save the interest." Unlike most local retailers, he seldom works with midrange dealers on a commission basis. One exception is a Pepsi Cola cooler. Since cold drinks are his highest volume item, he also has a privately owned cooler. His usual markup is from 10 to 20 percent, low enough to compete with or even go below stalls (and, of course, his profit margin is higher). On items popular with foreigners, his markup can be higher. A lucrative sideline is selling to local retailers to whom he sometimes gives credit (at interest) "if I know the person well."

Asked to comment on the subject of women and paid work, he made these points: "Now the type of work Tepoztecan women perform does not really matter, anyway not as it did in my father's day. All employment is equally respected." Still, "machismo is present in our daily lives. It is one of our traditions, something like our fiestas."

The sun was setting as this interview ended. The stark granite cliffs framing El Centro were blazing. Armando paused and made a sweeping gesture: "How could I want to leave all this?" Passing the shop, I often saw him standing at the door, chatting in his usual easygoing way and taking obvious pleasure in the exquisite setting and business arrangements of the mercado landmark tiendita (little shop).

Fixed Trading Gendering Trends

Logistically compared to nonfixed merchants, fixed traders are more vertically dependent on transnational trading networks, meaning they require more and more continuously available operating capital. Social capital is no less critical than financial capital since ultimately political influence conditions productivity options. Reservoirs of both are functions of family contributions of time, skills, money, and political connections, often market women's only support system. Accordingly, using the market to achieve the primary neoliberal goal of economic self-sufficiency makes fixed traders more dependent on family and community. On the other hand, labor market conditions and political uncertainties make steady income more essential to sustaining the cooperative unit. In sum, familism remains analytically relevant but new interdependency dynamics require a reconceptualization of this organizing system.

"The traditional family has never served everyone's interests equally, and has served certain groups very poorly" (Bergmann 1995:141). Many feminists continue to view the patriarchal organization of the traditional family as fundamental to gender inequality. Arguing functionality and presupposing patriarchy, economists interpret a family economy as a unitary for-profit "firm" staffed by the ideal sex- and age-stratified labor force (Becker 1991). Indeed, the evidence on fixed trading seems to support the model. The ability to control a differentiated labor pool depends on being able to assign specific tasks and functions to individuals. Authority remains an operational precondition. Now, however, authority is better understood in the commodity-culture terms stated by Cook: in Mexico, family-firm managers and workers are "creatures of the labor process in their industries" (1986:78).

This bottom-line reality explains how women often ascend without great to-do to the working status of honorary patriarch. The management function is a pragmatic, consented to response to the going-out and peeling-off choices members are compelled and enticed to make. Indeed, a paradox integrated into late familism is the requirement to facilitate the combining of non-family with family business interests by the labor pool. At some level, the future of each member is integrated into a collective for-profit enterprise, which Alfred Gell (1992:114) explores as patterned on the household ethos that reconciles contradictions by "bringing together disparate elements."

However, the case studies in this chapter testify not only to the mutuality but also the inevitability (and, likely, intensification) of the rationality of flexible familism in units under pressure to structurally adjust. Paradoxically, for many individuals the option of atomization may be possible only in the context of family capitalism. In fixed trading enterprises organized by late familism, consent prevails over despotism. Yet the resource of kinship/gender has never been more instrumental. The productivity focus must then be on the gendering of consent, on gender as it flows across domains "as a place, as a set of resources, and as an available labor force" (Pearson et al. 1991:xv).

Chapter Eleven

A Postindustrial Market System

> It is structural change itself in modernization that so to speak forces agency to take on powers that heretofore lay in social structures themselves.
>
> —Scott Lash and John Urry, 1994

Hirschman (1958) argued that for "latecomer" economies, preserving the low tech, preindustrial sector was the necessary condition for implanting the high tech, industrial sector. Up to this point, this study of Tepoztlán's market has validated his theory that development—economic growth with structural modification—required a meshing of the modern/forward and the traditional/backward. However, framed by a neoliberal project that destabilized industrialization, the global has not replaced but provoked the local. The result is the configuration interpreted by Daniel Bell (1973) as postindustrialism. Although he argued "the end of ideology," in fact, the ideology of gender has been central to Bell's new "refraction" of capitalism. Consequently, the concern of this chapter is to contextualize subsystem-specific ways that women reorganize work processes to function as backward/forward harmonizers of a postindustrial market system. The chapter has two sections. Explored is entrepreneurship in two primary growth industries: the prepared food subsystem of the mercado and the weekend tourist market, the tianguis.

Reflexive Feminization

Labor feminization is a flexibility strategy that all market operations—whatever their size and degree of integration into the dominant economy—have been compelled to implement. Lash and Urry caution that approaches deployed to achieve flexibility should not be interpreted as reactive "but as something actively and strategically devised" by self-monitoring individuals "within particular local areas" (1994:283). For these reasons, they interpret reorganized capitalism as "reflexive accumulation," a syndrome analyzed here as women's awareness of the hegemonic nature of the risk/benefits of using a forward made by and for powerful men. As I map the two industries, I will be foregrounding ways in which reflexive accumulation and reflexive feminization articulate.

THE PREPARED FOOD SECTOR

Each time I returned to Tepoztlán, I found that the food services industry had both expanded as new businesses opened and contracted as existing ones went under. So a branch of a trendy Mexico City restaurant opened and a sushi operation replaced last season's popular pizza restaurant. The usually local family-operated restaurants serving staple favorites every day and throughout the day had endurance advantages. While several of these enterprises did not survive the 1995 recession, I observed a far greater rate of failure for the innovative successes of previous seasons. All were operated by foreigners for foreigners, a combination predicted to produce optimal results.

Evolving as cogent responses to waves of new consuming populations, the sector became, and remains, the growth industry par excellence of Tepoztlán in general and the mercado in particular. Doña Josefina, a still-active industry pioneer, told me that into the 1950s there were no sit down eating-places in El Centro. The first enterprises appeared with commercial agriculture and imported laborers in need of someone to make their tortillas. The first entrepreneurs were homemakers who mainly invested their skills and infinitely elastic labor power. "We prepared larger proportions of what we cooked at home."

Since even now Tepoztecans rarely choose to or cannot afford to dine out, tourism triggered the expansion and complexity of the present sector. Upscaling is a major factor; in 1995, there were five expensive to very-expensive El Centro restaurants. Each opened only on weekends or for fiestas. In 2000, only three had survived; but by 2002, four new ones had opened. Even in modest establishments, selections are design intensive.

Of course, this expansion pattern was anything but a panacea for capital constrained Tepoztecas. Faced with ever more asymmetrical competition, protected by restrictions that kept foreigners out, and the strong association of typical market women and typical market food, Tepoztecas developed an enclave sector inside the mercado. This enclave was the high degree of feminization. However, the vitality of the sector in tandem with the deterioration of male salaries and migration difficulties has begun to attract an inflow of Tepoztecos, who also benefit from use restrictions. The result is that Tepoztecos, not outside capital, have invaded a growth sector once all but exclusively dominated by Tepoztecas. Since women are still at least 80 percent of the workforce, it is necessary to go inside "workplace and organizational arrangements" to expose incipient "gender scrambling": female-typed jobs that no longer require women (Adkins 2001:673).

Food Operations

In this section, I examine eating establishments located inside the mercado. For fare made on site, finished off, or heated, permits to operate on a daily basis are restricted to the mercado and to stakeholders. The types of operations are small restaurants, small cafes (*fondas*), smaller cafes (*fonditas*), and stalls (*puestos*). Like all prepared food operations, all mercado enterprises rely heavily on the patronage of distinct classes of foreigners.

Restaurants and cafes specialize in combination plates (*platos*). Restaurants and fondas have kitchens divided from the dining area. Fondas and fonditas have communal seating. Some food is prepared on propane gas-fueled burners. Complex dishes may be prepared or partly prepared off site. Fonditas are one or two-person operations.

Tortillas-based Mexican fast foods (*antojitos*) are the principal product of stalls. Seating is communal. Staffs range from usually two to (rarely) as many as eight. *Antojitos* are by far the leading item sold in the mercado. The dough, *masa*, and a large, standardized selection of some twenty or so fillings are pre-prepared, assembled to order, and heated on a griddle (*comal*) on a brazier. To augment antijitos, on Sundays and special days, an increasing number of stalls bring in high-demand slow food, thereby putting stalls into direct competition with restaurants and cafes.

Mercado Prepared Food Sector Patterns

Box 11.1 records representative patterns of activity in the sector. Revealed is a mosaic of subjective and objective factors that affect male/female participation ratios and their positions in the sector. Men and women inhabit the sector under substantively different circumstances. Thus what stands out is the high degree of task gendering.

In 1996, the three restaurants inside the mercado were male operated. Local men of substance owned two; they also owned the block of buildings in which the restaurants were located. The third belonged to a prominent local woman, but for reasons related to her Golf Club politics was currently leased

BOX 11.1
Food Sector Gendering Trends

Observing and participating in the daily operations in the food sector, I isolated the following profit-enhancing factors that go far toward explaining earnings disparities:

—The number of customers who can be served at one time
—*Platos* (combination plates) other than tortilla-based items
—Rapid on site preparation of *platos*, especially meat-based dishes and seasonal specialties
—Serving beer, cold drinks, and fruit juices
—Salaried labor
—Purchasing supplies in cost-reducing ways
—Staying open longer hours

Resource and constraint differences in establishments were too great to allow more than a few direct comparisons of the variables underlying advantages and disadvantages. Still, each factor was far more common in male-dominated businesses—not surprisingly, since each ultimately is a function of access to liquid capital in which men have a comparative advantage. Monitoring daily operations confirms that this empowering advantage reflects the asymmetrical gender division of social power; but what I want to stress is that advantage and disadvantage surface as the ability to control objective situations. For example, several women reported that attempts to innovate did not work for them; in fact, they lost clientele; and because of their greater dependency on daily sales to fulfill domestic obligations they did not have the time luxury of establishing themselves in new formats. It seems then that innovation is yet another male-gendered resource. In sum, the greatest advantage comes from not being a homemaker charged with the daily reproduction of both a household and a business. Nevertheless, except for a few women who retired or voluntarily exited, in 2000 all but two of the food services entrepreneurs present in 1996 were still managing to maintain structure. In large part, they did so by reflexively capitalizing the backward in order to create the forward.

to a Mexico City man. It was only in this restaurant that women worked as wait staff; the same women also staffed the kitchen and cleaned the restrooms, which was not the case for the male wait staff at the other two restaurants.

In contrast, fonditas were exclusively female operations. (Only once did I observe a man even temporarily helping-out in a fondita.) One fonda was male-owned, the other female-owned. One fonda and the restaurants had the most gender-mixed staffs, and also the most gendered task divisions. On a daily basis, stalls were overwhelmingly female dominated in both ownership and staffing. In 1996, one man did own and operate a stall (with his mother), and two young men regularly worked part-time in family businesses they are likely to inherit.

As a rule of thumb, as operational complexity increases, so too do variants of task sex typing closely and negatively tied to job quality. For example, the Sunday increase in male participation in stalls reflects the switch to barbecue service. Male specialists brought in barbecue (usually goat). Men carved and women served. Opportunistically, women do sometimes carve; but, as is the case throughout this division, male carvers rarely serve customers.

Even where staffing was gender mixed, tasks were rigorously gendered. For example, except in two restaurants with male chefs, women prepared the food, on or off site. In the two restaurants, men worked as waiters, as was the case in all upscale restaurants. Exceptions were the elegant dining rooms of the two leading hotels. In 1995, one hotel dismissed its male waiters—except for the barman—and required female cleaners to double as waitpersons without a salary increase. The Mexico City owner told me that the reason for preferring women was that "the women are not going to get drunk and not show up for work." The women on the dinner shift were particularly unhappy because most had to walk home at night. (Older children often insisted on accompanying them.) The second-ranked hotel soon followed suit.

A defining aspect of the food industry is its resistance to laborsaving technologies, especially when hands-on labor is the most cost-effective and consumer-preferred way of operating. Indeed, the homemade quality is what most diners desire to buy when they eat in the mercado. (Of course, there are also people who refuse to eat there because of the ambiance.) The demand for authenticity limits out-of-sight preparation; makes face-to-face interaction a crucial aspect of doing business; intensifies transformation labor; promotes unpaid or very low paid household activities: in short, it predicts the feminization of the labor force. Burns on the hands and arms of (usually young) women tending grease-splattering grills testify to the hazards of this heat-index raising stage. To call attention to the homemadeness that is the major draw, grills are in the forefront of most operations where comalistas have no protection from an afternoon sun that becomes brutal during the period of greatest attendance. (One of their assignments is to banter with passersby.)

While restaurants could substitute conveniences such as privacy and larger selections for the human touch, for the more traditional venues, the homemade ambiance is the competitive advantage and women are the natural bearers of these mothering-quality touches. However, Arlie Hochschild's "emotional labor" (1983) is also a feature of most upscale restaurants. Even in the posh French restaurant, on display is a typical woman in a gingham apron handmaking tortillas.

In stall operations, nothing is more important than that each selection is prepared in the precise variation ordered. (In one study of an hour of orders, during which I consumed a staggering number of quesadillas, no two were exactly alike; indicating the importance of point of sale displays and attentiveness.) The designing of quesadillas, the most popular item, to a client's specification is often a lengthy cooperative stage that consumers take very seriously. Saucers and bowls of the numerous mandatory filling choices all require chopping, seeding, peeling, cooking, grating, and so on and on. It is at this stage that paid and unpaid, seen and unseen family members, generally female and often children are most likely to contribute their labor power. That stalls have a near monopoly on filled tortilla offerings has much to do with the labor intensity, the fact that many ingredients are costly and cannot be carried-over to the next day. In the first case study, the side-by-side location of two cafes—one female owned and the other a joint male operation—make possible a rare comparative examination of the gender dimensions of the organization of the food sector. The second activity study maps the reflexive ways a successful female stall operator purposefully feminizes her operations.

Food Industry Activity Studies

Adela Flores, Sole Proprietor of Fonda Adela's and Caesar Sandoval and Jorge Mendoza, Co-proprietors of Fonda Marta's

Doña Adela, a self-employed, seventy-something widow, and Don Caesar, age forty-one, married, no children, and Don Jorge, age thirty-four, married with three children, operate adjacent enterprises in a heavily trafficked area. At first inspection, production facilities appear identical. Unlike the market's more numerous fonditas, the two fondas are equipped with chairs as well as benches. Each also has two oilcloth-covered tables that can accommodate around eight clients. A waist-high counter separates the kitchen from the dining area and serves as a staging area. Menus for the day are chalked on blackboards. It is with these menus that the central role of gender in the managerial strategies between the two operations begins to come into view.

Most days, Adela's board announces four main dishes, always a selection of the most popular class regional fare. Cesar and Jorge's offerings fill three boards. On one appears a seasonal selection of five local favorites. A second board lists two egg dishes, pork cutlets, and beefsteak with fried potatoes. The third board details the three-course vegetarian meal. Catered by two women from the foreign colony, it is offered daily along with wheat tortillas and optional alfalfa juice. Even the most renowned restaurants do not have such menu depth.

Adela's

Adela was "a good student," and her first and still lamented, ambition was to be a teacher. When she was in her first year of teacher's college, her father died and her schooling ended because "My mother either would not or could not give me money to continue my studies." A year later, she married a local farmer with whom she was to have ten children. ("YES, ten!" Adela somewhat defiantly reiterated.) It was to provide family necessities that she began attending Cuernavaca market days. She dealt variously in wearing apparel and foodstuffs.

The fonda is the culmination of a market career that began in the 1970s. At first, she sold only on special market days. Increased attendance convinced her of the feasibility of a continuous operation. Noting a shortage of prepared food service, she decided to open a stall. Though most earnings went toward family needs, she managed to earmark a portion to fund the present operation.

A prime corner location allows Adela's clients to savor the most popular local favorites while viewing market floor activities. Her *comida corrida* (main meal, served between 12:30 and 4:30) menus reflect the preferences, means, and hearty appetites of a clientele drawn mainly from working and laboring class men, less affluent visitors, and market personnel. Prices and portions on such standard fare as peppers stuffed with white cheese, a casserole of pork meatballs, and lentil soup are uniform across the market. Uniformity is a function of vender agreements that while informal carry harsh penalties for infringement. Customers are a rapid alert system to violations. Adela told me, "My customers always let me know if someone is charging less or giving bigger portions."

In 1995, the cost of combinations plates accompanied by a half-liter bottle of Coke and a basket of tortillas ranged from 10 to 12 pesos. Prices have consistently been creeping upwards, "creeping" because during this recession period, although profit margins are perilously thin, even a simple meal is a luxury for many Mexicans whose buying power has diminished by 75 percent since 1975. Vendors report that tourists who might formerly have ordered a main dish now combine free sightseeing with a cold drink, an ice cream, or a quesadilla. To compensate for missing customers, parsimonious orders, and spiralling overhead and purchasing costs, vendors artfully scale down portions. (As I discovered while working in a food operations, just as artfully, consumers detect this form of cost cutting.)

The backward and forward of New Economy tortillas are crucial to her operating costs. The most important aesthetic and material product in mercado food enterprises (already a combination that tends to depress the price of any female-gendered item) it is impossible to go against custom and charge for refills of the basket that comes with all meals. With the deregulation of flour, tortillas have become as significant a fixed cost as labor.

An important feature of Adela's operation that directly links her to the U.S. consumption economy is an upright cooler that is the property of a Cuernavaca Coca-Cola distributor. She does a steady business supplying market personnel with cold drinks. Often vendors dispatch children to buy a cold drink (the half-liter returnable bottle is the favorite). Not only are the sodas a favorite treat—Mexicans may have the world's largest per capita consumption of cold drinks—but buyers get change, always in desperately short supply because of the micro-size of most purchases. After subtracting a commission of 15 percent, when labor and other costs added in, she may well be losing money on the transactions.

Her only employee is her cousin Lupe, age thirty-nine. She does most of the kitchen work and receives a weekly salary, described by Adela as "an amount of money." She is also entitled to a comida, which she usually takes home. Adela's standard 10-hour workday proceeds as follows.

When not waiting on customers, setting up tables, attending to kitchen matters, or carrying out outside managerial activities, she engages continuously in interruptible labor-intensive preparation stages, such as chopping onions, sorting beans and rice, and charring peppers. Once a week, she travels to Cuernavaca to buy provisions in the wholesale district. (She also stocks a small table with candy and chips.) To save a porter's fee, she loads supplies on a dolly and wheels it herself the three long blocks from the bus stop to the market. But there is really little she can do to overcome the proliferation and diversification of competitors and escalating overhead. "Now after I pay for gas, tomatoes, onions, transportation, and my employee, I work only to eat. And even that is now in question."

For Adela, marketing was and indeed is still a materially essential form of mothering. Seven children live in Tepoztlán but she neither receives nor asks for financial aid from them; rather, she tries to help them financially. She explained the reasons why none of her children had come into the business. "Not only is there not enough business to support another person, none of them have an inclination for market work. Nor is it what I ever wanted for them."

As Mercedes González de la Rocha states, working-class women's primary resource of intensifying their labor may no longer be "theoretically or empirically viable" (2006:98). However, Adela remains firmly convinced that it is essential for women to have an independent income and to avoid complete dependency on a mate. For her, business has always been about struggle, but also about achieving clearly defined goals. When asked to sum up her career, she replied, "Business has been and still is a joy because my customers cheer me up. In the market, I am never bored and never old."

Cesar and Jorge's Operation

The "Doña Marta's" placard that hangs at the entrance to the adjacent cafe testifies to the fact that the space formerly belonged to Don Cesar's aunt. Finding that teaching no longer yielded an acceptable wage, when the aunt retired, he took it over and converted it from a fruit and vegetable stall into a fonda. Don Jorge joined the business when his craft production business collapsed. His responsibility is to supply the food. He accomplishes this by tapping into his large family of women known for their culinary expertise. The complexity of functions demands the synchronization of the inputs of both men and a secure supply of minimum waged women with the right skill sets. Since it is unusual for two primary earners to expect to gain a livelihood in a mercado operation, it seems that from the start, they had intended to combine their resources and achieve profitability through innovation: the "specific tool" entrepreneurs use to "exploit change as an opportunity for a different business" (Decker 1993:20).

Throughout the varied workday, either or both Jorge or Cesar are on hand. It is not customary to serve breakfast in the mercado. Women vendors must get children off to school and provision for the day ahead. But Cesar and a cook are present by seven: the cook in the kitchen; Cesar often playing chess—for which he has a great passion—with a client. Thus, some three hours before Adela has even completed her daily start-up chores in preparation for serving lunch, at Marta's orders are being filled.

By midmorning, Jorge has replaced Cesar who reportedly invests the time in other business interests. He checks supplies, brings in required ingredients, chalks the daily fare on the menu blackboard, and collects dishes prepared off premises. Generally, both are present for the peak comida hours. Cesar and a cook are on hand in the early evening, several hours later than at other eating-places. They do not have many evening clients, but usually enough to deplete the day's fare. By 7 p.m., Cesar generally has little left to serve, or he simply refuses to go to the trouble or interrupt his chess. Turning away a client is a practice unlikely to occur in an establishment operated by a woman.

From about 12:30 until 4.00 p.m., there is usually a full house and sometimes even a waiting line. In a period of recession, Fonda Marta has increased market penetration by serving vegetarian fare mainly to health conscious resident foreigners and high demand, hard to find regional and Aztecan specialties to weekend tourists, often including members of Mexico City's artistic and academic elite. Regular diners include a local intelligentsia, prominent political activists, and men from an increasingly out gay community. Of course, the crowd itself draws customers, emboldening even U.S. tourists to eat in the market.

Operations demonstrate that Schumpeter's (1950) paradigmatic interpretation of entrepreneurship—"the creating of conditions an enterprise can exploit"—in practice means extending operating hours, laying out financial and human capital, supplying relatively scarce items that have selling price elasticity, and having dependable access to a skilled and cheapened labor force. A primary enabler of these exploitable conditions is Jorge's aunt Doña Minerva, age fifty-six, previously employed as a cook in several top local restaurants. She comes in around 11 and does most of the on-site cooking and finishing off. Various catering, serving, and maintenance duties are carried out by women from Jorge's reservoir of female relatives who seamlessly fill-in for each other, two of whom are usually present at peak hours. I did not find out exactly how much Doña Minerva was paid. However, a niece believed her salary would have had to be in line with the around 150 pesos local male cooks receive in nonmarket establishments. She surmised the other women would not be working if they were not earning somewhat more than standard market wages.

There is a pattern to the men's on site contact with the food and the clients. I never observed either man preparing or even supervising food preparation (though Jorge told me he is "an excellent cook"). They do take orders and sometimes pass plates to diners (especially the vegetarian dishes), and on rare occasions, clear tables. I have seen Cesar (but never Jorge) with pail in hand making trips to the communal water supply. In 1994, as a rule, Jorge fetched beer and juices from other merchants; in 1995, they stocked these items.

An Epilogue of Reversal

By 2000, three comparatively large senior male-dominated spaces had been converted from produce operations into eating establishments. A notable increase in the sector's male population has continued at a time when competition has never been fiercer or more unlevel. As men entered the food sector, I detected a trend for categories of operations to become blurred. Now it is difficult to type either the labor force or enterprises. Were women being "written out" of this once female-gendered production system, as Lisa Adkins (2001:692) describes the trend she calls "cultural feminization," the substitution of males for females in a number of jobs? The following epilog of reversal to the tale of the two fondas complicates this feminization process within the process.

In terms of mercado operations, Marta's was a success. Even so, Jorge found that his input was too great for the rewards, diminishing as others began to duplicate his innovations. Doña Minerva retired and the supply of women willing to be exploited has all but dried up. Key family members wanted more modern type jobs. For his part, Cesar desired a lifestyle that would allow him to play a great deal more chess. He now rents the highly valuable space to Jorge who has converted it into the market's only coffee house. A female relative in the bakery business provides the cakes, pies, and cookies in the two refrigeration cases that have replaced the kitchen. There is now little to distract Cesar from his passion and with most of the business being take out, there are plenty of empty tables for the non-stop chess games.

About the same time, Adela broke her leg and a daughter who had lost her job took over. With her came her daughter who had just completed a course run by an NGO in commercial food preparation and management. Now at most sessions there is feverish activity at Fonda Adela. They had added a fast food operation and modernized the menu board. Adela still comes in though not every day. I asked her how she liked being semi-retired. "I like it well enough because I have become very active in the green movement."

How to account technically for this shift of a shift? The pattern is for technological changes to spread rapidly throughout a sector. Survivors are those who adjust to them. Then what differentiates operations is the quality of services that are not added into the customer's cost. It was this hands-on service that in the end Cesar and Jorge were glad to leave to women of the market. The requirement to create ways to make labor-intensity profitable undermines yet another orthodox paradigm, namely that backward enterprises hinder rather than advance the process of development.

Mirna Lau, Proprietor of a Food Stall

Doña Mirna, age thirty-one, mother of two boys, operates one of the most successful food stalls. In her serviceable (not cheap) cotton dress, apron, long braid, and can-do attitude, she is very much the ideal Mexican market woman. She is short and rather portly, self-assured, and clever. Though highly efficient, she disguises her managerial role and maintains a calm, somewhat ironic demeanor no matter how chaotic the day.

"We are a market family," Mirna told me. "After finishing tenth grade, I went to work full time in mother's fruit and vegetable stall." When her mother's high blood pressure and diabetes forced her to retire, Mirna purchased the space and immediately switched to a food operation. As her business thrived, she enlarged menu offerings. On Sunday and special days to the usual fare, she adds *pancita* and *pozole*, two complex stews that require mastering the art and several hours to prepare. Her reason for going into business was "to make money." The reason for changing the direction of the stall was that "It's hard work but easier than my mother's business and there is more money and less risk. It is really impossible for a mother of young children to go each dawn to Cuernavaca or, these days, even further away."

Her mother, an aunt, and an older sister work at various times in her stall. "Some receive a salary, others do not"; this was all she would say on this subject. But an employee told me that both the aunt and the sister make 30 pesos per day and a meal, a fair salary since some stalls were paying only 25 to 28 pesos and some do not include a meal. On Sundays, there are always several young women tending the grill. One, Eluaria, age 16, is present most days. She left school three years ago because "I didn't like it." She also earns 30 pesos per long day. She works cheerfully despite the splattering grease and heat. Compared to some shop workers, the body language of Mira's employees suggested either a higher degree of satisfaction or that they know that creating the right "feeling state" is critical to keeping the job.

On Sunday, Doña Velia, age thirty-eight, and Epi, age fifteen, both from San Andres, are non-family staff. The vivacious Epi "definitely" plans to continue her education. Her mother always comes to meet her. The frail and pallid Velia does much of the cleaning, fetching, and other menial tasks. A widow with six children, she receives 25 pesos, a meal, and the right to fill a pail with leftovers "for my dog."

At some point on Sunday, Mirna's husband David, a government employee, usually appears. Officially, a coproprietor, with great panache he briefly goes through the motions of helping out. However, Mirna does "borrow" from him from time to time, and she estimates that he supplies "60 percent of the household funds." (Her mother laughed derisively when she heard this.) When he arrives, Mirna usually goes home to see to the boys. (Her mother-in-law lives with the family and looks after them.) But another reason is that "two heads are not good for business," as Mirna told me one day as she departed shortly after the always natty David arrived.

The Sunday staff is at work by 7:30 a.m. Most early clients are locals who come for pancita, a great Sunday favorite. (Doña Louisa, Mirna's sister, age forty-five, a single mother of four, is famous for her pancita. She cooks it in her home kitchen and receives extra pay for this and for the other things she prepares off premises.) In the next wave is the first group of tourists and residents returning from jogging on the pyramid trail or men who have driven into town for the Sunday paper. The clientele is mainly drawn from day excursionists, many of them regulars.

Though traffic thins out around five, the staff works ceaselessly until around seven. It is rare for anyone except Mirna's mother to sit down. Closing time depends on traffic. A competitor estimated that Mirna cleared "up to 400 pesos on a good Sunday" but on the Sundays I worked in the stall it was certainly more; and on special days, perhaps even twice this amount.

Sunday is the make-or-break day for food services. While Mirna does more weekday business than many concerns, the peak-and-valley nature of tourism-dependent businesses makes economies of scale all but impossible. Often, she must buy supplies in small lots in the mercado. Generally, she has sufficient liquidity to pay cash, so at least she is not burdened with paying high short-term interest on a few onions or a packet of paper napkins. Because of the continuous operation rule of the mercado, unlike nonmarket establishments, she must remain open six days of each week. And when Mirna's is open, Mirna is generally present. Like many other vendors, she identified vanishing profits as her main problem. "Costs go up and up, but we can only gradually adjust prices." Still, she continues to enjoy being in the market: "I like the money and I don't like staying at home."

THE TIANGUIS

Each Sunday from around 11:00 a.m. to 7:00 p.m., the narrow, steeply sloping roadways leading in and out of Tepoztlán are, to the consternation of taxi drivers, literally clogged with thousands of tourists. All roads lead to the Revolution Avenue *tianguis*, the Indian name for a regularly scheduled market. Though it is Tepoztlán's most ancient resource for articulating into the exchange phase that links the production and consumption of a commodity, the tianguis is the trading system stakeholders have most zealously protected from imminent danger of takeovers. By continuously instituting structural adjustments, the pueblo has hung on to control overflows. That today's tianguis is not the market's most archaic venue but its most innovative subsystem is confirmed by deep product revisions between 1995 and 2000. Walking the end-of-the-millennium tianguis is therefore a way to integrate Tepoztecas into mobilities that gender the structures in which the globalized-local and the localized-global construct each other other.

In the 1980s, in response to unplanned growth, merchants pushed the idea of a Sunday market devoted to high-quality *arte típico*, Mexican crafts. To limit revenue leakage, they restricted vendors to artisan/dealers. Right away, it became apparent that the restriction was unenforceable. But since consumers were arriving, why not give them what they wanted to buy, even if crafted in a factory in Indonesia and distributed by chains of professional traders? In the last two decades, the municipio has encouraged diversity of trading partners as the means to bring outside commodity cultures inside.

While succeeding in drawing tourists, producer and dealer diversity has proven to be a highly contentious matter as it comes up against core civil society resource-sharing issues.

Trading Population and Operations

A Sunday-session is on its face an intensely gendered resource. As a day reserved for families to come together and share an elaborate meal, Sunday is the worst possible trading day for most wives and mothers. Yet women with the highest social standing many of whom would not wish to participate in the daily market are eager to participate in the tianguis, suggesting that as with all other exchange stages, not only is context everything, but contextualization is highly responsive to the consumer base.

In the beginning, there were only a dozen or so stalls, most operated according to plan. Soon, the unruly informal economy planners were so intent on excluding encroached more boldly at each session. Reorganization closely corresponds to the conditions that vastly increased the need for even two-income households to intensify cash-earning activities. Competition for space became a fiercely xenophobic issue as teachers, lawyers, homemakers, and other nonstandard market actors looked to global consumerism to supplement inadequate wages. The only way for most Tepoztecans to enter the tianguis effectively was with goods purchased in wholesale markets, an intrinsically gendered factor since merchant capital tended to be controlled by men.

Looking at 1995 as the ethnographic present, there are forty-nine male and one hundred female members of the United Association of Vendors and Artisans of the Revolution Avenue Tianguis. Of these, only five can legitimately claim to be producers of *arte típico*. The head town is the home of sixty-six (44 percent) members; of these, forty-eight are women. Thus community women are 73 percent of the total of citizens officially holding a space; and they are almost one-third of the members of the Association. Of the remaining eighty-three members, thirty-four (41 percent) are women. I determined that at least twelve of these thirty-four were crafter/traders who rotate around weekend craft markets. Some regular not local vendors are from Mexico City, Cuernavaca, and other towns; three are artisan families from Guerrero residing locally.

For a number of reasons, the vending population is never the same as the Association list. In the interests of diversity and novelty, the Hacienda holds some space to rent by the session. As in the other subsystems, spaces are routinely traded internally. Some local renters consign spaces to others, or consign stock to others to sell for them. In addition, since resident dealers tend to rotate family labor throughout the day, it is not always clear for whose account an individual is trading.

Of the forty-eight local women listed, fifteen are full-time teachers (as are five of the eighteen men). Still other women members are former or part-time teachers or qualified teachers looking for postings. Local teenagers and college students are a growing force in tianguis operations. Some sell stocks that belong to adult relatives; others purchase the goods with money earned at other part-time jobs or borrowed from a network of student moneylenders. For resident women, children from age ten upward are often on hand to help with setting up and taking down; only a few reappeared during the day to help out. Rarely were husbands in evidence.

Tianguis operations consist of tables and metal frames rented from a Cuernavaca contractor. A local company delivers the fixtures to the spaces very early in the morning. Prepayment is required. Since there is an extra charge for setting up, usually vendors do this. On Sunday, many stalls are not fully set up until around 11 a.m. Then there is a lull in traffic at dining time. Late afternoon is the peak time, interrupted frequently during the rainy season. Besides the stalls, shops, cafes, and hawkers, Revolution Avenue shops have extensive outdoor operations. A bit of window-space may be rented to, for example, a teacher selling handbags from China.

For stalls, stock estimates range from a low of 400 pesos to "many thousands of pesos." It is sometimes thought that people employ themselves in the street market economy because they can do so with small start-up investments; however, it was comparatively greater access to start-up capital that gave many tianguis vendors the idea of participating.

Dealers purchase stock for cash or on short-term credit. With interest a heavy burden, the pressure to move inventories is intense. The recession and drop in tourism during the Golf Club emergency caught most dealers. Sales melted away leaving them with stocks optimistically bought at credit rates that escalated with the collapse of the peso and deregulation of the credit industry. Displays of old stocks indicate the lack of inventory mobility during a time when products went out of fashion from week to week. Yet though desperate to get out from under mounting debts, even at the end of a bad day, official dealers were not corrupting the market process by deep bargaining.

Sales volumes vary wildly. Attendance is, of course, an important factor, but there can be a large crowd of spenders Don Carlos described as "having a fishhook in their pocket." One vendor of silver jewelry, the most expensive stall product, reported sales for four Sundays in one month (March 1995) ranging from a low of 300 pesos to a high of 2,500 pesos. A few dealers said they had sold "nothing" for the entire day. Some dealers cross themselves after the first sale of the day. Even on good traffic days, I observed dealers crossing themselves well into the afternoon. Take it from a onetime market vendor, vendors are notorious liars about sales, sometimes exaggerating, other times deflating results. But since I am reporting on activities during a extremely bleak period, there was probably little room to downplay sales.

Career street traders, most directly linked to craft-producing communities, increased markedly during my fieldwork. One merchandising format is for a kin group to rent a curbside space. Men roam but women and children are fixed and usually industriously engaged in painting ceramics shipped to them unfinished. Floor tax collectors report that some wandering traders do obtain a permit, but most are poachers with the skills to stay just out of their reach.

Free Marketing in the Tianguis

Even when traffic is heaviest, a non-shopper can walk the length of the tianguis in around five minutes, but this short route is a global odyssey. Early in the colonial period, Tepoztlán ceased to be a community of artisans; and even reputedly authentic locally produced crafts do not have indigenous origins. The craft most associated with Tepoztlán are the tiny wooden replicas of houses *(casitas)* built into the hills. Four generations ago, an artisan whose family still produces *casitas* brought the art to Tepoztlán, probably from Michoacán. One man, a teacher and member of a merchant family, makes an articulated bamboo skeleton that sells (once in a while) for between 200 and 500 pesos that he assured me is a "pure Tepoztecan" craft. (However, the item appears at many other markets.) A local workshop produces colorful wooden furniture. (The sister of the owner worked in the U.S. for the Lewis family.)

Numerous stalls have nearly identical displays of crafts, mainly made in Chiapas and Guatemala, generally purchased from dealers in Mexico City who buy goods from the makers or intermediary traders. (Their prices are lower than those charged by NGO sponsored cooperatives.) There are also resident Morelos craft producers using raw materials sent to them from Guatemala. (By 2000, these once ubiquitous items had fallen out of favor and all but vanished from the tianguis.)

A steadily increasing amount of space is devoted to cotton and synthetic clothing from India, Pakistan, China, Chile, and Indonesia, often produced by homemakers of those countries as piecework or by children in antiquated factories (Baud et al. 1993). Several new concerns vend neo-Mexican white cotton clothing costing considerably more than Asian clothes. A dwindling number of stalls specialize in *ropa típica,* ethnic dress. Imported clothing bought through importers undersells even these scandalously underpriced products (versus the production labor and skill). With *ropa típico* dealers having severe cash flow problems, they may voluntarily offer "a deal." Postindustrial items rapidly reaching a saturation point include semi-precious stones, embossed leather goods, tarot cards, incense, and natural beauty products.

Nervous sellers of silver jewelry generally have many toucher-feelers. Most jewelry comes from Taxco. Atelier reps call on dealers and offer combinations of purchase, commission, and short-term (usually ten days) credit. Selling prices seem to be only slightly higher than prices in the more than five hundred retail silver shops in Taxco.

In the afternoon, numerous women are in the Avenue selling such homemade delicacies as spinach quiche and cheesecake. Though these traders are primarily women from the foreign colony, there has been a marked increase of Tepoztecas.

Far and away the best seller is the ice cream vended from a mobile operation. In reality a national firm, the local names given to the flavors give the impression of a local operation. Some ten young adults (most from Cuernavaca, the company's headquarter) are eager to give you a taste of one of the thirty or so designer flavors, such as *Virgen de Navidad.* In one consumer survey, I found that thirty-five of forty tourists had purchased at least one ice cream. Indeed, vendors complained that many tourists buy almost nothing else.

Populations and activities must also be framed within the escalating conflict over land use as I discovered one Sunday morning when I arrived to find a major shifting of spaces. Fueled by the Golf Club struggle and encouraged by a clique of prominent market vendors, xenophobia had reached a new intensity. "Why should space be granted to foreigners when Tepoztecos are having such a hard time?" was the way one stakeholder seeking space stated the issue. On this day, five vendors in the group locals continue to refer to as "the hippies" had been displaced. Even though the outcasts were mainly dealing in Mexican crafts, the claim circulated that "gay hippies" were bringing in "unsuitable" merchandise and cheating people. In the musical-chair like reallocation of spaces, several long-time resident foreigners ended up in less desirable locations. Several women in this group were extremely distressed, but also extremely cautious in voicing complaints.

Tianguis Activity Studies

The neoliberal project has invaded the tianguis as exchange system variants: commodity production, private and family capitalism, and established local merchants. In all three, gender plays a decisive role in both adding and subtracting value to a commodity as it transits to the consumer.

Antonio Bello, Craft Producer/vendor

This interview took place just as the effects of NAFTA were surfacing in the free market tianguis as the escalating demand for designer goods. I had a conversation with Don Antonio, age fifty-five, a vendor from Cuernavaca of enameled wood products he and his wife produce in a home workshop. He took a 10-centavo coin out of his pocket. "Look," he said, "in your country you can buy something, not much, but *something* with ten cents. In Mexico, our pesos are almost worthless when you go to buy something. Imagine the days when a peso was worth more than a dollar!" "Will things get better with NAFTA?" "Perhaps," he replied, "but I doubt I'll live long enough to see it. So what good can come to me and my family?"

His hobby is now a critical backup livelihood resource. He is bitter about a number of internal tianguis problems he attributes to "Tepoztecan politics with the usual slant. This market was supposed to be for artisans, but we are being crowded out. Local people are taking the space and buying commercial things that are not even Mexican." (By 1998, he had given up on his wood items and instead was displaying T-shirts with Aztecs frolicking around local landmarks. A Cuernavaca workshop prints the designs on Hanes USA shirts. Clustered around his stall were U.S. students attending Cuernavaca language schools.)

Marta Roldán, Craft Vendor

Most local women participants are not full-time market traders. Doña Marta, age thirty-seven and mother of four, is the retail link of a family workshop. She sells miniature wooden houses (*casitas*) produced in a workshop operated for three decades by her husband's family. Prices range from 5 to 50 pesos. She also has silver jewelry from Taxco, priced from 10 to 1,500 pesos. She pays 6 pesos floor tax for her well-located stall.

Though she has a teacher's certificate, Marta has never had a full-time, secure local posting. Presently, she has a temporary position in a private school for children with Downs Syndrome. She earns 500 pesos monthly but considers it unlikely she will be rehired for another year.

Business is so slow for the workshop that for several years Don Camilo, her husband, has spent up to eight months each year working at various manual jobs in the U.S. Female and younger family members now participate in craft production and/or distribution phases formerly done by male adults. Camilo's grandmother and mother have side-by-side stalls, and two sisters are in the market. One sister returns each weekend from Mexico City, where she works in a bank, to sell (on her own account) in her mother's stall. All combine silver jewelry—the chief money making item—with other crafts.

So fierce is the competition that Marta counts herself lucky to sell even a few pieces. About "one weekend out of four" she sells enough jewelry to have "a very good day." Since she never visits Taxco, personal contact with workshop representatives is vital. It largely determines which vendors will be the first to have new fad items and get the most favorable credit terms. She gets from ten to fourteen days' credit on most items. She was not clear about how much interest she was paying, and, indeed, she seemed puzzled by the question.

One of her sisters shares the stall next to her that has a different product mix. Marta enjoys marketing, but is sometimes "really down" at the end of a slow day. She "loves" teaching. She considers Camilo the breadwinner, even though when he is away, often her earnings are the family's daily wage. "But now I barely make enough to keep us going. Perhaps I too will have to go to work over there, probably as a maid. Do you know of a job?"

Carmen Villamel, Craft Vendor

When Doña Carmen has the funds, she makes weekly visits to Mexico City dealers. She favors Chiapas crafts because while most items are utilitarian (items such as purses, vests, and backpacks), the workmanship and design are generally outstanding. But she also shops the vast wholesale district hoping to discover innovative stock that will distinguish her operation from the (too) many stalls that sell Chiapas crafts. In the last few years, with sales "300 percent down," she sometimes can go only once each month. She works around nine hours on Sunday and often on Saturday as well. She pays 3 pesos floor tax.

Carmen, age forty-three, was born in Mexico City. Her father had an influential circle of Tepoztecan friends. The family frequently occupied their Atongo Valley mansion and, unlike most villa occupants, mixed socially with local residents. At age twenty-two, she married a well-connected Tepozteco. After years of his blatant unfaithfulness, in 1996 they divorced.

In 1988, she opened a boutique on Revolution Avenue. "We sold perfume, jeans; almost anything with the right designer's name on it." For a time the shop thrived, but after three years, she had to close and "it broke my heart." She went into the tianguis because there was no other work and she had stock she urgently needed to sell.

About being an employed wife she said, "My mother's generation had no real options. My father would never have allowed her to work. In some ways, this made her choices easier. Work is liberating for women, but for middle-class Mexican women, it is a major domestic complication." Her husband used her work to excuse his unfaithfulness and to demand more attention to domestic obligations. "Before he would help me by fetching water, but after I went to work, he expected me to do everything." But sexual relations not housework were at the heart of their marital problems. "Husbands here expect to have sex several times a week. It doesn't matter how tired or out of the mood the wife is because her feelings don't count. Of my friends here, only one says she has a good sexual relationship with her husband; but he cheats too and she knows it. Another problem is that when you earn money, your husband gives you less. This means he has more to spend on outside activities that these days make you worry about what kind of diseases he could give you." Carmen fought to keep the family intact, even lending her husband money, though she suspected he would spend it on other women. In the end, he insisted on the divorce. Like his father, her son, whom she supports, deeply resents time she devotes to business.

In the depth of the contraction, there were days when her stall brought in as little as 100 pesos. "Some Sundays, I thought, 'I'm not going to sell anything today.'" When she can find the right new items, her sales greatly improve. For example, in a few hours, she sold 1,500 pesos worth of a new jewelry collection. By the next Sunday, two other dealers had the jewelry and her sales dropped. Carmen has other income sources, "But if sales don't improve I will have to find a full-time job, likely in Mexico City. Being 100 percent responsible for me and my son is very scary."

She followed her father's example of civic involvement. Still she was one of the dealers who lost space in the shakeup, and she worries about the growing anti-foreign sentiment. But since I don't want to leave Tepoztlán and there are no better work options for me, for now I persevere."

Marcela Gómez, Jewelry Vendor

Often now, households where both husband and wife are employed full-time must integrate regular part-time work. "My dream always was to be a teacher. Now that I am a teacher, it's almost a nightmare." Doña Marcela, age forty-one, and mother of three children, is a teacher and a tianguis vendor. The daughter of leaders of the Seventh Day Adventist community, she studied in a private Mexico City university. She is married to Don Gustavo, a lawyer, with a background almost identical to hers. Both are members of a generation that believed education would translate into upwardly mobility for themselves and their children. Inflation and loss of income have hit them hard. Gustavo is trying to secure a government job. "The pay is not good, but it is better work than selling ice cream in the Cuernavaca plaza. That is what I heard a classmate is now doing."

In 1993, Marcela entered the tianguis. Through family connections, she got a space and stocked it with silver jewelry. Marketing, she soon found, was also a perilous profession. As the crisis deepened, the inventory became a great burden. Marcela was extremely bitter. "On a teacher's salary, it is not possible to give my children a decent life. We can't travel or do any of the things we dreamed of. At this stage, it is only worthwhile to continue teaching to keep the benefit package. And with all the competition, there is little prospect of making enough to pay for my time. These days," she said, "it seems I'm always depressed."

Tianguis Gendering Trends

Some 150 surveys conducted with an eclectic range of tourist-consumers verified that the product most people shopping the tianguis hoped to encounter was authenticity: that "touristic make believe" that vendors and tourists "willingly, and often playfully, cooperate in" (Cohen 1989:31). Although the touristic "game" is perhaps the largest source of world trade, the nature of the product and its producer makes it analytically difficult for economists. However, Teresa Ebert's (1995:40) critical feminist tracking reveals "specific historical connections to the relations of production and the class struggle." Encountered at all phases of commodity production and distribution chains is the underpaid labor of women.

Astutely, Tepoztecan planners responded to revisions in modes and relations of production when they restructured the ancient tianguis with the aim of attracting new consumers eager to play the game. They opened Revolution Avenue to transactions that articulate the traditional but not precapitalist economy into postindustrial production-consumption capitalism. We find then that the New Economy tianguis Tepoztecas reflexively go to work in is an outcome of the under valorization of women's labor across multiple ever more determinatively intersecting commodity cultures.

Reflections on the Market

I return now to the feminization/marketization dialogic running through the market study: (1) how do actual market systems work for women in the time of global feminization through flexible labor; and (2) how do women make markets systematically structured by gender from the outside in and the inside out work for them as social actors and economic agents? Tracking gender as it manifests as worksite exchanges reveals that sex/gender divisions of labor and assets are crucial to every market process, whether on the floor itself or in a sweatshop in India. No sphere or aspect of market relations is isolated from the localization and globalization projects of privileged men. As I see it, there is an individual as well as a systems level answer. I draw on the experiences of octogenarian quesadilla entrepreneur Doña Leticia to speculate that an individual's art of using can have transformative implications for collective organization.

Even when she was the vivacious daughter of market professionals just married into another marketing family firm, Doña Leticia never stood as tall as five feet. Now a widow for forty years, she is wispy, taciturn, and bent almost double. But I never went into the market when she was not totally focused on business in her food stall. She had no employee, insisting on doing everything herself, brusquely refusing offers of help from colleagues even to carry pails of water.

"Much work, little profit" was how the legendary trader summed up her life in the mercado. But to other vendors, she is an astute merchant. Admiringly, Doña Adela reported, "Though she has no children, she lives quite well in her own home. She was the first to offer several of the now most popular fillings. She was also the first to put blue tortillas on her menu. Now everyone must offer them." On balance, Doña Leticia also judged her career a success. "It's not a bad life for women like me, women who have a taste (*una afición*) for marketing." I met other—though none more tenacious—"natural" market women. However, even for them, socio-economic and historical differences are more determinative than individual attributes or inclinations. At a general level, for the most undercapitalized, organizational differences are critical because they are unlikely to be able to capitalize sufficiently to increase productivity.

As to collective action, to attain the neoliberal goal of economic self-sufficiently, women are hugely and increasingly dependent on social capital controlled by empowered men. This dependency makes women with needs highly effective as local/global mediators, a fact not overlooked by the microfinance industry. But continuously since the first wave of globalization, for Tepoztecas protection of their economic resource base has been the battle cry. Most women I consulted agreed with Palmer's (1991) analysis that even though gender is enforced and often strengthened by the terms of their participation, greater still are the inequalities visited upon economic women in the absence of competitive markets. Their collective resolve supports Narotzky: "we have to think of economic processes as embedded in social and cultural processes" (1994:222). Specified in the next chapter are ways that these processes come together when Tepoztecas engage their third unequal challenge, the challenge of "community management" (Moser 1993).

Chapter Twelve

Feminization and Community Survival Struggles

> [T]he practical positions any group of workers adopt seem to be less a matter of discursive constructions than of their immediate pragmatic problems as social agents in a capitalist economy.
>
> —John Gledhill, 1994

"Without the women, the *lucha*, the struggle, would have fallen apart" (Don Lázaro). "The women were manlier than the men" (Don Gerardo). These comments from two movement leaders refer to the front line roles taken on by women throughout Tepoztlán's perilous *No al Club de Golf struggle*. The transformation of a seemingly underdeveloped plot of communal land into an elite tourism and commercial enclave was the objective of a coalition of awesomely empowered national and international "developers."

Tepoztecas, of all ages, economic status, and social orientations were the foot soldiers of a social protest movement that is still one of the few civil society victories over rampant Free Marketization. Indeed, it has become a model for grassroots resistance to projects to take over the resource bases where people create fully late capitalist "commodity cultures" (Cook 2004). That increasingly women are on the front lines of overmatched struggles to survive global commercial invasions prompts Saskia Sassen's (2002:90) call for a new mapping of "systemic links" among local and global economic agendas and the feminization of community survival struggles. To locate women in Gledhill's "immediate pragmatic problems," the commodity culture[s] women were defending, this chapter maps particular Tepoztecas and groups of Tepoztecas into the work processes of the No to the Golf Club struggle.

FOOT SOLDIERS IN THE GLOBAL COMMERCIAL INVASION

A counterhegemonic movement "requires the projection of 'sameness'" from which the demands of the collective can be seen to stem, writes Lynn Stephen (2005:66). Throughout the lucha, the readily "understandable" communication system of gender—the way a society constructs and enforces power differences between men and women—functioned as Stephen's essential "coherent social location." Evident at every point was the informed calculation with which Tepoztecans cooperated to mobilize the compelling imagery of stalwart campesina homemakers defending their caring labor resource base. Performances of gender sound bites were astutely designed to entice the media and provoke outside sympathy and support, thereby externalizing some of the mounting costs of overcoming. And internally for stakeholders on the edge, gender idioms powerfully evoked institutions that had never been at a higher threat level. Thus, though this was Tepoztlán's first wired lucha, as in monumental struggles past, narratives that rationalize gender systems functioned again—and, as before, functioned effectively—as simultaneously an offensive and defensive weapon.

In 1994, as the confrontation heated up, almost daily Morelos newspapers were headlining grotesque crimes, including kidnappings and murder, blatantly perpetrated against ordinary citizens. Testimonies of victims, witnesses, and anonymous insiders established the deep implication in these crimes of PRI operatives aggressively pushing the Golf Club. Why then did the pueblo allow women to be consistently out front in boldly public demonstrations against a criminal regime closely monitoring their activities? I put this question to the only woman in Tepoztlán with formal political standing. "Because women do not work."

I draw on participant observation and interviews to document contrary "systemic links." Women's valiant interventions expressed the reality that they do work; and work in and against an economic idea in which individual and collective strategies of survival and transformation are more fused than ever before. Each fusion proved to be intensely but not randomly regulated by gender constructs. To critique the centrality of Tepoztecas to a paradigmatic post-NAFTA New Social Movement (NSM)—actions "that connect the *micro* concerns of social life to the *macro* processes of social change" (Foweraker 1995:1)—I interface the two sides of the "gender politics" (Dore 1997) of community survival. On one side, gender structured what Heather Williams (2001:7) identifies as the "aggregate conditions that lead to collective action"; on the other side, I investigate gender as Williams' "disparate points of departure."

No to the Golf Club

"Tepoztlán is not for sale! Tepoztlán will not surrender!" This was the *grito*, the rallying cry, of the No to the Golf Club struggle. Resounding across the municipio from the end of 1994 into 1999, it expressed the fervent resolve of citizens to block a 500 million dollar scheme to develop a seemingly (to investors) nonproductive plot of land repeatedly designated by the municipio as communal property. Christened *El Club de Golf El Tepozteco* by the investors, really it was a multifaceted project, including even a fiber optics facility. Clearly, sponsors intended that this emphasis on invigorating, five-star recreation for stressed out CEOs would mask the mega dimensions of the commercial invasion, thereby also obscuring what for citizens was actually at stake: strategic control of their patrimony and legacy.

That Tepoztlán's determination not to be taken over by men long unaccustomed to having their will to power thwarted would call for a new order of resistance and sacrifice was made clear with the release of the names of the investors. Members of the loftiest elite of the PRI were among the venture capitalists eager to transform 187.129 windswept hectares into Mexico's first PGA-approved "golfer's paradise." And if two of *Fortune* magazine's top fifty corporations, the world's (perhaps) richest man, and surrogates for two sacrosanct former Mexican presidents were not enough to impel consent, the ultra conservative Catholic bishop of Cuernavaca assured Tepoztecans that the development had celestial endorsement.

In a Sunday homily, the bishop—rumored to be an avid golfer—instructed his notoriously obstreperous flock to look upon the Golf Club as "a gift from God that has fallen from the heavens" to succor the "starving Tepoztecans." Tepoztecas responded by inviting one and all to a great feast in El Centro. Mothers organized a parade of decidedly robust children in angel costumes. One banner carried this injunction: "Your lordship, look at these little angels! Do they look like they are starving?"

Early on, citizens realized that this struggle would bring into the beautiful mountain pueblo new globally interlocked Goliaths unleashed by trade and investment liberalization. In his first address to a nation with a currency that had just lost half its exchange value, a beleaguered President Zedillo (1994–2000) anointed the Golf Club "a veritable model" for precisely the kinds of near last-rite reforms made possible by NAFTA.

The patriotic urgency of instituting radical social and economic reforms was to be used throughout by promoters to legitimate what some analysts interpreted as a new stage in an ongoing plot to colonize what remained of commercially underdeveloped northern Morelos. The arrival of the menacing PRI closer charged with realizing the Golf Club supported this conspiracy theory. The new governor (handpicked in 1992 by outgoing

President Salinas, who along with members of his family owned choice tracts of municipio real estate) was none other than an ex-general infamous for the brutality with which he put down a nonviolent student movement. But perhaps the strongest threat to forging and sustaining a pan-municipio coalition was this. In the time of Tepoztlán's deepest economic depression, enticements dangled by the developers perfectly matched the angst and aspirations of citizens struggling to position themselves effectively in a New Economy that even as the first stage of NAFTA came into effect on 1 January 1994 appeared to be going down for the last time.

The roster of investors left no doubt that the Golf Club was being channeled through "the network of state-society alliance underpinning Mexico's distinctive form of authoritarian rule": the coalition that to Middlebrook and Zepeda (2003:13) explains the rapid and extensive penetration of neoliberal structural adjustments so radically opposed to longstanding Mexican forms of refusals to be absorbed.

Mega Developments

By the fall of 1994, the proposal to construct a deluxe tourism complex on a profoundly eroded plateau on the northwestern fringe of the municipio had gone from the rumor to the imminent stage. The announced goal of El Grupo KS—a consortium of four Mexican companies—was to transform a seemingly (to the investors) nonproductive stretch of land into a First World model development. Earth moving machinery was already in place when KS announced that US$300 million had already been committed. Where cattle now roamed hopefully among the tumbleweeds and stunted mesquites, soon there would be a verdant, opulent, walled off retreat for Mexico's superrich and super-superrich.

The enclave would include:

- an eighteen-hole Jack Nicklaus Signature Golf Course
- an 8,000m^2 clubhouse in colonial style
- eight hundred detached chalet-condominiums
- a five-star hotel, heliport, casino, and tennis club
- numerous swimming pools, fountains, and two artificial lakes
- *El Recinto*, a facility for offices, a fiber optics operation, shops, and service providers.

In full color brochures (in English), KS proclaimed its goal of attracting 250 "true leaders" to the region's most "environmentally sound and open" project ever. The minimum investment (quoted in dollars) was a five-lot package valued at $555,000. A seat on the prestigious board was the perk for the purchase of five packages ($3.85 million). Switching to pesos, KS emphasized the local benefits that would accrue. Some 14,000 jobs would be created during the construction phase with almost 3,000 steady jobs to follow. The annual projected revenue of 800,000 pesos "represents more than twenty years of normal municipio earnings," asserted KS CEO Francisco Kladt Sobrino.

To be shared with citizens was a 30,000-kilowatt capacity substation and a network of roads linking Tepoztlán to major highways. On the Cuernavaca to Tepoztlán highway, KS billboards proclaimed that 75 percent would be green area planted only in endangered and locally extinct indigenous flora. They promised to fund several cherished youth projects. "Water," I was told, "water is always the issue between Tepoztlán and the PRI." As its clinching justification, KS certified that "hydraulic experts" had discovered an untapped water source that would supply critically water-deprived Tepoztlán as well as keeping the fairways and gardens green.

From start to finish, Don Francisco's condescending press releases—condescending because he considered the Golf Club a done deal—emphasized that the "real economy" of Tepoztlán was no longer small farming. "In truth it is tourism, commerce, and services." Thus "our thoroughly researched" project will revive rather than degrade Tepoztlán's economy.

Citizens' objections to the project were economically rational even by neoliberal dogma. Thus: "Of course we need jobs, but more cleaning and gardening jobs are not what we want for ourselves or our children" (Doña Gaby). "The workers they will bring in are so poor and desperate they will work for even lower wages than we earn" (Don Jerónimo). "Where will the workers live? There is no more space even for us." (Don Hernán). "What will happen to their garbage?" (Doña Olivia). "The investors are sure to enrich themselves and impoverish us" (Don Oscar). "The people staying there won't use my husband's taxi, eat in my sister's cafe, or buy my vegetables" (Doña Teresa). "That land is already being used by our ranchers. What is to become of them and their families?" (Don Milán). And this from civil engineer Don Mario: "That area is environmentally very sensitive. It is our only protection against floods and mudslides." Citizens reiterated this pattern of pragmatic objections throughout the lucha.

Taking the position that they already had legal titles to the land (for reasons explained in endnote 5), preliminary construction had already begun when, on 24 September 1994, KS formally notified local officials of the project. So confident was KS of their overwhelming power and the self-evident rationality of the development, at no time were citizens solicited for their support or for their opinions on ways to make the project more acceptable (Demesa Padilla 1996:27; and interviews).

"Tepoztlán Is All of Us"

The projected site has a centuries-deep provenance, as well as a turbulent twentieth-century history. The land lies within territory reclaimed from a plantation and formally restored to Tepoztlán in 1929. It is inside a national park, a federally protected biological corridor, and an off-limits archeological zone. All protections were destabilized when the crosscutting of the area by the Mexico City highway transformed it into highly valuable real estate. In 1963, it was the was the site of the aborted "Montecastillo," the first conspiracy to construct an eighteen-hole paradise.[1] Ever alert to the certainty that Montecastillo was only on hold, citing Article 115 of the Constitution, a 1993 municipio act restated in no uncertain terms the legal prohibition against the construction on the land of "any roads, clubs, residential, or commercial structures."

Leading the campaign to impose the Golf Club was Jorge Carrillo Olea, the newly elected PRI Governor of Morelos. Even before being sworn in, this former director of Salinas' menacing Security Agency with documented ties to drug dealers (Preston and Dillon 2004:348) published his "personal assurance" to KS: "the Golf Club will be built." Essential to the mission many believed Salinas had sent Carrillo to Morelos to carry out was to control the selection of municipio mayor. (His official title is *presidente*.) Carrillo's candidate was Alejandro Morales Barragán (Beto), the personable thirty-year-old scion of an affluent local family, though not one that had lived in Tepoztlán "forever."

Not only was the right of residents rather than a PRI caucus to select local leaders a burning political issue, many people mistrusted the candidate. Though seemingly overqualified for the office, the reluctance to accept Morales was widespread even among his many friends and in his own party, the PRI. In addition to considerable land holdings, he owned Tepoztlán's largest construction firm and agricultural supply business. Even some supporters believed that in administering a government seed-distribution program, Beto had profited personally by extorting payment from "our impoverished farmers."

On 29 January 1994, the governor granted citizens a public meeting (the only one he attended; cautiously, it was held in a site deeded to state police). Tepoztecans were prepared to go to the wall on two issues: the imposing by the PRI of any candidate and Morales' candidacy in particular. Right away, the ex-general informed Tepoztecans that he would not permit any questioning of his authority in this matter. Nevertheless, the representative of El Comité Mujer [Woman] Tepozteca (CMT) rose and in a calm voice quoted the PRI's own bylaws to outline the legal objections, evoking a fuming response by a red-faced, fist-pounding governor who vowed to "destroy utterly these tyrants in petticoats who represent no one but themselves." And not only did Carrillo contrive Morales' narrow election victory (the narrowest ever); he created the circumstances that lead to the demise of the CMT.

After this encounter, leaders opposing the Golf Club worked even more urgently toward the harmonizing of old and new political factions. Dominating the influential open-party activist group Coordinate Democratic Tepoztlán (CDT) founded in 1983 were men and women from the professional and commercial establishment. A Municipal Committee (CM) spoke for an ostensibly more democratic PRI. Formed in 1979; the CMT was a force, as were organizations of farmers and ranchers, merchants, footballers, restaurant owners, education workers, environmentalists, and numerous other special interest coalitions.

Beginning in the fall of 1994, representatives of all associations met nightly. Present at every session were CMT founders. Recognizing that (in the words of a CMT founder) "it had to be a complete project," there was a formal closing of ranks around the proposition that "We are all Tepoztlán and Tepoztlán is all of us." Eventually, all factions agreed to be absorbed into El Comité de Unidad Tepozteca, CUT

Three days after this meeting, in an open session, the mayor and his council voted to deny KS a construction permit, a deeply mistrusted edict since Morales was known to be in constant contact with Cuernavaca. The next day, a delegation of prominent male citizens confronted the mayor who again gave his word that he would not issue a permit to change the use of the land. Three hours later, meeting in camera, Morales and four council members "provisionally" authorized KS to proceed with the Golf Club.

Leaving the City Hall by a back door, Morales encountered Don Carlos, a close friend: "The minute he saw me, he blurted out what he had done. 'Beto,' I said, 'you have made a terrible mistake and you will never be able to live in this town again.' 'I know it,' he replied and then hurried off." Carlos rushed to inform the leaders of CUT; Morales left at once for Cuernavaca and an extended exile.

Our Traitors

Late on the afternoon of 24 August 1995, bells resounded across the town. The some (estimated) 3,000 citizens massed in the Plaza demanded the impeachment (and worse) of those who had "betrayed the interests of the pueblo." From this time, there were numerous protest marches. Staged every evening in front of the City Hall (Presidencia) were planning and information sessions. Anticipating (correctly) that Carrillo would call out the militia and the certifiably vicious state police, citizens erected blockades at all municipio portals and posted twenty-four-hour male and female guards. In response, Carrillo issued the first of more than one hundred arrest warrants for ordinary citizens that would remain in effect until 1999, including even the parish priest and several long departed citizens.

Questionably since by now open dissent was dangerous, polls indicate anti-Golf Club consensus at 90 percent and crossing all demographic lines. Aware that not only victory but also citizens' personal safety depended on attracting international as well as national attention and resources, leaders—who demonstrated a fine-grained knowledge of the tactics of successful nonviolent social movements—reached out through cutting-edge communication media. They relied upon television, wire services, faxes, telephone, and the Internet to propagate images of the seemingly hopelessly overmatched village in Mexico. Much public use was made of the legends and the festive rituals that attract multitudes of tourists to Tepoztlán. Gender is explicit in all these references.

The press turned out in mass to cover the dramatic events that began on 3 September. Early on this Sunday morning, state police numbering some 600 entered the town. They closed off the streets leading to a home where politicos were meeting with Tepoztecans thought to be still open to persuasion. When a taxi driver carried the news to the parish church, Father Fili—the parish priest who defied his bishop to support his flock—stopped the mass. Church bells alerted residents. María Rosas (1997:26–27) reports vividly on the passionate response. Combatants ranged from market vendors who left stalls unattended to "diminutive old women" she describes as having spent their whole lives cocooned in somber-hued *rebozos* (shawls). Men, women, and children poured into the streets and faced down the police. Some 800 Tepoztecans shouting defiant messages—some also making ribald gestures—armed with skillets, wooden spoons and kitchen knives, machetes, slingshots, and sticks broke through police lines to mass outside the house of treason.

The police withdrew in considerable disarray, as did all inside fortunate enough to escape. Citizens captured six PRI officials trying to reach cars presciently parked heading out of town. There followed a melee of stone and epithet hurling, and one prisoner (the head of the local PRI) ended up with a profusely bleeding wound on her forehead that required stitches. (An opposition party activist described it as a "scrape Diana got when she slipped.")

In the criminal complaint Diana Ortega took to court, she testified, "the women threatened to hang me but they were stopped by the men." (She said there were only some fifty men.) What provoked this degree of rage was that this daughter of a former mayor would cooperate in bringing the enemy inside. The final act played out on in front of a neoclassical City Hall festooned with effigies of "our traitors" and received wide press coverage. While this episode made the "Golf War" even bigger news, on balance, it tended to give some support to Carrillo's characterization of protesters as a naïve rabble who were being stirred up by local individuals with vested reasons for wanting to block "progressive changes."

Since State Law 195 gives a "free municipio" the right to impeach and replace its elected officials, and states that in such matters the will of the citizens overrides that of the governor, citizens decided to elect a Provisional Council. On 24 September, Tepoztecans turned out in record numbers to vote. The closely scrutinized election was truly grassroots, and perhaps the first election in Mexico outside the party structure. (In Mexico, candidates must declare an affiliation with a registered political party.) Immediately, from the steps of the permanently renamed Presidencia Popular, the Provisional President stated three "nonnegotiable" demands: (1) a guarantee from KS of no construction of the Golf Club; (2) official recognition by the governor of the Provisional Council; and (3) immediate unconditional cancellation of all punitive and terrorist measures against Tepoztecans.

Martyrdom of "A man who always made me laugh"

By now, pungent *gritos* were inscribed on every possible surface and marked the cadence for numerous protest marches and rallies. But at 11 p.m. on 12 April 1996, from the ranks of citizens massed across El Centro, no battle cry resounded. Instead, silence enveloped a gathering of citizens said to be the largest assembly ever in Tepoztlán. Not even one peanut vendor from the usually ubiquitous army of street merchants worked the crowd. Children were not fidgeting; infants in their parents' arms did not even whimper. Families and close friends were noticeably drawn into tight units. The only sound was the relentless death knell tolling from the parish church and chapels across the municipio. Almost the only movement coming out of that pitch-dark sultry night was the funeral cortege led by the gallant Father Fili (now under warrant of arrest for treason against the state and threatened with excommunication).

The heartrending procession came into view. Puffs of myrrh and frankincense and a double file of twelve women in black weeds holding long white tapers preceded the cortege that with measured steps solemnly but resolutely descended from the barrio San Miguel Chapel along the steeply sloping Avenue Fifth of May to the Presidencia Popular.

With a chilling dignity, the pueblo received the unadorned pine coffin of Marcus Olmedo, a sixty-four-year-old Tepozteco known to all as "*il Tiburón*," the Shark. All his life had been lived in the lovely municipio hamlet of Ocotitlán. He was an authentic campesino who lived in an adobe home with his wife of forty-five years and four daughters now bonded together as a kind of living frieze of mourning women. To support the family, besides doing agricultural labor, each day he came to Tepoztlán to work in a tortilla factory where he earned less than US$4 per day. The founder of the local branch of the newly formed center-left PRD party, he was a fervent movement activist who carried a Zapata banner in the marches. And to his friend Doña Nuria, "a man who always made me laugh." Wednesday, 10 April 1996 was the day Don Marcus was martyred.

Things happened this way. On the morning of 10 April, he was one of a large group of excursionists composed mostly of seniors and mothers with young children, many in costumes. They were following a tradition of commemorating Zapata's assassination by retracing the Route of Zapata. They planned to end in Tlaltizapan where Zedillo was to deliver a commemorative address to a carefully vetted audience composed mainly of PRI old guard campesinos.

They intended to deliver a "respectful" petition signed by 4,000 citizens entreating Zedillo to order a halt to his "model project." Even as the caravan numbering several hundred (one press source estimated 500) left Tepoztlán, the head of Morelos Public Security was dispatching an armed detachment to head them off and prevent them and their petition from reaching Zedillo. The attack—vicious and brazen even in the bloody annals of Morelos—began when a three-deep contingent of some 300 elite security officers in riot gear blocked the procession on the outskirts of the town of San Rafael.

Nightsticks flying indiscriminately, and with some officers brandishing pistols, the police broke car and van windows and stormed the buses. Gunfire and occupants scrambled out and ran into the fields, pursued fiercely by the police. Many victims were beaten and kicked and some threatened by police pointing guns. ("I heard it when he cocked his pistol and I'll never forget that sound," said Doña Cynthia.) Diminutive Doña Graciela, age 77, had a patch of scalp pulled out by the officer who hauled her off the bus. The police dragged Tepoztecans unable to escape back to the highway. Some one hundred were women with children.

Throughout the afternoon, the captives were made to stand in the punishing April sun. Hats, water, and picnic lunches were confiscated. "A policewoman ate the lunch I packed," Doña Lorena recounted. "She was the worst of all. She taunted our children, who were crying because they were not allowed to break ranks even to urinate." A medical team arrived but was not permitted to attend even the grievously injured. Thirty-four Tepoztecans were held incommunicado at a Cuernavaca police station throughout the night. According to testimony given to a human rights commission conducting interviews in

Tepoztlán even children with bleeding head wounds did not receive medical treatment. Sketchy reports of the incident appeared in morning newspapers.

As the attack began, Don Marcus attempted to shield a woman from a police battering. Savagely, the officer leading the attack turned on him. He kicked and pushed Olmedo out of the bus. At least three shots were fired from the police ranks, hitting Olmedo in the neck and chest. "I saw the police put him into a police van," testified a CUT official. "I thought they were going to take him to the hospital. I thought he was still alive." Instead, stripped of identification, he was trussed up and stuffed into a duffel bag, discarded some 20 kms from the attack site. His fate was revealed two days later when a newspaper announced that an unidentified corpse had been found in a ditch.

The next day the governor went on the offensive on a popular TV news program. Carrillo began by denying that the incident could have taken place since "the police were not even armed." He contended that armed Tepoztecos had attacked the police at a "normal" highway inspection stop: "They just wanted to create a martyr." Then the station aired a video camera clip. A Tepozteco had filmed and sound recorded the start of the attack.

The next morning, Carrillo could not but acknowledge that the police had been carrying weapons ("for self-defense") and an unarmed man shot to death. He suspended four junior officers and promised a thorough investigation. Such was the force of the video even the steadfastly aloof Zedillo publicly condemned excessive police force in general; however, he did not then or ever have anything to say about the atrocities of the golf club.

Forthcoming was a KS press release (*La Jornada* 14 April 1996:5) announcing the project's "definite cancellation" because "circumstances have reduced the potential profitability of the Golf Club." To KS's CEO, "Our project was held hostage by history and by anarchists." Investors had had enough of the Tepoztecans. "The Board has voted to limit our losses to the six million dollars already spent." KS again enumerated the benefits the project would have conferred on Tepoztlán's "true vocation" of tourism, commerce, and services. The irrational millenarianism of the pueblo was the reason for ending the altruistic attempt to contribute to "the urban and social reordering of Tepoztlán."

For two days, *compañero* Olmedo lay in state. To the stream of Mexicans paying their respects and leaving tokens of affection what seemed to matter now was the unspeakable cruelty to a good man defending his patrimony. It was several days before Tepoztecans began to discuss the pyretic victory. Given the history of the site and perceiving KS's withdrawal with great skepticism in the words of one CUT leader, "The affair of the Golf Club is finished but not ended." Like many citizens, he viewed the outcome as a culmination of one phase only in an unceasing and likely intensifying stuggle.[2]

WOMEN'S DISTINCTIVE PATHS TO INVOLVEMENT

"By identifying women's movement location, we can explore ways in which women articulate their political movement standing and how such articulations can serve to transform the political contexts (Karen Beckwith 1996:1040).

"Here this, Senor Governor, for us, the women of Tepoztlán, our land is sacred! It is not for sale! No to the Golf Club!" Purposefully, though seemingly on cat's feet, a hundred or so Tepoztecas moved out of the front ranks of a well-disciplined throng of slogan chanting, banner and placard carrying citizens demonstrating in Cuernavaca's Plaza de Armas on 11 March 1995. In a matter of minutes, the women had formed into a chain, linked by their *rebozos* that encircled a state house hastily battened down when officials learned the Tepoztecans were on their way to present a petition. Standing as reverently as at prayer, holding the rebozos between them, the women proceeded to create a campesina happening that led evening news programs. It was not until the cameras stopped rolling that a CUT leader unobtrusively gave the signal for the chain to unlink.

On this occasion, even Tepoztecas who likely had had to borrow a suitably threadbare shawl presented themselves in this sanctified signifier of the self-abnegating campesinas. On other occasions, however, some of these same women made up mobs brandishing skillets and hurling stones and vulgarities. In both solemn and raucous demonstrations, they were situating their activities in a seemingly unified history of gendered struggles. Women's activities make clear that they understood the roles they, the foot soldiers, were expected to play when sent out to no-man's land. As well, they understood the absolute need for strict discipline when called upon, as in tumults past, to be "worse than the men." In all designated roles—from chucking tomatoes at the bishop's car to facing down state police—they relied on the myth of women's immunity to retribution rather than on black ski masks.

Mothering Is Problematic

"It is all very well to claim that the personal is political but the stress on 'motherhood' as the primary causal factor in women's collective action is problematic," argue Tessa Cubitt and Helen Greenslade (1997:56). Though militant motherhood remains a primary place women come out, rejecting the public man/private woman dichotomy, recent studies pay much more attention to the terms of the integration of new social actors—solidarities and individuals—into late commodity cultures (Harcourt and Escobar 2005). Protection of the resources required to carry out their domestic domain obligations was indeed the motivation many Tepoztecas cited for their courageous and physically burdensome activism. But from my fieldwork, I knew that the links in the *rebozo* chain represented many different New Economy production-reproduction challenges. Really, they expressed a multiplicity of motivations for carrying out the work processes of the third feminized challenge: frontline citizenship.

Never before had Doña Clara, a diminutive great-grandmother I saw at every demonstration, publicly protested any injustice or abuse. She was linked up to Doña Judith, age forty-five, a Sunday morning jogger, single, no children, and militant advocate for working class women's human rights. Teacher Leticia, age forty-two was there as well. A holder of an honors degree in biology who teaches an elementary school science class, she is a veteran of high union politics. A number of women had closed businesses in order to attend, though it was a time when no one could afford to miss even one sale. I saw Doña Elsa, real estate agent. Everyone says she has made a fortune brokering villas located on communal land. Doña Rosalie, the always impeccably groomed wife and daughter of men who owe their prosperity to the PRI, was another participant. Like many others, she too wore an apron, a semiotic confirming the labor intensity of the flexible specialization "woman of Tepoztlán."

Certainly, the Golf Club movement was "engendered in order to oppose what people perceive as threats to central values" (Nash 2005b:12), not all of which are economic. But as the struggle played out, women who shared and cherished much the same set of personal, family, and communitarian values followed many different paths to involvement. And paths followed are important because they contain within them the terms under which personal struggles becomes collective action.

Mobilization Pathways: The Committee of Women of Tepoztlán (CMT)

In 1979, a Morelos governor attempted to impose a "foreign person," a man from Cuernavaca, as municipio president. So outraged were citizens of all political persuasions they managed to come together to thwart the PRI. Since no Mexican municipio had ever defeated the PRI's candidate for this office, on the surface, the project seemed to be impossible, and all but a death wish for out front leaders. What made this unprecedented triumph possible was that for the first time a group of *mujeres grandes* (establishment women) organized to insert themselves as activists at the center of electoral politics. Citizenship not feminism was its reason for being.

Wisely taking Tepoztecans seriously, on Election Day the governor sent in troops. Photographs show women, most wearing aprons, handing out roses and snacks to battle-garbed troops, some with Uzis at the ready. The soldiers' assignment was to transport the ballot boxes to Cuernavaca for "safekeeping" before counting; but citizens with matrons at the fore, backed up by senior campesinos, refused to surrender the boxes. Newspapers across Mexico headlined the public counting of the ballots and the defeat of the PRI's carpetbagger. Although when the furor abated, a compromise mayor, a Tepozteco closely identified with the PRI, was installed, a new political force had emerged.

Though by 1979 Mexican women had begun to have a limited formal political presence in some regions (Fernández Poncela 1994; V. Rodríquez 1998), it was still not customary for proper Tepoztecas to engage publicly in old boy party politics. Now, however, the surprising success the women achieved in mobilizing other women made them interesting to politicians and made politics interesting to them. To one of its founders, CMT expressed two new dimensions uncovered when "we stood up to Cuernavaca." Women had the power to mobilize other women and to press certain issues—she mentioned improving the drainage system, raising school standards, and acquiring an ambulance—that are "far more important to women than to men."

The leader of the *comuneros*, farmers of communal land, whose power derived directly from the PRI, recognized the women's potential usefulness. "He regularly used them to deliver Tepoztlán to the PRI," asserted a PRD activist. She went on to characterize the CMT founders as "five women with power." "Most have personal incomes from shops, land, and houses they lease or have sold. They have family and material interests to protect, two good reasons for acting with the PRI." Thus the ironic trajectory of the CMT: it began and ended in a pitched battle against the PRI and in between depended on a clientist relationship with the Cuernavaca PRI. Yet, even if their power depended on corrupt PRI politics, this first coalition of Tepoztecas to openly (if not yet formally) act effectively in political matters must be judged a great advance in collective politics.

The roots of the high standing of four of the five founders ran back to the period when commerce became a road to political influence. It was customary for men with means to take advantage of the labor of their wives and daughters to establish businesses. From face-to-face interaction with consumers, the women, who in many cases actually ran the businesses, learned to find their way around in the El Centro commercial world. They built a constituency among women to whom they granted credit, lent money, or advised on ways to enter the cash economy. When husbands were politically influential, favor-seekers often solicited their wives to act on their behalf. Their children were the first post-highway generation of business and professional women. All had high status in the important politico-religious worlds of the barrios. Each was distinguished by the pueblo for the effectiveness with which she fulfilled her material and moral homemaking obligations. But even for these women of property and accomplishment, public-sphere empowerment diffused from men; and only when unmistakably not feminist did their activities not trouble the gender norms they too honored and, for the most part, abided by.

CMT never had a continuous organizational structure, a decisive constraint against accumulating independent power. It was a tactical tool for staking out a zone between formal and informal power. Toward this end, the leaders cultivated the image of an aggressive watchdog group that was above self-serving male politics as usual. While this position served to mobilize women disgusted by politicians, CMT never made the next step to a strategic base.

Eventually, CMT came to be known more for the over-the-top vehemence of confrontations with opponents than for initiating and sustaining progressive programs. In 1985, they staged a particularly strident campaign to oust the mayor. Although they charged him with drunkenness, entangled PRI politics were really at the heart of the matter. Their literally in-your-face activities included blockading the Presidencia for several weeks and a street corner physical attack on a journalist who had reported negatively on their activities. Such frenzy was decidedly off-putting for most Tepoztecas; the need to resort to such tactics reiterates the formal political weakness of the CMT.

Also damaging was the widely held belief that the PRI cemented the alliance by regular direct payments. (A CMT leader confirmed that this standard PRI cooptation practice was indeed going on. She also asserted that trafficking with the PRI were the Tepoztecan politics-as-usual terms they were forced to accept if they were to influence civic agendas.) Until the Golf Club, the CMT never again took a stand against the Cuernavaca PRI. Alliance with the PRI came ever closer to being CMT's reason for being as political influence shifted to more openly entrepreneurial women. Indeed, in 1994, the CMT leader was none other than the sister of the 1979 carpetbagger. Married to a local man, she owns a transnational restaurant chain.

Though it is difficult to tell since the CMT did not have regular meetings, by the time of the Golf Club, the number of women actively involved seems to have dwindled to fewer than a dozen. Then Carrillo's attack on political women rejuvenated the CMT. But to carry out this new mission, it had to dissolve into the ranks of the CUT.

None of these women had formal leadership status in CUT. However, a reliable source told me, "CUT seldom made a decision without consulting with CMT women." Nightly meetings in the Plaza seemed never to begin without at least one CMT woman present. I observed them as polite but bold and well-organized spokespeople in meetings in Cuernavaca. They were unfazed by the sublime arrogance of the Gucci-loafered PRI operatives standing in for always absent government officials with the power to act on issues. They stage-managed out-of-town demonstrations skillfully constructed to maximize impact while minimizing the danger to participants. The movement relied on private funding. CMT and other women individually or collectively persuaded merchants, well-to-do friends of Tepoztlán, and a maze of national and international organizations and institutions to donate materials, cash, and information.

What appeared to feminists to be a promising development was the effectiveness with which CMT women allied with student activists. Nevertheless, in 2000, one of the founding women explained, "Since we no longer have influence in Cuernavaca, the CMT no longer exists. Finished! But many of us have become PAN [the Right] activists." In short, while the governor did not succeed in imposing the Golf Club, he did fulfill his vow to "destroy utterly" the CMT. And the end came even as Tepoztecas were constructing their greatest political citizenship triumph.

The Teachers

In Tepoztlán, political power has mostly come from stakeholders set up to act on rather narrowly vested stakes. As people's problems change, so too do their politics. However, members of the teaching profession have single-mindedly channeled their political activities through the teacher's union (SNETE). Though in 1995, many *maestras*, teachers, earned less than male laborers, no special interest group has had more voice in child-centered Tepoztlán.

Morelos teachers have been going out on often-prolonged strikes since the 1920s to get payment of back wages, job security, cost of living increases, merit pay, social benefits, and pensions. The chief concern of the astonishingly corrupted longtime SNTE boss was to stay in favor with the PRI by repressing the demands of the teachers. He fermented internal division by segmenting women into lower professional ranks, thereby limiting their power to change the system. At the level of the setting of high personal standards, teachers have made significant contributions. But government policies (Villa Lever and Rodríguez Gómez 2003) enforced by a male hierarchy have constrained their ability to make progressive changes, and their personal empowerment limited by the meagerness of their salaries, insecure status, and the overuse of their labor time.

On the other hand, many teachers have converted the high regard Tepoztecans have for the profession into a base for collective and self-serving interventions. In the fall of 1980, when they joined colleagues across the region to close down the schools for a month they evidenced the caliber of their power (and angered many parents). They demanded reforms in working and instruction conditions and in SNTE. Being largely unsuccessful, they established a splinter group, the organization through which education workers articulated into the Golf Club.

While many teachers had already come out as citizens, the arrest inside his Cuernavaca union office of Gerardo Demesa, a movement leader and a teacher's union official, brought teachers out as teachers, and as members of Latin America's largest union. The governor did not attack them in the fist-pounding way he went for the CMT. Instead, except for closing down a major highway and blocking ten busloads of teachers coming to join the march, he publicly ignored and thus trivialized the most massive protest ever staged in Morelos (23 January 1996). The protests gained momentum but a seriously ill Don Gerardo stayed in jail until 1998. So, although teachers mobilized as members of a formal, high-status group, their collective participation too was feminized by the convergence of personal and political sex/gender inequalities.

Women of the Pueblo

Given the importance Tepoztecans ascribe to comforting foods, it was not surprising that one of the first movement facilities to be up and smoothly running was the public kitchen. On the night of the setting of the barricades, a detachment of women simply showed up, Doña Camela toting her largest casserole. They tied on their aprons and organized a field kitchen on the porch of the Presidencia. A big pot of beans was on the simmer until the last barricade came down in 1997. At any hour members of the guard posted at all municipio portals could partake of a bracing plate of beans and rice accompanied by tortillas and finished off with a stiffening cup of locally grown coffee. The kitchen immediately became a center for information coming in from and going out to the field and a hub of movement operations. Twenty-four-hour shifts seamlessly replaced each other. And as is usual for that most feminized of central places, the non-commercial kitchen, what mattered to citizens was that it was there always, rather than how the women staffing it came to be there. When I asked Doña María Jose, a volunteer adding seasoning to a vat of beans, what particular organization the group working that shift represented, her immediate reply was "We are women of the pueblo."

I learned that many women of the pueblo had histories of participation in protests organized around a range of civil society problems. These histories verify Judith Hellman's argument that in Mexico, ways of mobilizing from below have more elements of continuity than of rupture (1995:172). It is then all the more important to document the heterogeneity of the labor processes of coalitions that form on demand and just in time and then disperse into everyday practices.

While continuing to regard their households as their principal work site, their paths to involvement, and the placards they carried in the marches, indicated the importance they now assign to productive employment. Though the importance of the waged work many women perform is disguised by working conditions, as shop owner Doña Herlinda put it, "Tepoztecas do not sit around watching soap operas; everyone works at something." However, because of domestic obligations, the private/public complex of social constraints, and a general mistrust and disdain for old boy politics, many of these women had never before participated in a sustained political action. On the other hand, none had been personally excluded from the fundamental structural adjustments in women's lives that had brought them into at least the fringes of the new working-class culture of resistance. Then, the terms of their participation can inform us about the formal ways they are reinventing gender politics.

Women and Labor Activism

As followers of Rubén Jaramillo, some local women integrated into his 1960s movement to improve living conditions for rural and working-class families (Hodges and Gandy 2002). In the 1970s, some women were active in militant union activities directed against national and international industries where husbands and a few local women worked. A strike at a nearby sugar cooperative brought out many Tepoztecas to protest jobs lost by the numerous local men employed there. By this time, women were all too familiar with official brutality against groups organized to redress grievances that had become insupportable. Now, too, the formation of the PRD had revitalized the left faction that has long been a force.

Women and the Church

Tepoztlán was one of the first areas to be "Christianized." The local Church has always been a major political player in very Catholic (96 percent) Tepoztlán, but its polemics have varied profoundly in accord with the politics of the parish priest (Taylor 1996). Generally, priests have represented a Mexican Church, which far from excluding women from political roles has actively enlisted them as "family value" enforcers. The parish priest during the Golf Club, Filiberto González Moreno, led his parishioners in the direction of mutual aid, protecting women and children from all forms of violence and abuse, and treating alcoholism, depression, and poverty and its effects. In sharp contrast to his bishop, Padre Fili proactively supported the right of Tepoztecans to resist "tyranny." Interviewed at a ceremony at a barrio chapel, he said, "I deeply respect the unique local culture" and "Whatever the pueblo wants in the matter of the Golf Club, it is my duty not only to sympathize but to support them, militantly if necessary" (as he did, stalwartly). Most of the women he inspired came out through the barrio churches, which once again proved to be an effective means for structuring homemakers into high-risk collective action. More so, because wage-earning patterns mean women's engagement has seldom been directly with firms. On the other hand, they do have a history of militancy through and sometimes on behalf of the Catholic Church. Though the time now allocated to employment and gratis care giving has cut into active involvement, and the relationship has changed perhaps more subtly than other major influences on women's cultures of resistance, for many Tepoztecas the link continues to be strong. (In the 2000 elections, the link turned out to be decisive to victories of PAN, President Fox's socially conservative party [Delgado 2003].)

Don Sergio's Feminists

In fact, feminism has been inside since 1975. The movement has been the work of volunteers deeply involved in projects to aid poor and abused women and support liberation movements and a handful of full-time activists. For several decades, the major force promoting progressive changes was the legendary human rights advocate Sergio Méndez Arceo (1907–1988), bishop of Cuernavaca and one of Latin America's foremost proponents of the interventionist credo of Vatican II. Don Sergio (as he wished to be addressed), was the catalyst behind numerous human and political rights action groups. He was crucial to the founding in 1969 in Cuernavaca of a branch of the most important women's rights group in Latin America, known as CIDHAL, (Stephen 1997) and to Ecclesial Base Communities (CEBs) established to put the bottom-up ideals of liberation theology into practice. Numerous women of the pueblo actively support CEB projects; some also look to them for material and emotional support. Like Zapata, then, decades after his death Don Sergio's charisma and his message continues to motivate and direct involvement.

In 1982, the year a by now ultra-conservative Church forced him to resign, Don Sergio formally announced his "conversion" to feminism. Activist Doña Elvia explained to me what being "feminist" in Don Sergio's sense entails. "We work toward a transformation in the lives of women. We continue Don Sergio's struggle on behalf of men's as well as women's equality. At this time, our main preoccupations are the disastrous effects of the economic crisis on households and we support indigenous rights movements wherever they occur."

Women who identify themselves as political feminists took on important jobs in the movement. They galvanized several informal and formal women's organizations already active in CEB projects. For the first time, they formed alliances with women who have a largely negative concept of feminism per se. In a 1995 interview, activist Doña Judith said, "Of course we continue to hope we can strengthen these ties; but up to now, we have not been very successful in converting Tepoztecas to feminism."

Women of the Barrios

The family/household continues to be institutionally protected as women's principal work site. Consequently, the political landscape many Tepoztecas articulated into was their neighborhood, the site of their practical activities. Recognized leaders were tapped as cadres, and a new generation of leaders came forward. These women participated in self-organized groups or as agents designated by CUT to arrange marches, mass meetings, and logistical activities such as making signs, directing traffic around the barricades, distributing CUT literature to visitors, and activating all possible networks. To maintain the public kitchen, each barrio rotated a week of responsibility. Women committed to eight-hour shifts and the obligation of soliciting supplies. Many had worked in villas; they now drew on these contacts to solicit funds and commodities. (However, most villa occupants opted to stay out of a confrontation with the PRI; indeed, some I interviewed supported the Golf Club. A number of members of the Association of Friends of Tepoztlán simply stayed away during this period.)

Actors Outside Structures

While social and economic diversity meant that some women peeled off into vested issue formations, mobility also meant that numerous women could not integrate into structures. Some of these women constructed ways to participate by simply taking upon themselves tasks that needed to be done.

One longtime foreign resident who hesitated to participate in public protests because of the anti-foreign sentiment abroad went daily to the Plaza to post published accounts of the movement, read avidly by residents who could not afford to purchase them. Two women who said they did not have time to go on marches came early each Saturday to scour Plaza meeting places. Women in food services invited press and dignitaries to sample local specialties. Several women who worked in offices in Cuernavaca were liaisons to the worldwide internet. When a thousand or so Zapatistas passed through on their way to a Mexico City conference, individuals cooperated to provide shelter and food. Women simply showed up to produce the bitingly satirical posters, graffiti, and perform multiple other tasks.

Formalizing Neighborhood Politics

Neighborhoods not the deeply mistrusted political parties functioned as centers for the landmark, first-ever truly democratic election. Municipios were the first political entities where (in 1947) Mexican women gained the constitutional right to participate as voters and candidates. Judged by the scale of women's participation in the special election, it seems that the neighborhood level of organizing gave Tepoztecas confidence to participate in the discredited political system. However, emulating the disappointing pattern of women's exclusion from other governance levels, glaringly neighborhood-based politics did not result in any Tepozteca being a candidate. This omission is not surprising given the social conservatism of many elected leaders, male and female, in charge of the neighborhood stage of the election. In sum, in Tepoztlán, as in Mexico in general, as at the national and party levels, at the municipio level the record of formal participation continues to be discouragingly minimal and constrained.

It appears to be in the nature of gender politics in Tepoztlán that resource inequality is never limited to one sphere. Gender courses through income allocation, property rights, our customs and needs, and perhaps most intensely and enduring through de Certeau's "murmurings" of the everyday, such as cooking and simply turning up. Yet it may well be that it is because of these microresistances that though hegemonic, feminization does not rule out the potential for the accumulation of agency—inversions of repression and oppression—through participation in an unjust system.

THE TRICKIEST QUESTION

I now take up Hellman's "trickiest question" about New Social Movements: "what is it they *do*"? (1995:174). Addressed is whether a movement so profoundly and successfully invested in all too readily understandable gender scripts can promote women's *empowerment*: a "slippery process," argues Kathleen Staudt (2002), because it is "both a goal and a project." Sen (1999:190) identifies the *goal* as women's "active agency" and the necessarily coordinated *project* as insuring women's "well-being" not only as advocates for others but as political persons in their own right.

As to well-being, even before the Golf Club wound down, Tepoztecans were committing themselves in meetings and position papers to using the movement to make structural adjustments to institutions that had long not functioned optimally for certain groups. The social costs of restructuring were falling untenably heavily on the most vulnerable citizens. The municipio had to be more active in finding ways to fill vacuums created by the massive retreat of the state and industry as social income providers. Of course, funding was the major priority. A number of NGOs had taken up the Golf Club cause. Now a consensus of leaders agreed these and other alliances should be cultivated and turned toward new ends. A decade after the Golf Club, there is much to suggest that alignments have had a huge and on balance positive impact in terms of the well-being of most citizens, including women.

It is also at the well-being level that women have gained administrative power. In 2005, women were 40 percent of the greatly expanded appointed municipio council. While a substantial increase over pre-Golf Club sex ratios, as before, they are in charge of "women's issues" (as is also the case for women employed by the NGOs). Since many of these programs are new, few women have actually replaced men as administrators. Women office holders I spoke to have close connections to established political families (one is the Mayor's wife). Though seemingly personally highly qualified, it appears that

BOX 12.1

Cooperative projects include expanded health care for women, young people, and especially for the rapidly expanding population of unprotected seniors. Among the public work projects in start up stages are water treatment facilities, solid waste disposal systems, more careful inspection of the meat supply, and public involvement in reversing environmental deterioration. The prevention of infirmities and diseases is the work of a full-time medical brigade. While most of the funds have come from outside donors, groups of citizens commit their labor to a number of civic projects. For example, in the Tierra Blanca neighborhood men work on Sundays repairing streets. In addition, much of the money earned abroad, still primarily by men, now goes to improve housing, a fundamental change in the redistribution pattern of male income, I was told. A sports complex—one of the inducements held out by KS—now exists. The impressive facility includes a swimming pool (school children are required to attend free lessons). Here too are the offices of professional counselors for children with learning and conduct problems and providers of a range of social and health services. "Before, most of the time my family did not have the time or money to get such high quality medical care," commented Doña Lucia. Doña Augusta, age 82, had her first ever eye exam and received her first pair of badly needed glasses. Treatment for depression and pap smears (but not mammograms) is provided, as is counseling on alcohol addiction and domestic violence, mandatory for known offenders Partly in response to the appearance of violent youth gangs, public order is another major concern. State police are again (cautiously) allowed to enter the municipio. The local police force has been expanded (in 2006, 7 percent of weekend detachments were women) and instructed to strictly enforce tough new ordinances. Taken very seriously regardless of the status of the offender are parking violations, public intoxication, and brawling.

they have advanced largely by utilizing male-dominated channels. Visibility has not yet translated into formal political power.

The devolution of the CMT illustrates the complexity of the agency issue. The need for consensus fostered disempowerment, paradoxically, so too did the diminished hold on power of the Cuernavaca PRI. A former CMT activist who is now a PAN activist reported that women have less influence in the PAN than they do in the "new" PRI.

"There would be no Tepoztlán without the economic contributions of women," a female city government employee told me. "Yes we value and respect the work of women," reads a poster on a back wall in a refurbished People's Presidencia. Billboards of the 2006 PRI (winning) candidate for mayor had these words ballooning out of his mouth, "I will not discriminate on the basis of gender." The men here are just too macho to vote for a woman" was a former CMT leader's explanation for why the Golf Club did not advance women in the political hierarchy. With a now far right Church, political feminists have also seen their support base greatly diminished. A leader of this group had this to say, "Although we have had some success in making many people more conscious that women have human rights—and women themselves conscious that they must insist upon them—we have failed to help women in the arena that is now most important to them. Jobs that pay enough for them to take proper care of their children are what women here need and want."

Clearly, the tourism industry—which Tepoztecans too recognize as the pueblo's "true vocation"—must be made more productive for individuals to be a bulwark against the next (and certain) invasion of commercial global capitalism. Evidently, a goal and a project with contradictory implications for women's agency and well-being, yet the arching issue of gender equity never made it into this discourse.

Three gender-mainstreaming issues solidified during the Golf Club: (1) Improving the quality of frontline service sector jobs; (2) Adding jobs suitable for a generation of more highly educated, career-minded Tepoztecas; and (3) Providing women rights and social protections that do not depend on their relationship to the protected, usually male, population. In all these matters, far from clear is that working women's agency corresponds in any straightforward way to programs promoting the well-being of the community. I argue then that the trickiest question in postindustrial Tepoztlán is this: Can the slippery process of empowerment and "Jobs! Jobs! Jobs!" be integrated in this time of the feminization of the work process of community survival?

In Tepoztlán, a successful struggle for control of the commons in which women came out forcefully as gendered actors succeeded in accomplishing socially shared objectives. But the feminization of the process and the outcome has not troubled many of the negative effects on women's work processes of the neoliberal project. The framework for asking the right commodity culture questions is the work processes Tepoztecas construct to manipulate "the range of choice open to the individual, *what* can be chosen, and what *is* chosen by the individual" (Marcuse 1968:7). The final chapter looks at the interplay of the contradictory pair of gendered options and gendered choices within those realms of policies and practices activated and protected by dominant paradigms: theirs and ours.

Chapter Thirteen

Gender Mainstreaming Insights

> It is context which determines the precise structural implications of particular counter-hegemonic acts, and we must analyze both their possibilities and limitations as practices contributing to systemic change.
>
> —John Gledhill, 1994

To begin to synthesize gender mainstreaming insights I gleaned from observing the work processes of Tepoztecas, I revisit Oscar Lewis' prediction (1951:319–20) that homemakers would be the first to use the new technologies to structurally adjust. Taking seriously the household as the primary unit of cooperation and contestation, he detected that "standards of behavior" were mutually contrived "social fictions" endangered by progress. Nevertheless, he assumed homemakers' adaptations would be within the "ideal patterns for the expected roles." They would invest "time saved" in visiting, napping, knitting, and such. But given their "strong preference" to work outside the home, they would also turn their "leisure" toward "gainful pursuits"; however, because they were not yet sufficiently hostile to ideologies of subordination, these too would be more of the same old limiting activities.

Instead, as this study has shown women's adaptations to and of "globalization scripts of powerful men" (Gibson-Graham 1996) have been reflexive, structurally significant, and, for the most part, out in the open. Of course, the impact on "our customs and laws" cannot be minimized. However, I do not interpret the "proletarianization of women" as does Lomnitz as "upsetting" the "Morelos peasant cultural ideal of reciprocity, family integration and communal life" (1992:126). After all, women's gainful pursuits have always anchored Tepoztlán's "intimate cultures" (Lomnitz's words). Rather, "the systemic logics" of Cook's post-NAFTA "commodity culture[s]" (2004:297) I encountered, as workplace transactions reveal, the fierce commitment of stakeholders to the most urgent project of the current age: the challenge of "transforming the local and the global into each other" (N. Rodríguez 2003:88); and, further, that they recognize that this mammoth project requires "all of us."

This study indicates that Gerda Lerner's (1986:231) appraisal of the "three-fold challenge" of the feminist enterprise—the challenge of correctly defining, of deconstructing existing theory, and of constructing new paradigms—remains highly relevant. Up to now, I have focused on contextualizing women's experiences as production-reproduction binding agents so that their work processes can become Nash's (2005a) "fount of insights" and "touchstone of reality." Now, I use women's ways of turning constraints into strategies to take up the two remaining challenges. First, I evaluate dominant development paradigms. A critique of feminist theorized approaches to global feminization through flexible labor follows. I use the demand (capital's strategies) and supply (labor is free to choose) format because it is the idiom of scientific analyses. And a feminist standpoint is *not* about rejecting value-free science. What it *is* about is opening gates long closed to the "most critical feminist insight: the relationship between power and knowledge" (Strassmann 1995:2) as it is also about the contradictory relationships of "love, agency, and politics" (Charushela 2000:58).

DOMINANT DEVELOPMENT CRITIQUES

Even the "letting-things-be" logic of Mexico's neoliberal development model allows government a role in certain labor-supply facilitating investments. However, privatized market forces must determine supply-and-demand-side issues. This laissez-faire polemic evidences the decisive triumph of Redfield's patriarchal modernization stance over Lewis' patriarchal dependency propositions. But scientific controversy stopped at the door of the household. Both theorized women's chores as a given and their marketed labor as of little *economic* value, a still pervasive analytical entry point.

Supply-side Paradigms

In the globally resounding words of Gary Becker, the economist most closely associated with the orthodox canon of *New Home Economics* (NHE): "The heart of the economic approach" is the combined assumptions of 1) maximizing behavior by empowered self-interested individuals; 2) the market's natural tendency to equilibrate supply and demand functions; and 3) a stability of preferences that can be taken for granted and thus outside analyses (1976:5).

Becker's (1991) foundational NHE model treats consumption labor (value is realized through use) and employment (value is realized through exchange) as equivalences. As to stability of preferences, since men can expect to earn more, the maximizing unit (firms, households, other social arrangements) men *prefer* to specialize in employment. Because of physiology, socialization, and intrinsic nature, women maximize by opting for unpaid domestic labor often in combination with time-flexible employment. Women then *prefer* to convert their nurturing skills into inequitable wages likely to be pooled inequitably within Becker's family firm. Thus, the institutionalization as the now globally dominant service sector of the caring labor conundrum: "that family work may sometimes be coerced rather than altruistic, and that the choice of paid occupation may sometimes be motivated by altruistic concern for other people" (Badgett and Folbre 2001:331).

Comments

Clearly, Becker's three "functions" figure crucially in labor allocation decisions of Tepoztecan households. But when laws and codes reinforce the gendered organization of society in an economy based on the comparative advantage to empowered actors of a class of "unfree labor" (Sen 1999), Becker's functions *must* recreate rather than diminish women's inequality at work.

In late Tepoztlán, labor controls involve segregating and segmenting the household labor force even as it renders its members more dependent on an internally differentiated cooperative unit. While recognizing a unifying dependency on productive and reproductive tasks, Tepoztecans do not assign the same *meanings* to them. The bottom-line allocation complexity underlying all "preferences" is that for most families even the combined wages of two full-time workers are structurally barred from being sufficient to keep up or in some cases even survive.

Moreover, the high degree of mobility (domain and territorial) makes it impossible for most households to be the normative, stable units essential to NHE analyses. They form and reform around the often contradictory requirement for cash for daily maintenance and to maintain a unit that can function cooperatively. Now that women's labor choices tend to respond less to life-cycle norms than to the availability of mostly low status jobs, the quality of jobs of all members dictates internal redistribution. In short, in a structurally dual economy, backward/forward combinations of a house's labor force *are* the only maximizing approach.

Wages earned outside the municipio are essential in many (likely most) households, but seldom sufficient or secure enough to sustain the enterprise of family. To become a survival strategy, staying on women must transform remitted wages into tradables. The uncertainty of remittances and structural limitations on their enterprises increase the danger of trafficking in the global market. For however localized and small-scale, no way of gaining a livelihood can be distanced from the post-NAFTA commodity economy. Indeed, small sellers and small buyers are far more likely than are firms to be compelled to compete in an unregulated market.

Once redefined as lifelong economic agents, the costs to women of being out of the labor market are huge. Yet women take fulfilling social obligations as critical to their economic capital, even though they frequently identified the marriage relationship as a primary locus of tensions. (In my sample, some 80 percent reported having experienced some form of abuse from a mate.) Women are more materially dependent than men are on "the traditional family," an institution which has never served their interests equally (Bergmann 1995:141).

On the other hand, I found considerable evidence that women are physically and because likely to be more materially successful, also emotionally better off when they subscribe to the patriarchal institution of the conventional family. Going out to work on a regular basis can intensify discord and not only in the most traditionally organized households. The friction-reducing options of putting "chores" ahead of "work" or leaving the labor force are costly in women's primary assets of time, energy, and capabilities. Still, all but one Tepozteca saw marriage as in her material interests. A divorce rate of 2 percent indicates that most married women pragmatically decided to remain even in coercive relationships. In part, this decision responds to the reality that partnerships are about motherhood, a métier that demands continuity in access to nurturing resources. Given that for an increasing proportion of people, Lewis' "traditional village family" model seems incapable of performing many of its support functions, Barbara Bergmann (142) declares Becker's "preposterous" NHE theories "probably harmful" because they do not help us to strengthen the institution.

Human Capital Theory (HCT) also follows logically from orthodox fundamentals. Defining human capital as productive investments embodied in individuals—education, on the job training, good health—the "problem" taken up by neoclassical/neoliberal theorists is the need to increase women's productivity. To these theorists, cultural norms mean that women enter the labor market lacking the right stuff. Melioration requires modifying women's behavior by societal changes in preferences and by equipping women with skills that enhance their productivity in specific growth industries.

Economists long assigned this socializing role to family and community. However, the ascendant "efficiency approach" (Moser 1995) of neoliberal HC theorists stresses that direct "investments in women" by governments and firms are rational when productivity enhancing. The technocratic state is encouraged to intervene aggressively to slot women into the labor forces of particular growth industries.

Comments

Assuredly, the strong investment the pueblo has long made in women's education is a driving factor in the notable increase of Tepoztecas in waged labor. Younger Tepoztecas believed that HC gains would help them get the decent jobs they keenly desired. (All expected to be lifetime monetary contributors; but for cogent social and material reasons they did not plan to be the primary wage earner, though they knew that this role was possible.) Most well-being measurements—notably fertility reduction (not unproblematic to multitasking homemakers)—correlate strongly with capability advances that often but far from inevitably enhance earning power. Why then do labor roles mainly reflect the expansion of a miserably waged service sector that turns women's human capital disadvantages into the comparative advantages of outsourcing capitalists? HCT does not address the reality that high demand for women's labor generally occurs when their vulnerabilities are firm-specific advantages. While humanistic gains do figure significantly in what many women perceive as progressive movement into wage earning, HCT does not tell us how in the push-pull contradiction gender interacts with the imperatives of firms that cap advantages to women. That households are aware of mobility constraints shows up as the weak tendency to invest in higher education unless productive jobs seem assured by the existence of social networks.

Education has enabled some Tepoztecas to advance into Mexican middle-class jobs even while it has not mitigated the job-related factors that often mask discrimination. Since the types of jobs that pay Mexican women comparatively high salaries do not exist in the municipio, highly qualified women must leave to profit from human investments (as must some marginally qualified women household heads). In practice, then, human capital attributes can even be labor market-direct constraints and because it is very difficult to return to low wages, HC gains can permanently drain away productive women.

Moreover, staying in school longer and later ages of marriage and maternity promote the overcrowding vicious circle in several ways: students, migrants, and increasingly local men compete for women's jobs, of which there are far too few jobs for the most qualified women. And when men crowd into the best jobs, they tend to profit more from even basic level education.

While there have been changes in occupation ratios, women's productivity gains have had little effect on labor market inequities. That there cannot be a linear connection between HC gains and career success is evidenced by the rigidly of sex-typed discrimination. Now even the best standard female jobs often go to men; and if women fill standard male jobs, working conditions decline. Even in the intensely feminized service industry, jobs that pay the most because they cater to foreigners often go to male students. (As noted, the gender-driven reasons for this include the fact that they are often associated with liquor, take place at night and on Sunday, and depend on tips, another highly gendered context.) Routinely, women inhabit lower-paying tasks even when productivity differences are impossible to isolate or when they obviously favor women. That the gender gap has narrowed in some occupations mainly reflects deterioration in job quality that can take the form of adding on female-identified tasks or redesigning the labor process.

The contradictions I observed undermine key HCT premises. It cannot be assumed that the market creates new jobs in order to place skilled workers, or there would certainly be more positions for badly needed teachers and nurses. When direct comparisons were possible, professional attributes seldom elevated women over men; when women did make gains within an organization, it was usually over other women. A key factor here as well is that many jobs are in the micro enterprises development agencies are now encouraging women of the South to start-up. The only labor that is cheap enough is their own or that of even more vulnerable women. Nothing in HCT—but much in the imperatives of firms acting like firms—explains why women are generally the first to lose good jobs in bad times and the first hired back when jobs are deregulated and degraded. Of course, it can be argued that the queue is such that the labor market cannot evolve into a meritocracy. In fact, firms are creating the types of jobs vulnerable women compete with each other to fill. Specific adjustments have both stimulated the employment of "unemployed" homemakers and made investments in their human capital less rational.

Cleavages both within and outside the household are "sets of processes concerned with the production and distribution of goods and services" (Fraad et al. 1998:2). In Tepoztlán, cleavages bring into existence a working class defined by its dependency on exogenous wages. But what most predicts a truly globalized female working class is the expansion of low status but increasingly unregulated caring labor jobs. And in these "natural" industries (cleaning, hospitality, food), skills go unrewarded even though the intense competition for these slots means that they generally go to workers who have a high level of "cognitive skill in working knowledge" (Baba 2003:19). But even firm-specific skills are rarely rewarded when such jobs become available in the socially constructed labor market.

As the literature made it impossible to dismiss gender gaps "out of hand as some vague, lingering, premodern cultural ghost" (Tomaskovic-Devey

1993:137), a decisive shift came with the endorsement by donor agencies of the *Participatory Development* approach. Increasingly, these projects take the form of microloans from private financial institutions and even venture capitalists. The loans are widely heralded as enriching for both capital and labor.

Comments

Since 2000, increasing numbers of Tepoztecas have enrolled in microfinance programs. Established are close links between the programs and community status. The flaw is that insufficient attention has been given to the reality that "'the community' was all too often the male community" (Maguire 1996:30). Today ultimately global market forces condition all wages. And the historical unlikelihood of a women's small-scale entrepreneurship/state-capital alliance partnership being equal leads some to fear that the complexities of women's "needs and contributions to development" are being obscured in a strategy rapidly being adopted by major financial institutions (Guijt and Shah 1999:1). Critics argue that loan programs make women more dependent on dependency capitalism.

Similarly, analyses of the neoclassical subdiscipline of *New Institutional Economics* (NIE) (also closely associated with Becker) speak directly to the intersection of gender discrimination at work and profit maximizing by firms. The category of analysis is the transaction cost (an approach that focuses on the structuring role of institutions [Blau et al. 1998:45–48]). Gender infiltrates the power-free institution of the market because contracts securing property rights do not cover all market-driven contingencies. Thus the NIE argument: discrimination is rational for firms when sex typing is the outcome of "the nuts and bolts" decisions economic men organized as firms are "*supposed* to make" (Solow 1993:156). Though high risk, self employment is the dream job of many Tepoztecas. And self-employment at minimal levels is a nuts and bolts option for workers that make sense for scope-seeking firms.

The self-employment choice may be a woman's response to opportunity: acquiring disposable income that can be converted into start-up capital or detecting a niche firms do not want to fill. Its flexibility may recommend it at times when it is too costly to reduce reproductive labor.

Self-employment at the level in which women accumulate without capitalizing has huge advantages for producer/distributors. Balancing disadvantages for women include dealing in goods that are perishable and require transformation. Others—such as no social security; insertion into the most competitive sectors for sourcing and trading; the need to make labor elastic; and Tepoztlán's investment in popular tourism—predict the extremely high rate of self-employment-centered inequities. The transaction cost that looms largest of all is women's unequal responsibility for the timely and continuous production of care. That NIEs explain away the fact that costs accrue to firms as greater profitability makes clear that discrimination explained away as rational opportunism is rarely rational for women. If there is more to "institutional formation than utilities, then we have to look much more closely at the *process* and not just the outcome of change" (Adelman 2001:44). Together, "lingering premodern cultural ghosts" (Tomaskovic-Devey 1993:137) and reorganized capitalism support the argument that women's inequality at work is the source rather than the consequence of the most rapidly expanding global market sectors not excluding the microfinance industry.

Demand-side Paradigms

Demand-side hypotheses revolve around the relationship of human labor to capital accumulation. All integrate some variant of Marx's Reserve Army thesis. The supply (reserve) is inexhaustible (thus, disposable) because a worker's control over the means of production decreases as firms use income not paid as wages to grow. Meanwhile, workers invest their earnings in reproducing the next generation of laborers. In this cycle, wages inevitably flow back to capitalists.

Comments

Certainly, Tepoztlán has a female reserve army. But gender-blind readings of its formation do not apply once one sees that gender creates the status differences that in turn create asymmetrically different labor forces. Moreover, women workers are assuredly not disposable. The hallmark of postindustrial capitalism is that firms relocate to take advantage of surplus labor forces. Vulnerable aggregates have been consolidated (to Pearson [1989], "greened") by many different distortions, from the corruption of unions to fruitless searches for decent jobs. The labor market shows the flaws in a doctrinaire misreading of women's situations at this time of economic change in the context of deep crises. It is not women's rotation out but rather their influx into low-status labor, which serves as both a primary demand-side as well as a primary supply-side text/context.

The focus of Harry Braverman's (1974) still influential "degradation of labor" paradigm was the *deskilling* of particularly abundant and unmoored classes of labor. New technologies replace accumulated expertise, allowing for infinite redundancy in displaced labor forces.

Braverman's deskilling model fails to describe the skills appropriate to economies that produce through interactive services, now globally the largest sector. Thereby he excludes the growth area of micro entrepreneurship in which service providers are at once the producer and the product.

Conclusions

Approaches considered up to this point fail to integrate crises-driven realignments that have reverse effects on the flow of gendered labor in and out of the labor market. Now women are arranging their lives around the goal of having real careers; demand-side propositions must incorporate labor processes that remain inequitable even though they are waged and continuous rather than cyclical. Instead of leaving when they are pushed out of an occupation, women are pulled into (often) more precarious jobs. Feminization means that the placement and proportion of women in the labor force cannot be explained by the axiom that economic growth (decline) increases (decreases) the participation and status of working women. Instead, primary theoretical consideration must be given to employed caregivers who cannot earn an independent livelihood.

FEMINIST PARADIGMS

This section focuses very incompletely at a general level on results to date of the challenge to construct better paradigms. Pivotal to these propositions is the discovery that "neoliberal structural adjustment policies lead to a feminization of the labor force" (Cagatay and Ozler 1995:1883) but rarely in uncontested ways. What these challengers have in common is that they take women's arts of combination as properly economic; and they call for alternative approaches that extend legal protections and entitlements to the nonstandard work arrangements that have become standard.

Significant advances have come from studies of the personal/political tensions of combining consumption and production. Thus, Inez Smyth (1993) revisits the heavily subscribed to proposition that women's role in reproduction lies at the root of their subordination. Smyth concludes that now that jobs are out there, in many societies only "marriage and the presence of children can give women more personal freedom" (108). She finds, however, that jobs bring new problems along with new options.

On the one hand, many theorists reject the deterministic position that patriarchy inevitably originates in the inevitably patriarchal household. Against this premise is the body of research that has isolated the punishing forms in which women's dyadic economies organizationally link up to Cook's neoliberal project. For example, Jasmine Gideon (1999:8) shows that capital's overuse of women's power to labor means they have "less time to maintain social networks and norms and attend to the social needs of their families and communities" thus making them simultaneously more dependent on firms and on male "household heads" and communities of men.

Highly useful in sorting through and contesting new labor/capital relations is the question economist Diane Elson (2000) puts and begins to answer. Seeking to specify which structures are in fact adjusting and who is benefiting, she identifies three biases directly linking global feminization through flexible labor to reorganized capital's strategies and interests: the deflationary, the breadwinner, and the marketization biases. Thus, she is also identifying the structures that must be reconstructed at macro as well as micro levels as if the totality of women's work counted.

In Mexico, the *deflationary bias*—achieved mainly by wage constraints—is the outcome of government's response aimed at gaining credibility in financial markets in order to receive credit-restoring loans and attract foreign investors. Women have paid a hugely disproportionate share in the daily-life costs of stabilizing the money supply. As penny capitalists, they have had to substitute even more of their labor for increasingly scarce operating capital. To diminish risks, they rely on goods that are the cheapest and most widely available and thus the most competitive. And note a feedback effect: the degrading of women's labor encourages firms to expand into areas in which earning wages increases a woman's dependency on global investors.

The *breadwinner bias* endures even while globalizing, as evidenced by labor arrangements grounded still in the social fiction that women are supplementary workers. And when labor is masked as use-value, what is hidden is the overuse and underpayment of women's labor to produce exchange-value.

The *marketization bias* conditions all exchanges because it sets the prices for all commodities and wages. Compelled to buy most consumables, women go into the labor market at a time when it is intensely degraded. But diminished social income means that they must continue to supply caring labor gratis. Recent studies confirm that as gendered actors homemaking Mexican women are the most negatively affected by neoliberal budgeting (Katz and Correia 2001; Hofbauer et al. 2002; Colinas 2003; Hite and Viterna 2004). This bias directly subsidizes firms by disadvantaging those consumers who are most dependent on daily wages.

Returning to these issues, Elson 2006 makes the case that the achievement of substantive equality for women requires government action to ensure that the technocratic state functions without discrimination against women and that it works to overcome inequality in households, communities, markets and businesses. Specifically, government budgets must be no less concerned with budgeting for human rights than for stabilizing the money supply. Because it is impossible to identify at a distanced level the programs that benefit or harm women with specific sets of needs Elson's (67) central argument is that "It is necessary to investigate the content and impact of programs in special social and economic contexts" from a gender-focused standpoint.

The largely unexamined enthusiasm for microfinance projects had led many feminists to examine closely the impact on women's well-being and agency of these programs. Often brought to light by the studies are the high transaction costs for women, including an increase in violence against them when they refuse to re-lend the money to men. Though in many cases, the production-centric vision of these programs has been achieved, there are important unresolved empowerment issues that urgently need to be addressed in future research (Zeller et al. 2002).

Feminist studies have established that at the core of market driven transactions that organize Mexican women's subordination in the global economy, gender segregation and segmentation articulate as the most important factor enforcing women's inequalities at work (Fernández-Kelly 1983; Pedrerro et al. 1997; for Morelos, Tapia Uribe 1994). In Tepoztlán, job gendering is a situated process likely to take root at any point along a crosscutting continuum of commodity culture[s] relations. It is primary to the "unfreedoms of poverty as well as tyranny, poor economic opportunities as well as systematic social deprivations, neglect of public facilities as well as intolerance or over-activity of repressive states" (Sen 1999:3). To act against gender at work, it seems that Tepoztecans must emulate Don Sergio and "convert" to his interventionist brand of feminism.

In Tepoztlán, as across the global economy, segregation and segmentation articulate as the most rigid factors enforcing women's inequalities at work. The case studies presented here contextualize the infinity of combinations of backward/forward forms of gendering that work dialogically on each other to make gender fundamental to all commodity culture transactions. Support by the new state government, local policies, and central Mexicans' taste for popular class excursions has bolstered the tourism industry. However, expansion has solidified occupational segregation and in some cases even increased it since productivity has intensified competition from outsiders, students, and local men. As a source of jobs that work for many women because they are feminized, whether expanding or contracting, tourism has an uneven impact on women's agency. In sum, for staying on women, the immediate problem is not limited to the shortage of decent jobs, but making existing jobs decent.

Journalist Doña Inga expressed the feminist challenge in these words: "We need to get across that women's liberation is also the liberation of families and the pueblo. The reason we have not been able to enlist more Tepoztecas who can move the cause forward is that in these hard times, women simply don't have time to become involved." However, many women of the pueblo remain determined to reorganize around specific practical issues and advance Don Sergio's vision into the twenty-first century.

This study has put into motion as workplace transactions some of the scientifically most difficult feminist standpoint questions. Can the pueblo sustain popular tourism and thereby maintain relatively autonomous control over the commons without the triple exploitation of women's labor? Can households continue to absorb "development, change, near catastrophe, poverty, and sometimes grinding misery" (Selby et al. 1990:53) and maintain the structure that even Monterrey industrialists credit with having "saved" Mexico? And the complexity that is potentially the most customs shattering: In whose vested interest is it for the male-dominated pueblo to refuse to allow in big capital that may well be the only agency with the assets required to hack away at a (the?) central problem of free market capitalism, namely the recursive association between women and poverty?

What Is to Be Done?

It is all but certain that to be acceptable to Tepoztecans changes must be evolutionary rather than revolutionary. At the top of a short list of mainstreaming "doables" is the formalization of women's nonstandard participation, including homemaking. Other systemic corrections include making available affordable, higher, and less paternalistic education; a much more activist approach to women's health issues, childcare, and sanitary arrangements; the creation of career-track jobs reserved for women; and the politics for enforcing these and multiple other doables: "doable" for sure because even more has long since been done for privileged men.

In Mexico, change at the margins has tended to empower the already empowered who are likely to be men, a result that increases while justifying asymmetry. Once identified and matched to specific policy decisions, changes in the gendered organization of work become more imaginable. The Golf Club protest demonstrated that Tepoztecans are fully up to bearing the stresses of making social and technological changes in commodity culture norms and priorities. While nothing is more urgent than "Jobs! Jobs! Jobs! Decent jobs!" the devastating and intensely gendered effect on Tepoztecos of the neoliberal project means that nothing is more potentially hazardous to syntheses. So the challenge ahead for the pueblo is to reconstruct ways to act together to let the globalized outside come inside but in forms that protect the needs and interests of the most vulnerable. This challenge requires a refusal to be divided: a refusal that is "a personal decision—but then a social action" (R. Williams 1990:89).

Appendix A

Participant observation data, 1993–1998. Sums are in pesos unless dollar sign ($) appears; exchange rate, 10 pesos per USD. Unless otherwise indicated, earners are Tepoztecans residing in Tepoztlán when interviewed.

MALE EARNINGS

Contract farm laborer, age thirty-six, worked three months in Virginia and earned USD 300 per week. He paid travel expenses and most living costs; he described conditions as "very grim."

Another man, age forty-seven, made the same wages but the second year he received a bonus of $150; he described conditions as "good." (Perhaps it is important that the satisfied worker spoke English.)

Greenhouse manager, age forty-three, 70 pesos per day. Two migrants from Guerrero working there average 30 to 45 pesos daily.

Married man, age twenty, one child, works at hardware store. In 2000, earning 200 pesos per twelve hours. Pays medical insurance but has a "kind boss" who pays him a "bonus" of 20 per week, which goes for this insurance.

Taxi owner/driver, age fifty-two, nets 300 to 500 pesos weekly (in 1999) if working ten hours and a seven-day week. (On special event days he can clear 500 pesos.) Permit to operate a cab, 80,000 pesos. Drivers not owning a taxi must pay the owner and buy gas; they earn as follows. A man, thirty-four, driving an uncle's taxi earns 70 pesos for "a very long day." Two younger men made 40 to 50 daily. A teacher, age thirty-eight, on an all-night shift (an unpopular activity) charges more and makes around 100 pesos per night.

A bus driven, age thirty-seven, assigned to the high prestige but stressful Cuernavaca route earns 112.50 pesos for five round trips. He considers himself underpaid but benefits make him "fairly content" with his job.

Popsicle vendor, age twelve, charges 1.20 per stick and nets 12 centavos per item.

Construction worker, age forty, makes 70 pesos per eight-hour day. (He made 100 pesos when he worked in the state of Michoacán, where he said that there were almost no men left in the dry season.) A much older, skilled laborer makes 30 per day working "as often as I can." He thankfully walked eight miles to a job.

Porter in his forties makes 10 per dolly load anywhere in the downtown area.

Lavish villa watchman, age thirty-nine earns 100 per day and 200 per night. His wife who regularly "helps out" receives no wage.

Retired market vendor in his seventies comes early each day to the food stall a son now operates. He brings food prepared by his wife in the home shared by the two families and prepares the stall to open. No cash wage is involved; "it is work for the household," he informed me.

Waiter/bartender at the three-star Tepoztlán Hotel makes 25 pesos per day and works two meals; at the four-star Posada, the position pays 450 per week including tips. (In 1995, first the Posada and then the Tepoztlán replaced the male wait staff with women at a lower salary.)

Men are generally the waiters at full-service restaurants. In a restaurant popular with middle-class clients, one man, age twenty-one, made 35 pesos per day. If more affluent clients but less turn over, the usual wage is 40 pesos. Most upper-end establishments open only on weekends and they often employ male college students. Because of tips, restaurant jobs are highly desirable.

Tips are supposed to be pooled with kitchen personnel. The only male Posada waiter gives "a little" to the female cook. One student, age twenty-two, is paid 30 per eight hours but with tips often makes as much as 400 pesos. (A kitchen woman at this restaurant complained that she never received a just share.) Waiter at the local branch of a restaurant cleared 250 to 500 per weekend day. When at the Cuernavaca branch he took home 1,500 per week working from 8 a.m. to 8 p.m. University student is a Friday-Sunday waiter/wine steward at a branch of an upscale Mexico City restaurant. With tips, he can make around 500 pesos; most of this sum he lends to other students at an interest rate of 20 percent per month.

Sunday morning setting up at the craft market, I counted thirty-two boys helping a female relative (generally their mother) to construct the booth. None that I asked either received or expected to receive a wage.

Three staff/owner brothers of a bakery divide profits "evenly." Daily gross is 500 to 700; wages of two apprentices, 35 and 20; a twelve-year-old relative makes 15 for tending the charcoal oven and wiping carbon off each roll.

Coworkers of a groom played and sang at the wedding reception and received meals and drinks.

Man, around eighty years old, makes daily rounds buying stale tortillas. He sells them as food for pigs and dogs at 1 peso per plastic bag and makes "enough to buy my tortillas."

FEMALE EARNINGS

Local woman, age twenty-four, working at a border apparel factory made 8 pesos per hour (vs. 12 for males). At a Cuernavaca sewing factory, she made 6.30 pesos per hour.

Secretary, age twenty-six, at the Posada earns 50 pesos per day. Secretary, age forty-five, at the local branch of a Mexico City architect earns 1,200 pesos per two weeks.

Neighborhood store operator nets 10 to 20 percent depending on the item and buying terms.

Woman, age eighty-two, gathers brush in a field on the outskirts of town, loads it on her donkey. "I try to sell what I don't use." On this excursion, she was out for six hours.

For a ten-hour shift, tortilla factory worker makes 25 pesos and two kilograms of tortillas.

Daughter, age twenty-three, tends the grill in her mother's food stall and receives around 1 MS "whenever it is possible." Daughter, age ten, is not paid for work in her mother's vegetable stall, but "I always buy her lunch and drinks."

Widow (from rural Guerreo) with three young children works as a rent collector in the municipal market and makes 20 pesos for three to five hours daily.

Saleswoman with five years tenure in stationery shop receives 35; pharmacy attendants, 35 and 45 pesos.

Sunday market vendor, age twenty-five, manages a jewelry stall for a Mexico City firm makes 35 for ten hours.

Over three months in 1995, a longtime market produce vendor had negative profits. In better times, her income was from 350 to 500 pesos per month. Profits for a smaller operation ranged from "barely any" to 335 pesos per month.

Highly popular snack stall nets 2,000 pesos upward per week.

Market sweet roll vendors (4:30 to 10 p.m.), paid by per item sold, usually earned 20 pesos.

Woman, age fifty-two, travels to the border to buy used clothing. "At the very least I double my money."

Eleven-year-old babysitting a nephew is paid in gifts. (She was very unhappy when socks were the gift.) A neighbor pays her five per hour. Teenage nanny working weekends at a villa makes 100 for two days and one night.

Profits of a weekend market seller of sandals, age forty, were between "nothing" and 1,500 pesos gross. She had just opened a well-stocked shop which was bringing in less than her stall. (Sadly, her shop failed within a year.)

Head cook, age eighty-two, after fifteen years at the Posada was making 1,200 pesos every two weeks. She retired in 1998 and draws a pension of 1,000 per month.

Posada waitress earns 25 pesos and tips; laundress, 25 pesos per day. Room maid at Tepoztlán Hotel receives 35 for eight hours; at the three-star Posada, the pay is 400 per week and salary goes up to 450 after two weeks but there are no more raises. Both are entitled to one meal; both report receiving few tips. At a third, no-star hotel, maid, age seventy-two, gets 35 pesos, with no meal, and often works ten-hour days on weekends. She is not paid overtime and is "never" tipped. Tepozteca receptionist, age twenty-six, at the two-star Hotel Tepoztlán made 270 pesos per week. The Mexico City woman who manages the Posada for absentee owners makes 650 per week.

Domestic worker, age thirty-eight, in a local household (in 1993) received 1 MS (the lowest salary I heard about). A foreigner pays 50 pesos for five hours for two weekend days of work. Woman caring for villa (whose owners rarely come) receives 500 per month. Atongo Valley housekeeper receives 70 pesos per day. If she works more than eight hours, she receives 5 pesos per hour. Guests give her "good" tips. She works only if the family is in residence. Often they do not come for long periods.

At the end of a selling day, market vendor exchanged fruits with woman vending bread.

Nurses earn 650 pesos weekly versus 750 in Cuernavaca.

Primary school teacher with fifteen years tenure earns 1,486 pesos per two weeks; another with less tenure, 1,200; a temporary in a rural school, 400 per week. A full-time first-year elementary teacher of English received 850 pesos per thirty-six-hour week. All teachers have hefty deductions taken out; for example, the teacher making 1,200 nets only 900 pesos. Local woman teaching Spanish in a U.S. school earns $1,500 every two weeks.

Home piece worker from Guatemala now settled in Tepoztlán produces T-shirts with front and back designs. She sells three per week for 60 pesos to an NGO that pays on delivery if the product is satisfactory and sells abroad though the Catholic Church at USD $18 per item. The shirts, from Hanes-Mexico, cost 13 pesos; thread, 3; transportation, 10; production time, ten to twenty hours (she works only three days each week). On costs of 26 pesos, she earns 34 pesos.

Owner of a downtown snack stall can make up to 400 on Sunday; otherwise, 70 to 90 pesos. Teenage daughter working for her makes 100 pesos per weekend. "She is of an age now when she needs clothes *a la moda* and if I don't pay her, she will get a paying job and I need her here and helping me at home." (The wage sounds far too high.)

Notes

INTRODUCTION

1. All Spanish words are italicized on first use, including those that have passed into English if only to remind us how many have become standard English. Italics are then dropped for some frequently used words. Italicized words inside quotations are by the source quoted.

2. Michel de Certeau (1925–1986)—a French non-conformist Jesuit priest, historian, and anthropologist—taught in Cuernavaca during the time that Ivan Illich (1926–2002), a Viennese philosopher and priest, lived and taught there. Illich frequently resided in nearby Tepoztlán and several people remembered that de Certeau visited him. Both men worked toward a revolutionary revision in the education system that used people's experiences of dysfunctional and corrupt institutions to formulate what Illich called "the right questions." This association led me to study and utilize some of the still highly influential ideas of de Certeau, especially, and increasingly Illich.

3. "Liberal" as in "neoliberalism" does not carry the same meaning as in U.S. politics. Rather, it is a belief system deriving from classical/neoclassical laissez-faire, or letting-things-be, economic doctrines. These principles embody the assumption that prices (supply-and-demand) are set by exchanges in unfettered markets; and thereby express the rational (i.e., self-interested) choices of individuals and inevitably must result in competitive practices. Therefore, governments should not interfere in private economic decisions. However, governments must intervene in the money supply. Neoliberal economists calling themselves "monetarists" assert a direct link between the rate of the supply of money and inflation, making general equilibrium impossible to achieve. The remedy is that the money supply must increase (decrease) at the same rate as production (output) rises (falls). Judged essential is to drastically cut social spending, stimulate investment through incentives to entrepreneurs and firms, and privatize all industries and delivery systems.

4. I made certain that everyone interviewed knew that the information imparted was intended for publication. Translations of conversations (and other Spanish texts) are by me unless otherwise noted. Names are fictional except for a few public figures and people who asked me to use their names. Multiple interviews may have been condensed. In some case studies, changes in details have been made to protect the privacy of individuals.

5. Statistical data comes mainly from Mexico's National Institute for Statistics, Geography, and Information (INEGI). The bibliography references specific sources utilized.

CHAPTER 1

1. The dollar sign ($) indicates U.S. dollars. (In Mexico, it also indicates pesos.) Between 1993 and 2000, the exchange rate hovered around 10 pesos to USD 1. Otherwise, the sums are in pesos and centavos, the Mexican currency.

2. There are two categories of material assets that can be converted into cash. "Real assets" include land, a house, machinery, jewelry, and other possessions. "Financial assets" include such things as stocks and pensions.

CHAPTER 4

1. In a 1928 shootout that took place in the Plaza during Carnival, twenty-two bystanders—sixteen were women and children—were killed in the crossfire exchanged by the Bolshevik campesino faction and the men of the commercial center. Though occurring during his fieldwork, Redfield does not mention the event.

CHAPTER 12

1. Since the 1950s, Tepoztlán has been a prime target for take-over projects. In 1956, a local man enticed sixty-three families to transfer titles to land destined to be bisected by the Mexico City highway. He transferred the titles to the Golden Bear Corporation of Florida. By the time the scheme became known, already under construction was "Montecastillo," a lavish resort whose crowning glory would be Mexico's first 18-hole golf course. At the groundbreaking ceremony, citizens armed with sticks and *machetes* succeeded in blocking the project. However, land titles remained on file in Cuernavaca. In 1993, Montecastillo returned as El Club de Golf El Tepozteco. Meanwhile in 1976, came the plan to connect the highway by cable car directly to the sacred mountains, meaning visitors might never enter the town. Convening as a Popular Assembly, citizens voted "No al *teleférico*." In 1986, a proposal for a ring road that would bypass the town and feed into a network of mountain roads was again rejected by voice vote. In 1992, citizens said "No to the scenic railroad," yet another

plan to highjack tourism. Numerous national and international firms continue to request permits to establish local businesses. To date, none has been granted. However, like all rights to use the land, the leasing of space is a very murky area.

2. The PRI forced Carrillo Olea to resign before his term ended but not because of the Golf Club. The evidence was strong that he had conspired with Morelos security forces in a series of kidnappings that terrorized Morelos. He was exonerated by a PRI-dominated committee. Later on, with a change in administration, he was found guilty of charges unrelated to the Golf Club. (For more on the Golf Club and its aftermath see Perutz 2003; Stolle-McAllister 2005; J. Martin 2006).

References and Bibliography

Besides references cited in the text, this bibliography includes sources drawn upon for statistics as well as for historical, demographic, and other general and background information not cited in the main text. I utilized considerable material privately published by the municipio. In addition to interviews, I also drew on oral memoirs, photographs, old and recent local publications, and memorabilia.

Abu-Lughod, L. 1990. "The Romance of Resistance: Tracing Transformations of Power through Bedouin Women." *American Ethnologist* 17(1):41–55.

Adelman, J. 2001. "Institutions, Property, and Economic Development in Latin America." Pp. 27–54 in *The Other Mirror: Grand Theory through the Lens of Latin America*, eds. M. Centeno and F. Lopéz-Alves. Princeton: Princeton University Press.

Adkins, L. 2001. "Cultural Feminization: 'Money, Sex, and Power' for Women." *Signs* 1(3):669–96.

Aguilar, S. 1992. "Geografía fisica y ecología del Estado de Morelos." *Ciencia y Desarollo* 18(104):75–85.

Alatorre, J., G. Carega, C. Jusidman, V. Salles, C. Talamante, and J. Townsend (eds.). 1994. *Las Mujeres en la Pobreza*. México: El Colegio de México.

Alba, F., and G. Cabrera (eds.). 1994. *Población en el Desarrollo Contemporáneo de México*. México: El Colégio de México.

Albelda, R. 1997. *Economics and Feminism: Disturbances in the Field*. New York: Twayne Publishers.

Anker, R. 2001. "Theories of Occupational Segregation by Sex: An Overview." Pp. 129–56 in *Women, Gender and Work*, ed. M. Loutfi. Geneva: International Labor Organization.

Antrobus, P. 2004. "A Caribbean Journey: Defending Feminist Politics." Pp. 138–50 in *Developing Power: How Women Transformed International Development*, eds. A. Fraser and I. Tinker. New York: The Feminist Press.

Appadurai, A. 1992. "Introduction: Commodities and the Politics of Value." Pp. 3–63 in *The Social Life of Things: Commodities in Cultural Perspective*, ed. A. Appadurai. New York: Cambridge University Press.

Arias, P., and L. Bazán. 1977. CIVAC: *Un Proceso de Industrialización en una Zona Campesina*. México: Cuadernos de la Casa Chata, 1, Centro de Investigaciones superiores del INAH.

Baba, M. 2003. "Working Knowledge Goes Global: Knowledge Sharing and Performance in a Globally Distributed Team." *Anthropology of Work Review* 24(1–21):19–29.

Badgett, M., and N. Folbre. 2001. Pp. 327–46 in *Women, Gender and Work*, ed. M. Loutfi. Geneva: International Labor Organization.

Bakhtin, M. M. 1981. *The Dialogic Imagination*, ed. M. Holquist.; trans. C. Emerson and M. Holquist. Austin, TX: University of Texas Press.

——. 1984. *Problems of Dostoevsky's Poetics*, trans. C. Emerson. Minneapolis, MN: University of Minnesota Press.

Baron, A. 1991. "Gender and Labor History: Learning from the Past, Looking to the Future." Pp. 5–25 in *Work Engendered: Towards a New History of Labor*, ed. A. Baron. Ithaca: Cornell University Press.

Barta, R. 2002. *Blood, Ink, and Culture: Miseries and Splendors of the Post-Mexican Condition*, trans. M. Healey. Durham, NC: Duke University Press.

Basu, A., I. Grewal, C. Kaplan, and L. Malkki. 2001. "Editorial." *Signs* 26(4):943–48.

Baud, I. 1993. "Gender Aspects of Industrialization in India and Mexico. "Pp. 79–96 in *Gender, Small-Scale Industry and Development Policy*, eds. I. Baud and G. de Bruijne. London: IT Publications.

Becker, G. 1976. *The Economic Approach to Human Behavior*. New York: Columbia University Press.

——. 1991. *A Treatise on the Family*. Cambridge: Harvard University Press.

Becker, M. 1995. *Setting the Virgin on Fire*. Berkeley: University of California Press.

Beckwith, K. 1996. "Lancashire Women Against Pit Closures: Women's Standing in a Men's Movement." *Signs* 21(4):1034–68.

Beechey, V. 1986. "Studies of Women's Employment." Pp. 130–59 in *Waged Work, A Reader*. London: Virago Press.

Bell, D. 1973. *The End of Ideology*. Cambridge: Harvard University Press.

Bello Villamil, F. *Informe: 1997–2000, Presidente Municipal*. H. Ayuntamiento Municipal. Tepoztlán, Morelos.

Benería, L. 1992. "The Mexican Debt Crisis: Restructuring the Economy and the Household." Pp. 83–104 in *Unequal Burden: Economic Crises, Persistent Poverty, and Women's Work*, eds. L. Benería and S. Feldman. Boulder, CO: Westview Press.

——. 2001. "The Enduring Debate Over Unpaid Labor." Pp. 85–110 in *Women, Gender, and Work*, ed. M. Loutfi. Geneva: International Labor Organization.

——. 2003. *Gender, Development, and Globalization: Economics as if All People Mattered*. New York: Routledge.

Benería, L., and M. Roldán. 1987. *The Crossroads of Class and Gender: Industrial Homework, Subcontracting, and Household Dynamics in Mexico City*. Chicago: University of Chicago Press.

Benhabib, S. 1999. "Sexual Difference and Collective Identities: The New Global Constellation." *Signs* 24(2)335–61.

Berdan, F. 1985. "Markets in the Economy of Aztec Mexico." Pp. 339–68 in *Markets and Marketing*, ed. S Plattner. Lanham, MD: University Press of America.

Bergeron, S. 2006. *Fragments of Development: Nation, Gender, and the Space of Modernity*. Ann Arbor: University of Michigan Press.

Bergmann. B. 1995. "Becker's Theory of the Family: Preposterous Conclusions." *Feminist Economics* 1(1):141–50.

Bernholdt-Thomson, V. 1991. "Subsistence Production and Extended Reproduction." Pp. 41–54 in *Of Marriage and the Market: Women's Subordination Internationally and Its Lessons*, eds. K. Young, C. Wolkowitz, and R. McCullagh. London: Routledge.

Blau, F., M. Ferber, and A. Winkler. 1998. *The Economics of Women, Men, and Work*. Upper Saddle River, NY: Prentice Hall.

Bose, C., and E. Acosta-Belén. 1995. "Introduction." Pp. 1–14 in *Women in the Latin American Development Process*, eds. C. Bose and E. Acosta-Belén. Philadelphia, PA: Temple University Press.

Boserup, E. 1970. *Women's Roles in Economic Development*. New York: St. Martin's Press.

Braverman, H. 1974. *Labor and Monopoly Capitalism*. New York: Monthly Review Press.

Brumfiel, E. 2006. "Cloth, Gender, Continuity, and Change: Fabricating Unity in Anthropology." *American Anthropology* 108(4):862–77.

Burawoy, M. 1991. "Introduction." Pp. 1–7 in *Ethnography Unbound: Power and Resistance in the Modern Metropolis*. Berkley, CA: University of California Press.

Butler, J. 1990. *Gender Trouble: Feminism and the Subversion of Identity*. New York: Routledge.

Cagaty, N., and S. Ozler. 1995. "Feminization of the Labor Force: The Effects of Long-Term Development and Structural Adjustment." *World Development* 23(11):1883–94.

Cameron, J. 1996–1997. "Throwing a Dishcloth into the Works: Troubling Theories of Domestic Labor." *Rethinking Marxism* 9(2):24–44.

Cardona, Gloria (ed.) 1994. *Manuel del Taller de Educación Ambiental Corredor Biológico Chichinautzin*. Cuernavaca: Servicios Gráficos de Morelos.

Cardoso, E., and A. Helwege. 1995. *Latin America's Economics: Diversity, Trends and Conflicts*. Cambridge, MA: MIT Press.

Carrasco, D. 1990. *Religions of Mesoamerica*. San Francisco: Harper and Row.

Carrasco, P. 1982. "Estructura familiar en Tepoztlán en siglo XVI." *Nueva Antropología* 18.

Carrier, J. 1995. *Considering the Market*. Paper delivered at American Anthropology Association 94th Annual Meeting.

Castells, M., and A. Portes. 1989. "World Underneath: The Origins, Dynamics, and Effects of the Informal Economy." Pp. 11–37 in *The Informal Economy Studies in Advanced and Less Developed Countries*, eds. A. Portes, M. Castells, and L. Benton. Baltimore, MD: John Hopkins University Press.

Centeno, M. 1994. *Democracy Within Reason: Technocratic Revolution in Mexico.* University Park, PA: Pennsylvania State University Press.
———. 2001. "The Disciplinary Society in Latin America." Pp. 289–308 in *The Other Mirror: Grand Theory through the Lens of Latin America.* Eds. M. Centeno and F. López-Alves. Princeton, NJ: Princeton University Press.
Chant, S. 1990. *Women and Survival in Mexican Cities: Perspectives on Gender, Labor Markets, and Low-income Households.* Manchester: Manchester University Press.
———. 2006. "Contributions of a Gender Perspective to the Analysis of Poverty." Pp. 87–106 in *Women and Gender Equity in Development Theory and Practice: Institutions, Resources, and Mobilization*, eds. J. Jaquette and G. Summerfield. Durham, NC: Duke University Press.
Charusheela, S. 2000. On History, Love, and Politics. *Rethinking Marxism* 12(4): 45–61.
Chase, S. 1946 (1931). *Mexico: A Study of Two Americas.* New York: Macmillan.
Chaudhury, A. and A. Chakrabarti. 2000. "Market Economists and the Market Economy: Through the Lens of a Housewife." *Rethinking Marxism* 12(2): 81–103.
Chávez, C., A. García, and R. Oliver. 1990. *Plan de Manejo Integral para el Area de Protección de Flora y Fauna Silvestre Corredor Biológico Chichinautzin, Estado de Morelos.* México: UAM-X.
Chávez G., A. María, D. Moctezuma Navarro, and F. Rodríguez Hernández (eds.). 1994. *El Combata a la Porbreza en Morelos: Aciertos y Desaciertos de Solidaridad*. Cuernavaca: UNAM.
Chevalier, F. 1964. *Land and Society in Colonial Mexico: The Great Hacienda*, trans. A. Eustis. Berkeley, CA: University of California Press.
Chilcote, R., and J. Edelstein. 1985. *Latin America: Capitalist and Socialist Perspectives on Development and Underdevelopment.* Boulder, CO: Westview Press.
Chiñas, B. 1993. *La Zandunga: Of Fieldwork and Friendship in Southern Mexico.* Prospect Heights: Waveland Press.
Clendinnen, I. 1991. *Aztecs: An Interpretation.* Cambridge: Cambridge University Press.
Coase, R. 1937. "The Nature of the Firm." *Economics* N.S. 4: 386–405.
Código Civil para el Distrito Federal en Material Común y para toda la República. 1993. (I) México: UNAM.
Cohen, E. 1989. "'Primitive and Remote' Hill Tribe Trekking in Thailand." *Annals of Tourism Research* 16(1):30–61.
Colen, S., and R. Sanjek. 1990. "At Work in Homes, I: Orientations." Pp. 1–13 in *At Work in Homes: Household Workers in World Perspective*, eds. R. Sanjek and S. Colen. American Ethnology Society Monograph Series, No. 3. Washington: American Anthropological Association.
Collins, J. 1995. "Transnational Labor Process and Gender Relations: Women in Fruit and Vegetable Production in Chile, Brazil and Mexico." *Journal of Latin American Anthropology* 1(1):178–99.
Collins, P. 1997. Comment on Hekman's "Truth and Method: Feminist Standpoint Theory Revisited": Where's the Power? *Signs* 12(2):375–81.

Cook, S. 1986. "The 'Managerial' vs. the 'Labor' Function, Capital Accumulation and the Dynamics of Simple Commodity Production in Rural Oaxaca." Pp. 54–95 in *Entrepreneurship and Social Change*. Monographs in Economic Anthropology, No. 2, eds. S. Greenfield and A. Strickon. Lanham, MD: University Press of America.

———. 1993. "Craft Commodity Production, Market Diversity, and Differential Rewards in Mexican Capitalism Today." Pp. 59–84 in *Crafts in the World Market: The Impact of Global Exchange on Middle American Artisans*, ed. by J. Nash. Albany: State University of New York Press.

———. 2003. "Struggling to Understand Complexity: The Sociocultural Anthropology of Mexico at the Beginning of the Twenty-First Century." *Mexican Studies/ Estudio Mexicanos* 19(1):203–42.

———. 2004. *Understanding Commodity Cultures:Explorations in Economic Anthropology with Case Studies from Mexico*. Lanham, MD: Rowman and Littlefield.

Cook, S., and M. Diskin. 1976. "Peasant Market Economy of the Valley of Oaxaca in Analysis and History." Pp. 5–26 in *Markets in Oaxaca*, eds. S. Cook and M. Diskin. Austin, TX: University of Texas.

Cooper, J., T. de Barbieri, T. Rendón, E. Suárez, and E. Tuñón. 1989. *Fureza de Trabajo Femenina Urbana en México*. México: UNAM-Porrúa.

Crespo, H., and Brigida von Metz (eds.). 1984. *Morelos: Cinco Siglos de Historia Regional*. México: CEHAM.

Cubbit, T., and H. Greenslade. 1997. "Public and Private Spheres: The End of Dichotomy." Pp. 52–64 in *Gender Politics in Latin America: Debates in Theory and Practice*, ed. E. Dore. New York: Monthly Review Press.

Dalgic, D. 2007. "International Expert Organizations and Policy Adoption: The World Bank and Microfinance in the 1990s." *Cultural Dynamics* 19(1):5–38.

Debord, G. 1983. *The Society of the Spectacle*. Detroit: Red and Black.

de Certeau, M. 1984. *The Practice of Everyday Life*. trans. S. Rendall. Berkeley, CA: University of California Press.

Deere, D., and C. Doss. 2006. "The Gender Asset Gap: What Do We Know and Why Does It Matter?" *Feminist Economics* 12(1):1–50.

del Alba Acevedo, L. 1995. "Feminist Inroads in the Study of Women's Work and Development." Pp. 65–98 in *Women in the Latin American Development Process*, eds. C. Bose and E. Acosta-Belén. Philadelphia, PA: Temple University Press.

de la Peña, G. 1981. *A Legacy of Promises: Agriculture, Politics, and Ritual in the Morelos Highlands of Mexico*. Austin, TX: University of Texas Press.

Delgado, A. 2003. *El Yunque: La ultraderecha en el poder*. México: Plaza Janés.

Demas Padilla, G. 1998. *No Al Club de Golf: Tepoztlán, la Lucha del Pueblo Tepozteco Contra la Imposición de un Megaproyeto*. Published by the author.

de Sahagún, B. 1950. *Florentine Codex: General History of the Things of New Spain*, ed. and trans. by A. Anderson and C. Dibble. Salt Lake City, UT: University of Utah Press.

Díaz de Castillo, B. 1965. *The Conquest of New Spain*, trans. J. M. Cohen. Baltimore, MD: Penguin Books.

Diskin, M. 1976. "The Structure of a Peasant Market System in Oaxaca." Pp. 49–66 in *Markets in Oaxaca*, eds. S. Cook and M. Diskin. Austin, TX: University of Texas Press.

Dore, E. (ed). 1997. *Gender Politics in Latin America: Debates in Theory and Practice.* New York: Monthly Review Press.

Ebert, T. 1995. "The Knowable Good: Post-al Politics, Ethics, and Red Feminism." *Rethinking Marxism* 8(2):39–59.

Echeverría, E. 1994. *Tepoztlán: Que Viva La Fiesta!* Cuernavaca: Unidad Regional Morelos.

Edwards, R. 1979. *Contested Terrain: The Transformation of the Workplace in the Twentieth Century.* New York: Basic Books.

Edwards, S., and M. Naím (eds.). 1997. *Anatomy of an Emerging-Market Crash: Mexico 1994.* Washington, DC: Carnegie Endowment for International Peace.

Elson, D. 1992. "From Survival Strategies to Transformation Strategies: Women's Needs and Structural Adjustment." Pp. 26–48 in *Unequal Burden: Economic Crises, Persistent Poverty, and Women's Work* , eds. L. Benería and S. Feldman. Boulder: Westview Press.

——. 1995. Gender Awareness in Modeling Structural Adjustment. *World Development* 23 (11):1851–68.

——. 2000 The Social Context of Macroeconomic Policies. *World Development* 28(8):1347–64.

——. 2006. Budgeting for Women's Rights: Monitoring Government Budgets for Compliance with CEDAW. New York: UN/UNIFEM.

Elson, D., and R. Pearson. 1986. "Third World Manufacturing." Pp.67–92 in *Waged Work, A Reader.* London: Virago Press.

England, P. 1993. "The Separative Self: Androcentric Bias in Neoclassical Assumptions." Pp. 37–53 in *Beyond Economic Man: Feminist Theory and Economics.*, eds. M. Ferber and J. Nelson. Chicago: University of Chicago Press.

Epstein, G., J. Graham, and J. Nembhard (eds.). 1993. "Introduction." Pp. 1–18 in *Creating a New World Economy.* Philadelphia, PA: Temple University Press.

Esteva, G. 1983. *The Struggle for Rural Mexico*, trans. D. Castledine. South Hadley: Bergin & Garvey Publishers.

Feldman, S. 1992. "Crises, Poverty, and Gender Inequality: Current Themes and Issues." Pp.1–25 in *Unequal Burden: Economic Crises, Persistent Poverty, and Women's Work* eds. L. Benería and S. Feldman. Boulder: Westview Press.

——. 2001. "Exploring Theories of Patriarchy: A Perspective from Contemporary Bangladesh." *Signs* 26(4):1097–1128.

Ferber, M., and J. Nelson. 2003. *Feminist Economics Today: Beyond Economic Man.* Chicago: University of Chicago Press.

Fernández-Kelly, M. P. 1982. *For We are Sold, I and My People: Women and Industry in Mexico's Frontier.* Albany, NY: State University of New York Press.

Fernández-Kelly, M. P. and S. Sassen. 1995. "Recasting Women in the Global Economy: Internationalization and Changing Definitions of Gender." Pp. 99–124 in *Women in the Latin* American *Development Process*, eds. C. Bose and E. Acosta-Belén. Philadelphia, PA: Temple University Press.

Fernández-Kelly, M. P., and D. Wolf. 2001. "A Dialogue on Globalization." *Signs* 26(4):1243–50.
Fernández Poncela, A. (ed.). 1994. *Participación Política: Las Mujueres en México al Final del Milenio*. México: El Colegio de México.
Flores, J. 1991. *Propuestas generales para un Gobiernodemocrático, Tepoztlán Mor.* H. Ayuntamiento, 1991–94.
———. 1992. *Primer Informe Municipal 1991–94*.
Folbre, N. 1995. "'Holding Hands at Midnight': The Paradox of Caring Labor." *Feminist Economics* 1(1):73–92.
Foucault, M. 1993. *The Archaeology of Knowledge*. New York: Barnes and Noble Books.
———. *POWER/Knowledge: Selected Interviews*. 1980. C. Gordon, ed., trans. New York: Pantheon.
Foweraker, J. 1995. *Theorizing Social Movements*. London: Pluto Press.
Fraad, H., S. Resnick, and R. Wolff. 1998. *Bringing It All Back Home: Class Gender and Power in the Modern Household*. London: Pluto Press.
Fraser, N. 1989. *Unruly Practices: Power, Discourse, and Gender in Contemporary Social Theory*. Minneapolis, MN: University of Minnesota Press.
Freeman, C. 2001. "Is Local: Global as Feminine: Masculine? Rethinking the Gender of Globalization." *Signs* 26(4):1007–37.
French, J., and D. James. 1997. "Squaring the Circle: Women's Factory Labor, Gender Ideology, and Necessity." Pp. 1–30 in *The Gendered Worlds of Latin American Women Workers*, eds. J. French and D. James. Durham, NC: Duke University Press.
Friedmann, J., R. Abers, and L. Autler (eds.). 1996. *Emergences: Women's Struggles for Livelihood in Latin America*. Los Angeles: UCLA Latin American Center.
Froebel, F., J. Heinrichs, and O. Kreye. 1978. *The New International Division of Labor*. Cambridge: Cambridge University Press.
Gaceta Tepozteca. 1994. *Reglamento de Uso del Suelo e Imagen Urbana*. Organo informativo del H. Ayuntamiento de Tepoztlán.
Galeana de Valadés, P. (ed.). 1987. *Seminario: Sobre la Participación de la Mujer en la Vida Nacional*. México: UNAM.
———. 1993 *La Condición de la Mujer Mexicana*. México:UNAM.
Gamst, F. 1984. "Considerations for an Anthropology of Work." Pp. 56–62 in *Work in Non-Market and Transitional Societies*, ed. H. Applebaum. Albany: State University of New York Press.
García, B., and O. de Oliveira. 1994. *Trabajo y Vida Familiar en México*. México: El Colegio de México.
Gell, A. 1992. "Inter-tribal Commodity Barter and Reproductive Gift-exchange in Old Melanesia." Pp. 142–61 in *Barter, Exchange and Value*, eds. C. Humphrey and S. Hugh-Jones. Cambridge: Cambridge University Press.
Gerhard, P. 1972. *A Guide to the Historical Geography of New Spain*. Cambridge: Cambridge University Press.
Gibson-Graham, J. K. 1996. *The End of Capitalism (as We Knew It): A Feminist Critique of Political Economy*. Oxford: Blackwell.

———. 2005. "Building Community Economics: Women and the Politics of Place. Pp. 130–57 in *Women and the Politics of Place*, eds. W. Harcourt and A. Escobar. Bloomfield, CT: Kumarian Press. Minneapolis, MN: University of Minnesota Press.

Giddens, A. 1984. *The Constitution of Society*. Berkley, CA: University of California Press.

Gideon, J. 1999. "Looking at Economics as Gendered Structures: An Application to Central America." *Feminist Economics* 5(1):1–28.

Gillespe, S. 2000. "Rethinking Ancient Maya Social Organization: Replacing 'Lineage' with 'House'." *American Anthropology* 102(3):467–84.

Glazer, N. 1996. *Women's Paid and Unpaid Labor*. Philadelphia, PA: Temple University Press.

Gledhill, J. 1994. *Power and Its Disguises: Anthropological Perspectives on Politics*. London: Pluto Press.

———. 2005. "'Disappearing the Poor?' A Critique of the New Wisdoms of Social Democracy in an Age of Globalization." Pp. 382–390 in *The Anthropology of Development and Globalization: From Classical Political Economy to Contemporary Neoliberalism*, eds. M. Edelman and A. Haugerud. Malden: Blackwell.

Goetz, A. M. 2001. *Women Development Workers: Implementing Rural Credit Programs in Bangladesh*. Thousand Oaks, CA: Sage Publications.

Goffman, E. 1959. *The Presentation of Self in Everyday Life*. New York: Doubleday Anchor.

González de la Rocha, M. 2006. "Vanishing Assets: Cumulative Disadvantages Among the Urban Poor." In *Out of the Shadows, Political Action and the Informal Economy in Latin America*, eds. M. P. Fernández-Kelly and J. Shefner. University Park, PA: The Pennsylvania State University Press.

González Marin, M. L. 1996. "Mujer y Trabajo." *Momento Económico* 84:5–8.

González Martínez, A. (ed.) 1992. *Tepoztlán: Hacia un manejo participativo de sus recursos naturales*. Grupo de Estudios Ambientales A. C. El Comité de Barrios, Pueblos, y Colonias on Estudio de Impacto Ambientale. México: GEA.

González Montes, S., and V. Salles (eds.). 1995. *Relaciones de Género y Transformaciones Agrarias: estudios sobre el campo mexicano*. Mexico: El Colegio de México.

Gramsci, A. 1971 (1929–1935). *Selections from the Prison Notebooks of Antonio Gramsci*, ed. and trans. Q. Hoare and G. Smith. New York: International Publishers.

Granovetter, M. 1990. "The Old and the New Economic Sociology: History and an Agenda." Pp. 89–112 in *Beyond the Marketplace: Rethinking Economy and Society*, eds. R. Friedland and A. Robertson. New York: Aldine de Guyter.

Griffin, H., and A. Ickowitz. 2003. "Confronting Human Development." Pp. 577–95 in *Confronting Development: Assessing Mexico's Economic and Social Policy*. eds. K. Middlebrook and E. Zepeda. Palo Alto, CA: Stanford University Press.

Grindle, M. 1991. "The Response to Austerity: Political and Economic Strategies of Mexico's Rural Poor." Pp. 129–54 in *Social Responses to Mexico's Economic Crisis of the 1980s*, eds. M. González de la Rocha and A. Escobar Latapí. San Diego, CA: University of California Center for U.S.-Mexican Studies.

Grint, K., and S. Woolgar. "On Some Failures of Nerve in Analyses of Technology." Pp. 48–75 in *The Gender-Technology Relation*, eds. R. Gill and K. Grint. London: Taylor and Francis.

Grossberg, L. 1988. "Putting the Pop Back in Post Modernism." Pp.166–90 in *Universal Abandon? The Politics of Postmodernism*, ed. A. Ross. Minneapolis, MN: University of Minnesota Press.

Guijt, I., and M. Shah (eds.). 1999. *The Myth of Community: Gender Issues in Participatory Development*. London: Intermediate Technology Publications.

Gutierrez, L. 2007. Solutions, Sustainability, and Non-Violence Research Newsletter. See www.pelicanweb.org.

Harcourt, W., and A. Escobar (eds.). 2005. *Women and the Politics of Place*. Bloomfield, CT: Kumarian Press.

Harding, S., 1991. *Whose Science? Whose Knowledge?* Ithaca: Cornell University Press.

———. 2000. "Gender, Development, and Post-Enlightenment Philosophies of Science." Pp. 240–61 in *Decentering the Center: Philosophy for a Multicultural, Postcolonial, and Feminist World*, eds. U Narayan and S. Harding. Bloomington, IN: Indiana University Press.

Harding, S. and K. Norberg. 2005. "New Feminist Approaches to Social Science Methodologies: An Introduction." *Signs* 20(4): 2009–16.

Hart, K. 1990. "The Idea of Economy: Six Modern Dissenters." Pp. 137–62 in *Beyond the Marketplace: Rethinking Economy and Society*, eds. R. Friedland and A Robertson. New York: Aldine de Gruyter.

Hartmann, H. 1979. "The Unhappy Marriage of Marxism and Feminism." *Capital and Class* 8:1–33.

Hartsock, N. 1997. "Comment on Heckman's 'Truth and Method: Feminist Standpoint Theory Revisited': Truth or Justice?" *Signs* 22(2):367–74.

Haskett, R. 1991. *Indigenous Rulers: An Ethnohistory of Town Government in Colonial Cuernavaca*. Albuquerque, NM: University of New Mexico Press.

———. 1997. "Activist or Adulteress? The Life and Struggle of Doña Josefa María of Tepoztlán." Pp. 145–64 in *Indian Women of Early Mexico*, ed. S. Schroeder. Norman, OK: University of Oklahoma Press.

Hassig, R. 1993. *Trade, Tribute, and Transportation: The Sixteenth-Century Political Economy of the Valley of Mexico*. Norman, OK: University of Oklahoma Press.

Hawekesworth, M. 1997. "Confounding Gender." *Signs* 22(3):649–86.

Hay, C. 1995. "Rethinking Crisis: Narratives of the New Right and Construction of Crisis." *Rethinking Marxism* 8(2):60–76.

Hellman, J. 1995. "Power, and Inequality in Latin America." Pp. 165–184 in *Wealth, Power, and Inequality in Latin America*, eds. S. Halebsky and R. Harris. Boulder, CO: Westview Press.

Hernández Chapa, G. 1995. *Herencia e Identidad: Santa Catarina un Pueblo Náhuatl*. Cuernavaca: SUR.

Hicks, F. 1994. "Cloth in the Political Economy of the Aztec State." Pp. 89–112 in *Economies and Politics in the Aztec Realm*, eds. M. Hodge and M. Smith. Albany, NY: University Press at Albany State.

Himmelweit, S. 2002. "Making Visible the Hidden Economy: The Case for Gender-Impact Analysis of Economic Policy" *Feminist Economics* 8(1): 49–70.

Hirschman, A.1958. *The Strategy of Economic Development*. New Haven, CT: Yale University Press.

———. 1970 *Exit, Voice and Loyalty*. Cambridge, MA: Harvard University Press.

Hirschmann, D. 2006. "From "'Home Economics' to 'Microfinance': Gender Rhetoric and Bureaucratic Resistance." Pp. 71–86 in *Women and Gender Equity in Development Theory and Practice: Institutions, Resources, and Mobilization*, eds. J. Jaquette and G. Summerfield. Durham, NC: Duke University Press.

Hirth, K. 1984. "Early Exchange in Mesoamerica: An Introduction." Pp. 1–15 in *Trade and Exchange in Early Mesoamerica*, ed. K. Hirth. Albuquerque, NM: University of New Mexico Press.

———. 1998. "The Distributional Approach: A New Way to Identify Marketplace Exchange in the Archaeological Record." *Current Anthropology* 39(4):451–76.

Hite, A., and J. Viterna. 2004. "Gendering Class in Latin America: How Women Effect and Experience Change in the Class Structure." *Latin American Research Review* 40(2):50–82.

Hochschild, A. 1983. *The Managed Heart: Commercialization of Human Feeling*. Berkeley, CA: University of California Press.

Hofbauer, H., G. Lara, and B. Martinez. 2002. *Health Care: A Question of Human Rights, No Charity*. Cuernavaca: FUNDAR, Center for Analysis and Research.

Hodges, D., and R. Gandy. 2002. *Mexico Under Siege*. London: Zed Books.

Hondagneu-Sotelo, P. 1996. "Domestic Workers and Their Employers." Pp. 44–47 in *Women and Work*, eds. P. Dubeck and K. Borman. New Brunswick, NJ: Rutgers University Press.

Howell, J. 2002. "Of Servanthood and Self-Employment in Southern Mexico: Changing Patterns of Domestic Service in Southern Mexico." *Urban Anthropology* 32(3/4):389–422.

Humphrey, C., and S. Hugh-Jones. 1992. "Introduction." Pp. 1–10 in *Barter, Exchange and Value*, eds. C. Humphrey and S. Hugh-Jones. Cambridge: Cambridge University Press.

Illich, I. 1981. *Shadow Work*. Salem, NH: Marion Boyars Publishers.

Institutio Nacional de Estadistica Geografia E Informatica (INEGI). 1980. X Censo General de Población y Vivienda, Morelos.

———. 1990. XI Morelos Resultados Definitivos.

———. 1995. Resultados Preliminares, Tabulados Basicos.

———. 1997. Anuario Estadustico del Estado de Morelos.

———. 2000. XII Tabulados Básicos, Morelos, I, II.

———. 2000. XII Censo General de Población y Vivienda

———. 2004: Encuestra Nacional sobre la Dinámica de las Relaciones en los Hogares, 2003.

———. 2005. Mujeres y Hombres en Morelos.

International Labor Organization. 1999. *New Challenges for Employment Policy*. Geneva.

Jain, D. 2005. *Women, Development and the UN: A Sixty-Year Quest for Equality and Justice*. Bloomington, IN: Indiana University Press.

Jaquette, J., and G. Summerfield. 2006. "Women, Gender, and Development." Pp. 17–52 in *Women and Gender Equity in Development Theory and Practice: Institutions, Resources, and Mobilization*, eds. J. Jaquette and G. Summerfield. Durham, NC: Duke University Press.

Jennings, A. 1993. "Public or Private? Institutional Economics and Feminism." Pp. 111–30 in *Beyond Economic Man*, eds. M. Ferber and J. Nelson. Chicago: University of Chicago Press.

Jhally 1990, S. *Cultural Politics in Contemporary America*. New York: Routledge.

Jones, W. T. 1975. *The Twentieth Century to Wittgenstein and Sartre*. New York: Harcourt Brace Jovanovich.

Joyce, R. 2000. *Gender and Power in Prehispanic Mesoamerica*. Austin: University of Texas Press.

Judisman, C., and M. Eternod. 1995. *La participation de la población en la actividad económica en México*. Tomo VI. Morelos, México: INEGI.

Katz, E., and M. Correia, (eds.). 1997. *The Economics of Gender in Mexico: Work, Family, and Market*. Washington, DC: The World Bank.

Kearney, M. 1996. *Reconceptualizing the Peasantry*. Boulder, CO: Westview Press.

Keating, C. 2004. "Developmental Democracy and Its Inclusions: Globalization and the Transformation of Participation." *Signs* 29(2):417–37.

Knight, A. 2001. "The Modern Mexican State: Theory and Practice." Pp. 177–218 in *The Other Mirror: Grand Theory through the Lens of Latin America*, ed. M. Centeno and F. López-Alves. Princeton, NJ: Princeton University Press.

Kopytoff, I. 1992. "The Cultural Biography of Things: Commoditization as Process." Pp. 64–94 in *The Social Life of Things: Commodities in Cultural Perspective*, ed. A. Appadurai. Cambridge: Cambridge University Press.

La Botz, D. 1990. *Mask of Democracy: Labor Suppression in Mexico*. Boston: South End Press.

Larkin. P. 1988. *Collected Poems*. New York: Noonday Press.

Lash, S., and J. Urry. 1994. *Economies of Signs and Space*. Thousand Oaks, CA: Sage Publications.

Laurell, A. 2003. "Transformation of Social Policy in Mexico." Pp. 320–49 in *Confronting Development: Assessing Mexico's Economic and Social Policy* eds. K. Middlebrook and E. Zepeda. Palo Alto, CA: Stanford University Press.

Lavrin, A. 1992. "Introduction: The Scenario, the Actors, and the Issues." Pp. 1–43 in *Sexuality and Marriage in Colonial Latin America*, ed. A. Lavrin. Lincoln, NE: University of Nebraska Press.

Lefebvre, H. 1991. *Critique of Everyday Life, I*, trans. J. Moore. London: Verso.

Lerner, G. 1986. *The Creation of Patriarchy*. New York: Oxford University Press.

LeVine, S. with C. Correa. 1993. *Dolor y Alegría: Women and Social Change in Urban Mexico*. Madison, WI: University of Wisconsin Press.

Lewis, O. 1951. *Life in a Mexican Village: Tepoztlán Restudied*. Champaign, IL: University of Illinois Press.

———. 1959. *Five Families: Mexican Case Studies in the Culture of Poverty*. New York: Basic Books.

———. 1960. *Tepoztlán: Village in Mexico*. New York: Holt, Rinehart and Winston.

———. 1964a *Pedro Martínez: A Mexican Peasant and His Family*. New York: Random House.

———. 1964b "The Tender Violence of Pedro Martínez." *Harper's Magazine*. February: 54–60.

———. 1970. *Anthropological Essays*. New York: Random House.

Lockhart, J. 1992. *The Nahuas After the Conquest*. Stanford: Stanford University Press.

Lomnitz, C. 1982. *Evolución de una sociedad rural*. SEP/Fondo de Cultura Económica.

———. 1992. *Exits from the Labyrinth: Culture and Ideology in the Mexican National Space*. Berkeley, CA: University of California Press.

———. 2001. *Deep Mexico Silent Mexico: An Anthropology of Nationalism*. Minneapolis, MN: University of Minnesota Press.

———. 2004. "Nationalism as a Practical System: Benedict Anderson's Theory of Nationalism from the Vantage Point of Spanish America." Pp.329–60 in *The Other Mirror: Grand Theory through the Lens of Latin America*, eds. M. Centeno and F. López-Alves. Princeton, NJ: Princeton University Press.

Lopez, S. 1995. "The Politics of Service Production: Route Sales Work in the Potato-Chip Industry." Pp. 50–73 in *Working in the Service Society*, eds. C. Macdonald and C. Sirianni. Philadelphia, PA: Temple University Press.

Lorber, J. 1995. *Paradoxes of Gender*. New Haven, CT: Yale University Press.

Loutfi, M. 2001. "Introduction." Pp. 3–20 in *Women Gender, and Work: What Is Equality and How Do We Get There?* Ed. M. Loutfi. Thoudans Oaks, CA: Sage Publications.

Lustig, N. 1998. *Mexico: The Remaking of an Economy*. Washington, DC: Brookings Institution.

Macdonald, C. and C. Sirianni (eds.). 1995. *Working in the Service Society*. Philadelphia, PA: Temple University Press.

Mackintosh, M. 1989. "Domestic Labor and the Household." Pp. 392–406 in *On Work: Historical, Comparative, and Theoretical Approaches*, ed. R. Pahl. Oxford: Basil Blackwell.

Malinowski, B., and J. de la Fuente. 1982. *The Economics of a Mexican Market System*, ed. S. Drucker-Brown. London: Routledge & Kegan Paul.

Marcuse, H. 1969. *One-Dimensional Man*. Boston: Beacon.

María Liberacion del Pueblo, the Staff. 1988. *María Liberacion del Pueblo a 17 Años*. Cuernavaca.

Martin, C. 1985. *Rural Society in Colonial Morelos*. Albuquerque, NM: University of New Mexico Press.

———. 1996. *Governance and Society in Colonial Mexico: Chihuahua in the Eighteenth Century*. Palo Alto, CA: Stanford University Press.

Martin, J. 2006. *Tepoztlán and the Transformation of the Mexican State: the Politics of Loose Connections*. Tucson, AZ: University of Arizona Press.

Massey, D. 1995. *Spatial Division of Labor: Social Structures and the Geography of Production*. New York: Routledge.

Mauss, M. 1925/1967. *The Gift: Forms and Functions of Exchange in Archaic Societies*, trans. I. Cunnison. New York: W. W. Norton & Company.

McClosky, D. 1993. "Some Consequences of a Conjective Economics." Pp. 69–93 in *Beyond Economic Man*, eds. M. Ferber and J. Nelson. Chicago: University of Chicago Press.

———. 2000. "Postmodern Feminism: Half of a Conversation with Gayatri Chakravorty Spivak." *Rethinking Marxism* 12(4):27–36.

Maguire, P. 1996. "Proposing a More Feminist Participatory Research." Pp. 27–39 in *Participatory Research in Health: Issues and Experiences*, eds. K. de Koning and M. Martin. London: Zed Books.

Meier, G., and J. Rauch (eds.). 2005. *Leading Issues in Economic Development*. New York: Oxford University Press.

Meissner, M., E. Humphreys, S. Meis, and W. Scheu (eds.). 1989. "No Exit for Wives: Sexual Division of Labor and the Culmination of Household Demands in Canada." Pp. 476–95 in *On Work: Historical, Comparative, and Theoretical Approaches*, ed. R. Pahl. Oxford: Basil Blackwell.

Middlebrook, K., and E. Zepeda. 2003. "On the Political Economy of Mexican Development Policy." Pp. 3–54 in *Confronting Development: Assessing Mexico's Economic and Social Policy*, eds. K. Middlebrook and E. Zepeda. Palo Alto, CA: Stanford University Press.

Middleton, N. and P. O'Keefe. 2001. *Redefining Sustainable Development*. London: Pluto Press.

Mies, M. 1986. *Patriarchy and Accumulation on a World Scale: Women and the International Division of Labor*. London: Zed Books.

Miller, D. and C. Tilly. 1996. "Editorial." *Journal of Material Cultural* 1: 5–14.

Mintz, S. 1976. "Foreword." Pp. xi-xvii in *Markets in Oaxaca*, eds. S. Cook and M. Diskin. Austin, TX: University of Texas.

———. 1962. "Peasant Markets." *Scientific American*, 203:112–22.

Mingione, E. 1991. *Fragmented Societies: A Sociology of Economic Life Beyond the Market Paradigm*. Oxford: Basil Blackwell.

Monsiváis, C. 2006 "Este País y el imaginario político." *Este País* (México 1991–2021) Abril 2006(181): 5–9.

Monteón, M. 1995. "Gender and Economic Crises in Latin America: Reflections on the Great Depression and the Debt Crisis." Pp. 39–62 in *Engendering Wealth and Well-Being: Empowerment for Global Change*, eds. R. Blumberg, C. Rakowski, I. Tinker, and M. Monteón. Boulder, CO: Westview Press.

Moore, H. 1994. *A Passion for Difference: Essays in Anthropology and Gender*. Bloomington, IN: Indiana University Press.

Morgan, S. 2002. "An Overview of the Impoverishment of Women." *Voices*, December, 2002:3–8.

Moser, C. 1993. *Gender Planning and Development: Theory, Practice, and Training*. London: Routledge.

Myles, J. 1990. "States, Labor Markets, and Life Cycles." Pp. 271–300 in *Beyond the Marketplace: Rethinking Economy and Society*, eds. R. Friedland and A Robertson. New York: Aldine de Gruyter.

Nadal, A. 2003. "Macroeconomic Challenges for Mexico's Development Strategy." Pp. 55–88 in *Confronting Development: Assessing Mexico's Economic and Social Policy*, eds. K. Middlebrook and E. Zepeda. Palo Alto, CA: Stanford University Press.

Narotzky, S. 1997. *New Directions in Economic Anthropology*. London: Pluto Press.

Nash, J. 1980. "Aztec Women: The Transition from Status to Class in Empire and Colony." Pp. 138–48 in *Women and Colonization: Anthropological Perspectives*, eds. M. Etienne and E. Leacock. New York: Praeger Publishers.

———. 2005a. "Women in Between: Globalization and the New Enlightenment." *Signs* 31(1):145–68.

———. 2005b. "Introduction." Pp. 1–23 in *Social Movements: An Anthropological Reader*, ed. J. Nash. Malden: Blackwell.

———. 2005c. "Defying Deterritorialization: Autonomy Movements against Globalization." Pp. 177–86 in *Social Movements: An Anthropological Reader*, ed. J. Nash. Malden: Blackwell.

Nash, J., and Helen Safa (eds.). 1980. *Sex and Class in Latin America*. Westport, CT: Greenwood Publishing Group, Inc.

Nelson, J. 2006. "Can We Talk? Feminist Economists in Dialogue with Social Theorists." *Signs* 31 (4):1051–74.

Netting, R. 1992. *Smallholders, Householders: Farm Families and the Ecology of Intensive Sustainability*. Palo Alto, CA: Stanford University Press.

Nuijten, M. 2003. *Power, Community and the State: The Political Anthropology of Organization in Mexico*. London: Pluto Press.

Oyewumi, O. 1998. "De-confounding Gender: Feminist Theorizing and Western Culture, a Comment on Hawkesworth's 'Confounding Gender'." *Signs* 23(4):1049–62.

Pablos, J. Tuñón. 1999. *Women in Mexico: A Past Unveiled*, trans. A. Hynds. Austin, TX: University of Texas Press.

Parpart, J. 2002. "Lessons from the Field: Rethinking Empowerment, Gender and Development from a Post- (Post?) Development Perspective." Pp. 41–56 in *Feminist Post-Development Thought: Rethinking Modernity, Post-Colonialism and Representation*, ed. K. Saunders. London: Zed Books.

Parpart, J., S. Rai, and K. Staudt (eds.). 2004. "Rethinking Em(power)ment, Gender and Development: An Introduction." Pp. 3–21 in *Rethinking Empowerment: Gender and Development in a Global/Local World*. London: Routledge.

Palmer, I. 1991. "Gender and Population in the Adjusment of African Economies: Planning for Change." Geneva: ILO

Pastor, M. 1994. "Managing the Latin American Debt Crisis: The International Monetary Fund and Beyond." Pp. 289–313 in *Creating a New World Economy*, eds. G. Epstein, J. Graham, and J. Nembhard. Philadelphia, PA: Temple University Press.

Pearce, D. 1978. "The Feminization of Poverty: Women, Work, and Welfare." *Urban & Social Change Review* 11(1-2):28–36.

Pearson, R. 1989. "Female Workers in the First and Third Worlds: the Greening of Women's Labor. " Pp. 449–68 in *On Work: Historical, Comparative, and Theoretical Approaches*, ed. R. Pahl. Oxford: Basil Blackwell.

Pearson, R., A. Whitehead, and K. Young. 1981. "Introduction." Pp. ix–xix in *Of Marriage and the Market: Women's Subordination in International* Perspective, eds. K. Young, C. Wolkowitz, and R. McCullagh. London: CSE Books.

Pedrrero, M., T. Redón, and A. Barrón. 1997. *Segregación Occupacional por Género en México*. Cuernavaca: UNAM.

Perutz, S. 2003. *Women's Work in Tepoztlán (Mexico): In the Time of Globalization*. PhD thesis. Dallas, TX: Southern Methodist University.

———. 2006 "Domestic Labor in Globalized Tepoztlán: From a Gendered Labor Process Standpoint." Pp. 241-60 in *Markets and Market Liberalization: Ethnographic*

Reflections, eds. N. Dannhaeuser and C. Werner. Research in Economic Anthropology (24). Amsterdam: Elsevier.

———. 2007. "A Tale of Two Fondas: Scrambling Gender in Tepoztlán in 'the Decade of the New Economy'." *Food and Foodways* 15(3–4):237–260.

Plattner, S. 1994. "Economic Behavior in Markets." Pp. 209–21 in *Economic Anthropology*, ed. S. Plattner. Palo Alto, CA: Stanford University Press.

Polanyi, K. 1944. *The Great Transformation*. New York: Holt, Reinhart, Winston.

Portes, A., and K. Hoffman. 2003. "Latin American Class Structures: Their Composition and Change during the Neoliberal Era." *Latin American Research Review* 38(1):41–82.

Preston, J., and S. Dillon. 2004. *Opening Mexico: The Making of a Democracy*. New York: Farrar, Straus and Giroux.

Pyburn, K. 2003. "Archaeology and the Gender without History." Pp. 3–18 in *Gender at Work in Economic Life*, ed. G. Clark. Walnut Creek, CA: AltaMira.

Pyle, J. 1978. "*Tianguis*: Periodic Markets of Mexico City." Pp. 132–41 in *Periodic Markets, Hawkers, and Traders in Africa, Asia, and Latin America*, ed. R. Smith. Vancouver, BC: University of British Columbia.

Radcliffe, S., N. Laurie, and R. Andolina. 2004. "The Transnationalization of Gender and Reimagining Andean Indigenous Development." *Signs* 29(2):387–416.

Redclift, N. 1989. "Gender, Accumulation, and the Labor Process." Pp. 392–406 in *On Work: Historical, Comparative, and Theoretical Approaches*, ed. R. Pahl. Oxford: Basil Blackwell.

———. 1997. "Conclusion: Post Binary Bliss: Towards a New Materialist Synthesis?" Pp. 52–64 in *Gender Politics in Latin America: Debates in Theory and Practice*, ed. E. Dore. New York: Monthly Review Press.

Redfield, M. 1929. "Notes on the Cookery of Tepoztlán, Morelos." *American Journal of Folklore* 42(164):167–96.

Redfield, R. 1972 (1930*). Tepoztlán, a Mexican Village: A Study of Folk Life*. Chicago: Chicago University Press.

———. 1961. *The Little Community and Peasant Society and Culture*. Chicago: University of Chicago Press.

Riley, G. 1974. *Fernando Cortés and the Marquesado in Morelos, 1522–1547: A Case Study in the Socioeconomic Development of Sixteenth-Century Mexico*. Albuquerque, NM: University of New Mexico Press.

Robles, U. H. 1975. *El Marco Socioeconómica de Tepoztlán, Estado de Morelos*. Thesis in Geography. FFL/UNAM.

Rodríguez, N. 2003 "The New World Order; The Globalization of Racial and Ethnic Relations in the Late Twentieth Century. Pp. 81–89 in *Perspectives on Las Americas: A Reader in Culture, History, and Representat*ion. Oxford: Blackwell Publishing.

Rodríguez, I. 1989. *Las tendencies de la descampesinización y el comportamiento politico del parcelero de Tepoztlán, Morelos*. Thesis in Sociology: FCPS/UNAM.

Rodríguez, V. (ed.). 1998. *Women's Participation in Mexican Political Life*. Boulder, CO: Westview Press.

Roman, R., and E. Velasco Arregui. 1997. "Zapatismo and the Workers Movement in Mexico at the End of the Century." *Monthly Review* 49(3):98–116.

Roos, P. 1985. *Gender and Work: a Comparative Analysis of Industrial Societies.* Albany, NY: State University of New York.
Rosaldo, M. 1980. "The Uses and Abuses of Anthropology: Reflections on Feminism and Cross-Cultural Understandings." *Signs* (5):400–36.
Rosas, M. 1997. *Tepoztlán: crónica de desacatos y resistencia.* México: Ediciones Era.
Roseberry, W. 1991. *Anthropologies and Histories: Essays in Culture, History, and Political Economy.* New Brunswick, NJ: Rutgers University Press.
———. 1995. "Latin American Peasant Studies in a 'Postcolonial' Era." *Journal of Latin American Anthropology* 1(1):150–77.
Ross, J. 1998. *The Annexation of Mexico From the Aztecs to the IMF: One Reporter's Journey Through History.* Monroe, MA: Common Courage Press.
Rothstein, F. 2000. "Flexible Work and Postmodern Culture: The Impact of Globalization on Work and Culture in Rural Mexico." *Anthropology of Work Review* 221(1):3–7.
Rubery, J. 2005. "Reflections on Gender Mainstreaming: An Example of Feminist Economics in Action?" *Feminist Economics* 11(3):1–26.
Rubin, G. 1975. "The Traffic in Women: Notes on the 'Political Economy' of Sex." Pp. 157–210 in *Towards an Anthropology of Women*, ed. R. Reiter. New York: Monthly Review Press.
Safa, H. 1995. *The Myth of the Male Breadwinner: Women and Industrialization in the Caribbean.* Boulder, CO: Westview Press.
Salas, C., and E. Zepeda. 2003. "Employment and Wages: Enduring the Costs of Liberalization and Economic Reform." Pp. 522–60 in *Confronting Development: Assessing Mexico's Economic and Social Policy*, eds. K. Middlebrook and E. Zepeda. Palo Alto, CA: Stanford University Press.
Salinas, M. 1981. *Historias y paisajes morelenses.* México: Imprenta Aldina, Rossel y Sordo.
Sánchez Ascencio, P. 1998. *Antología Histórica de Tepoztlán.* Cuernavaca: Morelos Museo y Centro de Documentación Histórica, Exconvento de Tepoztlán INAH Morelos.
Sanders, K. (ed). 2002. *Feminist Post-Development Thought: Rethinking Modernity, Post-Colonialism and Representation.* London: Zed Books, 2002.
Sanjek, R. 1994. "The Holistic Anthropology of Anthony Leeds." Pp. 27–45. *In Cities, Classes, and the Social Order.* Ed. R. Sanjek. Ithaca, NY: Cornell University Press.
Sartre, J. P, 1938. *Nausea*, trans. L. Alexander. New York: New Directions.
Sassen, S. 1999. "Service Employment Regimes and the New Inequality." Pp. 64–82 in *Poverty and the Underclass, A Reader*, ed. E. Mingione. Malden, MA: Blackwell.
———. 2002. "Counter-geographies of Globalization." Pp. 89–104 in *Feminist Post-Development Thought: Rethinking Modernity, Post-Colonialism and Representation*, ed. K. Saunders. London: Zed Books.
Schultz, T. P. (ed.). 1995. *Investment in Women's Human Capital.* Chicago: University of Chicago Press.

Schumpeter, J. A. 1950. *Capitalism, Socialism, and Democracy*. New York: Harper.

Scott, A. M. (ed.). 1994. *Gender Segregation and Social Change, Men and Women in Changing Labor Markets*. London: Macmillan.

Scott, J. 1991. "Gender: A Useful Category of Historical Analysis." Pp. 13–37 in *Women's Studies International*, ed. A. Rao. New York: Feminist Press at the City University of New York.

Selby, H., A. Murphy, and S. Lorenzen. 1983. *The Mexican Urban Household: Organizing for Self-Defense*. Austin, TX: University of Texas Press.

Semo, E. 1993. *The History of Capitalism in Mexico: Its Origins, 1521-1763*, trans. L. Lozano. Austin, TX: University of Texas Press.

Sen, A. 1983. "Development: Which Way Now?" *Economic Journal* 93:745–62.

———. 1999. *Development as Freedom*. New York: Anchor Books.

Shiva, V. 1999. "Diversity and Democracy: Resisting the Global Economy." *Global Dialogue* 1(1):19–30.

Shumway, D. 2000. "Fetishizing Fetishism." *Rethinking Marxism* 12(1):1–15.

Sikkink, L. 2001. "Home Sweet Market Stand: Work, Gender, and Getting Ahead among Bolivian Traditional Medicine Vendors." *Anthropology of Work Review* 22(3):1–6.

Skinner, W. 1964. "Marketing and Social Structure in Rural China (I)." *Journal of Asian Studies* 24:3–43.

Smeets, M. 1999. "Globalization: Threat or Promise?" *Global Dialogue* 1(1):10–18.

Smith, A. 1994. "New Technology and the Process of Labor Regulation: An International Perspective." Pp. 157–89 in *Workplace Industrial Relations and the Global Challenge*, eds. J. Bélanger, P. K. Edwards and L. Haiven. Ithaca, NY: ILR Press.

Smith, D. 1987. *The Everyday World as Problematic : A Feminist Sociology*. Maidenhead, UK: Open University Press.

Smith, J. 1984. "The Paradox of Women's Poverty: Wage-earning Women and Economic Transformation." *Signs* 10(2).

Smith, M. E. 1996. *The Aztecs*. Malden, MA: Blackwell.

Smith, M. P. *Transnational Urbanism: Locating Globalization*. Oxford: Blackwell. 2001

Smith, S. 1997. "Comments on Hawkesworth's 'Confounding Gender'." *Signs* 22(3):691–97.

Smyth, I. 1993. "Gender Inequality, Labor Market and Household Influences." Pp. 97–108 in *Gender, Small-Scale Industry and Development Policy*, eds. I. Baud and G. de Bruijne. London: IT Publications.

Solow, R. 1993. "Feminist Theory, Women's Experiences, and Economics." Pp. 153–57 in *Beyond Economic Man: Feminist Theory and Economics*, eds. M. Ferber and J. Nelson. Chicago: University of Chicago Press.

Spain, D. 1992. *Gendered Spaces*. Chapel Hill, NC: University of North Carolina Press.

Spivak, G. 2000. "Other Things Are Never Equal." *Rethinking Marxism* 12(4): 37–44.

Standing, G. 1989. "Global Feminization through Flexible Labor." *World Development* 17(7):1077–96.

Stark, O. 1992. "Nonmarket Transfers and Altruism." Pp. 9–20 in *Understanding Economic Process*, eds. S. Ortiz and S. Lees. Lanham, MD: University Press of America.

Staudt, K. 2002. "Engaging Politics, Beyond Official Empowerment Discourse." Pp. 97–111 in *Feminist Post-Development Thought: Rethinking Modernity, Post-Colonialism and Representation*, ed. K. Saunders. London: Zed Books.

Stephen, L. 1997. *Women and Social Movements in Latin America: Power From Below*. Austin, TX: University of Texas Press.

———. 2005. "Gender, Citizenship, and the Politics of Identity." Pp. 66–77 in *Social Movements: an Anthropological Reader*, ed. J. Nash. Malden: Blackwell.

Stern, S. J. 1995. *The Secret History of Gender: Women, Men, and Power in Late Colonial Mexico*. Chapel Hill, NC: University of North Carolina Press.

Strathern, M. 1987. "Introduction." Pp. 1–32 in *Dealing with Inequality: Analyzing Gender Relations in Melanesia and Beyond*, ed. M. Strathern. Cambridge: Cambridge University Press.

Stevens, E. 1974. *Protest and Response*. Cambridge, MA: MIT Press.

Stolle-McAllister, J. 2005. *Mexican Social Movement and the Transition to Democracy*. Jefferson, NC: McFarland & Company.

Strassmann, D. 1995. "Editorial: Creating a Forum for Feminist Economic Inquiry?" *Feminist Economics* 1(1):1–5.

Suárez Davila, F. 2006. "La economía 1991–2006: "del milagro al espejismo": ¿como retomar el camino hacía 2021? *Este País* 181:14–20

Székely, M. 2006. "Perspectivas sobre la pobreza y la desigualdad en México: 'hay que correr más rápido que el tigre'." *Este País* 181:26–30.

Tapia Uribe, M. 1994. *Mujer Campesina y Apropiación Cultural*. Cuernavaca: UNAM.

Távara, J. 1993. "Development Strategies in Latin America: Which Way Now?" Pp. 391–404 in *Creating a New World Economy*, eds. G. Epstein, J. Graham, and J. Nembhard. Philadelphia, PA: Temple University Press.

Tax, S. 1958 (1940). *Penny Capitalism: A Guatemalan Indian Economy*. Washington, DC: Institution of Social Anthropology, Smithsonian Institution.

Taylor, W. B. 1979. *Drinking, Homicide and Rebellion in Colonial Mexican Villages*. Palo Alto, CA: Stanford University Press.

———. 1996. *Magistrates of the Sacred: Priests and Parishioners in Eighteenth-Century Mexico*. Palo Alto, CA: Stanford University Press.

Thomson, G. 1987. *Needs*. London: Routledge & Kegan Paul.

Thompson, L. 1992. "Central Mexico: the Decline of Subsistence and the Rise of Poverty." Pp. 170–88 in *Creating and Transforming Households: The Constraints of the World-economy*, eds. J. Smith and I. Wallerstein. Cambridge: Cambridge University Press.

Tinker, I. 1995. "Beyond Economics: Sheltering the Whole Woman." Pp. 261–84 in *Engendering Wealth and Well-Being: Empowerment for Global Change*, eds. R. Blumberg, C. Rakowski, I. Tinker, and M. Monteón. Boulder, CO: Westview Press.

———. 2006. "Empowerment Just Happened: The Unexpected Expansion of Women's Organizations." Pp. 268–302 in *Women and Gender Equity in Development Theory and Practice: Institutions, Resources, and Mobilization*, eds. J. Jaquette and G. Summerfield. Durham, NC: Duke University Press.

Tomaskovic-Devey, D. 1993. *Gender and Racial Inequality at Work*. Ithaca, NY: ILR Press.

Tostado Gutiérrez, M. 1998. *Tepoztlán, Nuestra Historia*. México: INAH.

Torrado, S. 1978. *Sobre los Conceptos 'Estrategoas Familiares de Vida' y 'Proceso de Reprodución de la Fuerza de Trabajo': Notas teórico-methodológicas*. Buenos Aires: Centro de Estudio Urbanos u Regionales.

Truman, Harry. 1964. *Public Papers of the Presidents of the United States: Harry S. Truman*, Washington, DC: U.S. Government Printing Office.

United Nations Publications. Fourth World Conference on Women, Beijing 4–15 September 1995.

———. Economic and Social Council. 1997. Platform for Action.

———. 1999. *World survey on the role of women in development: globalization, gender, and work.*

Varela, R. 1984. *Expansion de Sistemas y Relaciones de Poder: Antropologia politica del estado de Morelos*. México: Universidad Autonoma Metropolitan.

Vaughan, M. 2001. "Modernizing Patriarchy: State Politics, Rural Households, and Women in Mexico, 1930–1940." Pp. 194–214 in *Hidden Histories of Gender and the State in Latin America*, eds. E. Dore and M. Molyneux. Durham, NC: Duke University Press.

Vázques, Sánchez E., R., S. Vázques, and J. Palanera. 1988. "Geologia de la Cuenca de México." *Geofísica Internacional* 28(2):133–91.

Villa Lever, L., and R. Rodríguez Gómez. 2003. "Education and Development in Mexico: Middle and Higher Education Policies in the 1990s." Pp. 277–319 in *Confronting Development: Assessing Mexico's Economic and Social Policy*, eds. K. Middlebrook and E. Zepeda. Palo Alto, CA: Stanford University Press.

von Werlhof, C. 1988. "The Proletarian is Dead: Long Live the Housewife!" Pp. 168–79 in *Women: The Last Colony*, eds. M. Mies, V. Benholdt-Thomsen, and C. von Werlhof. London: Zed Books.

Walby, S. 2001. "Reply to Harding and Sprague." *Signs* 26(2):537–40.

Waldrop, M. 1992. *Complexity: The Emerging Science of the Edge of Order and Chaos*. New York: Viking Press.

Warman, A. 1980. *"We Come to Object": The Peasants of Morelos and the Nation State*, trans. K. Ault. Baltimore, MD: John Hopkins University Press.

Waters, W. 1994. *Roads, the Carnivalesque, and the Mexican Revolution: Transforming Modernity in Tepoztlán, 1928–1943*. MA Thesis, Texas Christian University.

Weiner, A. 1976. *Women of Value, Men of Renown: New Perspectives in Trobriand Exchange*. Austin, TX: University of Texas Press.

Wilcox, C. 2006. *Robert Redfield and the Development of American Anthropology*. Lanham, MD: Lexington Books.

Williams, H. 2001. *Social Movements and Economic Transition: Markets and Distributive Conflict in Mexico.* Cambridge: Cambridge University Press.

Williams, M. 2003. *Gender Mainstreaming in the Multilateral Trading System: A Handbook for Policy-makers and Other Stakeholders.* London: Commonwealth Secretariat.

Williams, R. 1983. *Keywords: A Vocabulary of Culture and Society.* Oxford: Oxford University Press.

———. 1990. "The City and the World." 75–89. In *What I Came to Say.* London: Hutchinson Books

Wolf, D. 2001. "A Dialogue on Globalization." *Signs* 26(4):1243–50.

Wolf, E. 1957. "Closed Corporate Communities in Mesoamerica and Java." *Southwestern Journal* 13(1):1–18.

Womack, J. 1968. *Zapata and the Mexican Revolution.* New York: Vintage Books.

Zeller, M., and R. Meyer (eds.). 2002. *The Triangle of Microfinance: Financial Sustainability, Outreach, and Impact.* Baltimore, MD: John Hopkins University Press.

Zúñinga Navarrete, Ángel. 1984. *Breve Historia y Narraciones Tepoztecas.* Printed by the author.

Index

Note: Most terms and concepts highlighted and contextualized in the Introduction are not included in the index. Only some quoted and cited authors are indexed with particular concepts central to the text. All entries relate to Tepoztlán and Tepoztecans unless otherwise limited.